Communism
Ontologies

An Inquiry into the Construction of
New Forms of Life

Bruno Gulli and Richard Gilman-Opalsky

Minor Compositions

Communist Ontologies. An Inquiry into the Construction of New Forms of Life
Bruno Gullì & Richard Gilman-Opalsky

ISBN 978-1-57027-451-0

Cover illustration by Ashley Yeo
Cover design by Eve Yeo (www.eveyeo.com)

Interior design by Casandra Johns
Author photo by Joshua Kolbo

Released by Minor Compositions 2024
Colchester / New York / Port Watson

Minor Compositions is a series of interventions & provocations drawing from autonomous politics, avant-garde aesthetics, and the revolutions of everyday life.

Minor Compositions is an imprint of Autonomedia
www.minorcompositions.info | minorcompositions@gmail.com

Distributed by Autonomedia
PO Box 568 Williamsburg Station
Brooklyn, NY 11211

www.autonomedia.org
info@autonomedia.org

CONTENTS

JOHN HOLLOWAY
PREFACE 1

CHAPTER 1
PHILOSOPHY, THEORY, SOURCES. 3

CHAPTER 2
WORKS (DOING AND UNDOING) 58

CHAPTER 3
HUMAN BEING AND BECOMING 83

CHAPTER 4
COMMUNISM, COMMON, MARXIST TRAJECTORIES 116

CHAPTER 5
LIMIT POINTS AND STRATEGIC DEPLOYMENTS 181

CONCLUSION
MOVEMENTS TOWARDS NEW FORMS OF LIFE .212

JOHN HOLLOWAY

PREFACE

Two friends strolling through the agora, chatting, greeting and engaging with other friends as they go – Aristophanes, Hegel, Guy Debord, Angela Davis, Spinoza and a hundred more – talking of the affairs of the day, coming back again and again to the issue of revolt.

Communists. Of course. They are, we all are. Of course. It is the only way of being human: to refuse the inhumanity of capitalism, the inhumanity that destroys us today and threatens to annihilate us tomorrow.

To be communist is to be lost, looking for an answer, looking for a way out. Lots of "Exit" signs, but no exit. We must look for ourselves, create the exit ourselves. Ourselves, not just myself. Perhaps myselves, a discordant ourselves, talking, debating, discussing, disagreeing. Not a vacuous talking shop, but a real pushing to understand, for breaking capitalism is urgent. So we must discord, debate, disagree-and-agree. The throw-away irony by Subcomandante Galeano in the Fifth Part of the extraordinary series of Zapatista comunicados of a couple of years ago is all-important: "¿todavía hay debates?" …Are there still debates? Because if there are no debates, there is no communizing.

Anti-identitarian, therefore, breaking barriers. Identity, like an invasive weed, crawls into our resistances and rebellions, smothering them, strangling them, limiting them, giving them a fixity that has no place, creating separations that weaken and destroy them. The "we are" of the classic sectarianism of the Left, the "weareanarchistsyouarecommunists," the "wearetrotskysistsinourinfinitesubdivisions," and now all the "weares" of identity politics, fragmenting the unity of our "NO." No, we are not, we are more than that, we overflow. The philosophy of an anti-identitarian flow against the ideology of identitarian lines; to borrow Richard Gilman-Opalsky's distinction, philosophy questions, ideology asserts. Philosophy is a restless, tormented admission of inadequacy, a not-enough, not-enough, while ideology is a lazy oh-we-have-the-answers-already, we-do-not-need-to-think.

Asking we walk, the Zapatistas say. Asking we walk, because we do not know the answers. Asking we walk because it breaks the great Left tradition of monologue, takes us into a world of dialogue. Asking we walk because it prises open the world that is so rapidly closing around us. Asking we walk breaks the Party. The Party is a place of answers, of programs, of definitions. However revolutionary it claims to be, it is a symmetrical reproduction of the state. Asking we walk takes us to the other great organizational tradition of revolt: the commune, council, assembly, soviet, all those forms that are not instruments designed to achieve an end, but are in themselves ruptures of the society they reject, of the social organization that is both deadening us and killing us. The commune not as a place of unity, but of shared dissonance. Nothing worse than an imposed line, but also nothing worse than a polite we're-too-nice-to-express-our-disagreement, a refusal of debate that has done so much to fragment resistance in recent years.

Asking we walk, or, in this case, asking we stroll through the agora. The dialogue of debate does not usually take the form of a dialogue. More often, it comes in the shape of a statement, a "this is what I think" that then waits anxiously for someone to read it and come back and say either "Yes, I agree" or a "No, I think in a different way." The first statement comes in the shape of a monologue, but often it is a monologue that hopes to be drawn into dialogue. In this case, however, the book is an explicit dialogue between Bruno Gullì and Richard Gilman-Opalsky. It breaks with the monologue form, brings us away too from any monological concept of anti-capitalist politics. It is a stroll, a chat, a meandering that is extraordinarily rich and extraordinarily enriching. There is a questioning here all the time, a coming-and-going between the two participants. The chat is a constant weaving of different authors and ideas with recent events and political trends into some sort of fabric that is straggly and has loose ends hanging out, not a closed and neat texture. It stirs you up, makes you want to go back and ask "what did they say about this person or this event," or "who is that, I want to read them, they sound interesting." And always, always the central, all-important question of revolt, of refusal of the deadening, killing capitalism. A stroll by two communists, immensely rewarding, immensely subversive.

CHAPTER 1

PHILOSOPHY, THEORY, SOURCES

Bruno Gullì (BG) asks: I like the way you begin *Spectacular Capitalism* with a critique of ideology. I think this is a very important point, often overlooked. In your introduction, you say that you "make an effort to differentiate philosophical from ideological modes of thinking, and to emphasize the importance of that difference for politics."[1] This is one of the central moments in your book, and you accomplish your goal very well. Can you say more about the difference between ideology and philosophy and its importance for us today?

Richard Gilman-Opalsky (RGO) answers: Ideology is especially problematic whenever it is present from the start. It is much better to arrive at an ideological position after a long journey, than to start with ideology before the journey. We should think of ideology as a worldview, or as the more precise German term, a *Weltanschauung*. Ideology is a view of life, a way of looking at the world and interpreting what you see in the world. A person can carry ideology around like a pair of glasses through which they see the world in a particular way, or, for example, a communist group may wield its ideology by interpreting every problem as a problem of capitalism. On the other side, a conservative group may wield its ideology by viewing every problem as a problem of communism. I argue that we should avoid any *Weltanschauung,* resist all ideology, and even if we look at the world as communists, we must strive to avoid giving rote communist explanations for everything that we see. We will misunderstand many things that we see if we seek to understand them only from a communist, conservative, or liberal point of view.

---

1   Richard Gilman-Opalsky, *Spectacular Capitalism: Guy Debord and the Practice of Radical Philosophy* (New York: Autonomedia, 2011), 10.

One problem with ideology is that it can be given and deployed without easy detection. One can teach a child to interpret everything they see as the will of God or as the misdeeds of liberal politicians. In this way, a child begins to understand the world through a finished worldview, but in this case, the child skips over a difficult philosophical passage that should precede ideology. The philosophical side is no profession. It is, rather, the side of uncertainty. Philosophy is the place where we want to know what is happening, how to explain things in the world, but we are so *uncertain* about what is happening, or how best to understand it, that we have no choice but to think. If one thinks and thinks, and even ideally, learns how to take joy in the thinking, to take pleasure in the philosophical activity, they may inevitably arrive at particular ideological preferences, i.e., for a Marxist or a Christian or a feminist worldview. However, even then, if one is not simply ideological, the philosophical side will haunt their confident knowledge, pressing them to avoid automatic interpretation (that is, interpretation without the activity of interpretation). We could say that a specter haunts ideology, the specter of philosophy.

It is fair to say that philosophy works best wherever the answers are not clear, wherever we are not even certain about the questions we are asking and answering. Are they the right questions? Ideology is much easier than philosophy. Ideology can relieve you of the entire burden of thinking. If you are a Republican or a Democrat, you can simply go and find out what Republicans and Democrats have to say about any proposal. Then, you do not have to think about it yourself. You already know your ideological identity, and so you have committed yourself from the start, from before the start – *a priori* – to whatever position taken by those who share your worldview. That is why, if you watch C-SPAN, and you watch so many (indeed most) up and down votes in the Senate, it is almost perfectly predictable that the senators will behave like human switches, like a wall of switches. Look at the yay and nay votes, almost invariably mapped out on party lines, with the exception of one or two who "break ranks" like a Joe Manchin or a John McCain. The most bizarre part is that these unimaginative businessmen and ideologues will then be called "mavericks" for simply not going all the way with their party each and every time, even though they may go with the party ninety-nine out of a hundred times. With ideology, it is so easy to be a maverick.

A more insidious way of using ideology is to go on a search for only those facts that support your already-existing worldview. People do this all the time, which we see with ecological questions and perhaps most odd in the US, with QAnon conspiracies and the pandemic. It is not hard to go on the Internet and keep on looking until you find the evidence you want to find. All this so-called confirmation bias is ideological, yet none of it is philosophical. There is an absolute minimum of thinking. Ideology at its zenith is post-philosophical. So much of what we see on the political field is pre-philosophical and anti-philosophical too. We are talking about the adoption and deployment of a *Weltanschauung*.

Marx, in *The German Ideology* and to a lesser extent in his very short "Theses on Feuerbach," expressed repulsion at what he regarded a kind of "in vogue" Hegelianism of his generation in Berlin in the 1840s. He was so repulsed that he lumped philosophy together, in a rather polemical and derogatory way, with ideology. Perhaps no one captured this culture and *Gemeingeist* better than Bakunin who described it so vividly in *Statism and Anarchy*.[2] It is perhaps hard to imagine. You go to Berlin and become a political radical; everyone around you is engrossed in discussions to all hours of the night about *Sittlichkeit* and the unique role of the German spirit in world history; young people are convinced that they are making history by participating in the great German intellect's development. Then, all you see around this café culture is human suffering in burgeoning nightmares of industrial capitalism. One could sympathize with Marx's repulsion. Whenever I read the accounts, I certainly do.

However, no one today lives in Berlin of the 1840s. Can you even imagine a society with a youth culture paralyzed by an obsession with Hegelian philosophy? Unthinkable! Today, our problem is not too much philosophy, but too little. To be perfectly clear, by "too little philosophy," I do not mean I want to see a new Hegelianism in vogue (although some philosophers would quite like that). Instead, I want to see more subversive questioning of – and direct challenges to – the truth and justice of the existing reality. That is what good philosophy has always done, going all the way back to Socrates's encounter with Thrasymachus in *Plato's Republic*. It is why Socrates was afraid to speak. Socrates did not want to affirm the existing reality, but rather, he sought to throw it into question. For

---

2   Michael Bakunin, *Statism and Anarchy*, trans. Marshall S. Shatz (Cambridge and New York: Cambridge University Press, 1994), 130-133.

that philosophical activity, he eventually became an enemy of the state, sentenced to death. The point I want to emphasize is that none of this is about reading or writing philosophy, but about throwing the world into question. We need more of *that* philosophy, and less ideology. The philosophical questioning that often comes into the world by way of social upheaval can potentially break the ideological warfare of politics. We have to be careful because there is always a temptation to interpret every upheaval through an ideological lens. We know that when Black Lives Matter revolts rocked Minneapolis and Ferguson (and the country and other parts of the world), there were plenty of commentators on the left and right who had their ideological explanations ready to roll out. Both the liberals and conservatives agreed, as they often do, that revolt is violent and irrational (unless aimed at Putin or some other proverbial bad man). Many liberals allowed themselves to say that Black revolt sent a great message, but that the method of communicating the message was bad. However, what if instead of teaching revolts we allowed them to teach us, to change us, to alter our understandings of the world. Unfortunately, people often resist philosophy, both inside and outside of classrooms.

Ideology has proven impervious to facts and events. It can survive anything. Everything else burned down, scorched to a cinder, ideology lies shiny and unscathed in the ashes and rubble. We have to destroy it, and that is precisely what Debord understood best. In the preface to the third French edition of *The Society of the Spectacle*, Debord says, "This book should be read bearing in mind that it was written with the deliberate intention of doing harm to spectacular society."[3] When Debord says that his central aim is to destroy the society of the spectacle, he means precisely that he wants to destroy a world ruled by a capitalist *Weltanschauung*. Debord understood that ideology does not float above the world, but rather, makes – *materializes* – a world of capitalist ideology. That is what he meant by the term "ideology in material form," which was also the title of his final Chapter IX of *The Society of the Spectacle*. The society of the spectacle is a society materially structured to embody and reflect the interests of a capitalist ruling class. Ideology may be their weapon, and I would like philosophy (as defined and discussed above) to be among one of ours. We do not have the great arsenal we need. However, our enemy has no real interest in philosophy, and I think that is because they know it would not

---

3   See the 1992 preface to *The Society of the Spectacle* (New York: Zone Books, 1999).

be their ally in the end. Moreover, we cannot fight a Gramscian war of position against those who have perfected the technological weaponry of ideology and foreclosed its discursive spaces. Whether or not we could have used ideology differently in the past, today it is a fatal form of stupidity in politics.

BG asks: One of my first questions has to be about the passage from your first book, *Unbounded Publics*, to your second, *Spectacular Capitalism*. They are very different books, yet there is also some continuity between them, perhaps "the continuity of discontinuity," to use Nishida Kitarō's wonderful phrase to speak about time.[4] One thing to notice is the presence of the neither/nor of transgression, as defined by you in *Unbounded Publics*, for instance, in relation to the ideologies of capitalism and bureaucratic socialism, to their spectacular character. As you say they work *a priori*, just like all ideologies.[5] Obviously, neither ideology is the answer to the question posed by Guy Debord's "practice of theory" and radical philosophy. This means that neither ideology is the answer to the question of truth. As you say in Chapter 4, "Truth is a matter of both theory and practice."[6] You continue saying that despite "Baudrillard's obfuscation on the subject, truth can be discerned, although never very easily, and never as a *purely theoretical* or as a *purely practical* matter."[7] And you add: "Truth is not *a priori* or *a posteriori*, for it is both…"[8] –both, or perhaps neither/nor. Can you say something about the relationship between *Unbounded Publics* and *Spectacular Capitalism*? Can you describe the process that brought you from one project to the other? After all, *Spectacular Capitalism* is all about the idea of transgression, which is a basic concept in *Unbounded Publics* as well. But there are many differences between the two projects. Can you address that?

RGO answers: We will discuss Jean Baudrillard more fully below, so for now, I will focus on your central question about the transition from and relation between *Unbounded Publics* and *Spectacular Capitalism*, and will elaborate on what I mean by "the practice of theory." The most obvious

---

4   Nishida Kitarō, *Ontology of Production: 3 Essays*, trans. William Haver (Durham and London: Duke University Press, 2012).
5   Gilman-Opalsky, *Spectacular Capitalism*, op. cit., 10.
6   Ibid., 114.
7   Ibid.
8   Ibid.

and perhaps even jarring difference between *Unbounded Publics* and *Spectacular Capitalism* is stylistic and structural. *Unbounded Publics* developed out of my Ph.D. dissertation at The New School for Social Research, and I did its research according to the formal expectations for a Ph.D. dissertation. I had always thought of it as a future book and was encouraged to think of it as such by several mentors. Therefore, after it was finished and defended as a dissertation, I reworked it significantly in an effort to make it more appealing to a general readership beyond my dissertation committee. One of the chief problems with *Unbounded Publics*, from my perspective today, is that it is by an author who did not yet have a voice. I wrote it, yes, but I was not yet a writer.

Up to that point, I had done some political and activist writing for various left-wing magazines and journals, but none of that was part of my theoretical work, which really began with *Unbounded Publics*. Even now, I would say that *Unbounded Publics* is the grounding for all of my theoretical work since, though when I wrote it I was in the early stages of becoming a writer. That is partly why I do not think *Unbounded Publics* would be a pleasure to read, and I scarcely recommend it. One of the immediate striking differences between that book and *Spectacular Capitalism* is that the latter is a very short book. Stylistically, *Spectacular Capitalism* is the first one written in the voice of the writer I am today. It is a creative book. For example, the last chapter is a détournement of Marx's "Theses on Feuerbach." It probably goes without saying that détournement would not have been an acceptable method for my dissertation committee. (As an aside, Bruno, one of the things I always loved about reading your books, is that they all bear the mark of a realized author with a developed and unique voice. That is not the case in my body of work.)

Nonetheless, the reason I regard *Unbounded Publics* as the grounding for all of my work to come is that, in it, I was already committed to theorizing a politics from below. That is, I was already committed to a concept of politics that pushes professional politicians and the ruling class far into the margins of thought, and centers a very different focus on those typically viewed as *outside* the domain of politics and power. *Unbounded Publics* was about thinking politics from below and about thinking of a politics insubordinate to nation-state framings of global affairs. I already wanted to think about the politics of other places, other ways of doing politics than through conventional modalities, and I wanted to think about a politics that could link up beyond nation-state framings because I was always convinced by Marx's early claim that the problems of capitalism are not obedient to national borders. I think *Unbounded Publics* establishes this very well, so for all of its faults and limitations, it enabled me to go on to deal with other modes of politics in other places in many different ways.

However, how does any of this lead to Guy Debord? It is not simply a clear straight line from Kant and Habermas to Debord! I should first say that *Spectacular Capitalism* stems largely (and quite independently) from my frustrations with both reading Debord and reading other peoples' readings of him. Debord was, for me at least, very difficult to understand. After a long time of failing to understand him, I discovered that the task was much easier after I had studied quite a bit of Hegel, Marx, and Lukács. Reading early Baudrillard and Lefebvre also helped. Debord is full of uncited and non-specific references to most of these thinkers and the theoretical discourses they spawned. I was never assigned Debord in any university class. I discovered his work in anarchist circles entirely outside the university, but in many ways, I could not understand him without the university. The university helped me to contextualize, approach, and ultimately comprehend Debord's project, even though it is undeniable that, in France in the 1960s, many young radicals and revolutionaries found inspiration in his work without Hegel, Marx, Lukács, or the university. I should perhaps be ashamed of the fact that I needed so much philosophy to get into Debord, though I am not too ashamed to confess it. I think, however, that Debord himself (and perhaps many of his early activist readers) did not fully appreciate how much philosophy he was doing, how serious his work was from a philosophical point of view that he did not want to take as his own.

Debord reminded me a bit of Marx who, in the preface to the first German edition of *Capital, Volume 1*, said: "With the exception of the section on the form of value, therefore, this volume cannot stand accused on the score of difficulty. I assume, of course, a reader who is willing to learn something new and therefore to think for himself."[9] This statement by Marx is demonstrably absurd and always makes me laugh. *Capital* has been the subject of diverse debates, multifarious interpretation, and wide-ranging misunderstandings since its publication, and by countless thoughtful

---

9   Karl Marx, *Capital, Volume 1*, trans. Ben Fowkes (London and New York: Penguin Books, 1982), 90.

readers. The fact that Marx could even suggest that it is not a difficult book to read (aside from one section, which he admits is a bit tough) shows how far removed he was from appreciating the complexity of his own work. Bakunin also observed this about Marx in *Statism and Anarchy* and, much to the surprise of Marx when they lived and argued together, Bakunin characterized Marx as an academic philosopher far away from the basic sensibilities of everyday people.[10] Marx knew, of course, that he was a doctor of philosophy, but could not quite see this. Debord was also engrossed in deep theoretical work, but perhaps like Marx, could possibly not appreciate the complexity, difficulty, and seriousness of his own writing. It is probably true that Middle School children could read Marx and Debord and get some powerful ideas out of the effort, but I wanted to help more fully appreciate in Debord what so many others have tried to help do with Marx. That is partly what I wanted to do in *Spectacular Capitalism*. However, as mentioned above, I was also frustrated with *readings of Debord*, which mostly treated him as a curious footnote to the events of the May-June 1968 rebellion in France, or only on aesthetic terms, almost as if we should only appreciate his work as a part of art history. To all of this, I wanted to scream "NO!" Debord's theory of the spectacle was profound, theoretically developed, and crucial to a good analysis of contemporary capitalist society... It still is! I wanted to bear out the relevance of Debord's theory for radical and revolutionary socialist philosophy and for *new* revolutionary thinking for the twenty-first century.

Finally, I shall say something about the practice of theory and the relation to *Unbounded Publics*. Debord was convinced that revolt and other disruptions, riots and uprisings, social movements engaging in creative, illegal actions of civil disobedience (or what is today often called "culture jamming") were modalities of theory in the world, which is to say, that all such upheaval directly questions and challenges the justice and reality of the existing world. I was and remain very drawn to the idea that – inasmuch as philosophy raises questions and challenges the justice and reality of the world – revolt does it better. This notion of ideas written and published by and in the uprisings of everyday people traces straight to my earlier interest in the example of the Zapatistas that was so crucial to *Unbounded Publics*. With the Zapatistas, I found an actual theorization of

---

10   See, for example, Michael Bakunin, *Statism and Anarchy*, trans. Marshall S. Shatz (Cambridge and New York: Cambridge University Press, 1994), 141-142.

the public sphere that came out of their uprising, a theory that was absent in the philosophical texts of public sphere theorists from Jürgen Habermas to Michael Warner. This is where you can see a seamless and even organic development from *Unbounded Publics* to *Spectacular Capitalism*. Aside from other differences, a central question in both books and one that remains for me now, is the question of who can do theory besides the theorists. Who does philosophy other than the philosophers, and from what other places and locations can revolutionary ideas spring up and alter understandings of the world and ourselves?

These central questions remain for me even now, and frame everything I do, including in *The Communism of Love*, where I am also looking for other locations for the theorization of communist forms of life than locations found in the books of socialist philosophers. Of course, it was no small point for me that Debord was himself not accepted as a philosopher by professional philosophers who ignored him and mostly continue to do so. Debord was never taken seriously enough as a great philosopher by philosophers, by even himself, when in fact he was. In a very clear way, then, and from the very start, with both *Unbounded Publics* and *Spectacular Capitalism*, I write books as a philosopher who ultimately wants to turn our attention away from the books of philosophers.

RGO asks: In the early chapters of *Earthly Plenitudes*, you begin to think about individuation and singularity in relation to human dignity and universal aspirations. This interest is sustained also in your later books, *Humanity and the Enemy* and *Singularities at the Threshold*. It is hard to resist reading you as a humanist, and more precisely, as a Marxist-humanist. Humanism is in the margins of a lot of Marxism. We can find Marxist-humanism in France in Jean-Paul Sartre and Maurice Merleau-Ponty, in German critical theory from Herbert Marcuse and Erich Fromm, and in the US from Raya Dunayevskaya and Peter McLaren, and also, variously, in C. L. R. James, Frantz Fanon, Eugene Kamenka, Paulo Freire, and others. You engage McLaren and Fanon and the Frankfurt School (and some others too), but it is safe to say that Marxist-humanists and Marxist-humanism do figure prominently in your work. I would like to know more about the relation of your philosophy to humanism? Do you or would you consider yourself a humanist? If not, why not?

BG answers: It is difficult to say whether I consider myself a humanist or not. I guess my most spontaneous answer would be "yes," but then it would have to be qualified. First of all, I resist accepting ready-made categories; and second, I have an eclectic approach to research and writing, which means that I never stay in one place only. The reason for this is that what I value most, more than the rigor, is the *agility* of thinking. I think this is important because it helps us avoid falling into stifled and ossified modalities, into narrow ideological and dogmatic positions. But to answer your question, let me begin by commenting on a view that strongly opposes humanism and Marxist-humanism. I am thinking of Louis Althusser's notion of Marx's theoretical, or philosophical, anti-humanism. Although there are many interesting points Althusser makes, I ultimately find them unconvincing. To begin with, I reject Althusser's claim of an epistemological break in Marx in 1845. From what I saw in *The Communism of Love*, you and I agree on that. No doubt, there is an evolution in Marx's thinking, but not to the point of completely abandoning problems and concepts that concerned him before, as Althusser claims. His new project of the critique of political economy that culminates with *Grundrisse* and *Capital*, does not have that meaning. For instance, he does not abandon his interest in the question of alienation, which is one of the main points made by Althusser, though he no longer insists on using the word. Marx's language and method do change profoundly, but I don't think that justifies the distinction between a humanist and scientific period in Marx to the extent described by Althusser, who refers to the concept of alienation as a "pre-Marxist ideological concept."[11] Perhaps one could say that it is Althusser himself who fetishizes science. His distinction between science and ideology is also problematic, and humanism is of course for him an ideology. This leads him to dismiss ethics, which is certainly central to any humanist approach to thinking. But, once again, I don't find his argument compelling. What I think is important in Althusser's discussion of Marxism and humanism is the idea that it is "impossible to *know* anything about men except on the absolute precondition that the philosophical (theoretical) myth of man is reduced to ashes."[12] This is central to his notion of Marx's theoretical anti-humanism, and it is related to his claim that in 1845, "Marx broke

---

11   Louis Althusser, "Marxism and Humanism," in *For Marx*, trans. Ben Brewster (London: Verso, 1990), 239.
12   Ibid., 229.

radically with every theory that based history and politics on an essence of man."¹³ However, these ideas do not necessarily have to yield a notion of anti-humanism, whatever that means. If one thinks of Jean-Paul Sartre's position on humanism, one can see that the real problem is that of positing or not positing the idea of the essence of 'man' (that is, the human being). However, if instead of a human essence, one thinks of the human condition, as Sartre does, then things are completely different. One can still think in humanistic terms without having to give science such a disproportionate role – also because science itself is an ideology. Below, I will go back to Sartre's thought, which was perhaps the main influence on me when, as a teenager, I started studying philosophy – and I still retain important elements of that influence.

Before doing that, I want to deal with another attack on the idea of humanism. I am thinking of Martin Heidegger's important "Letter on Humanism," a direct response to Sartre's *Existentialism is a Humanism*. What's important in Heidegger's essay is his critique and deconstruction of "the dominance of subjectivity,"¹⁴ "the modern metaphysics of subjectivity,"¹⁵ and I completely agree with that, as is shown in my *Singularities at the Threshold*. In a sense, Heidegger's critique of humanism is close to Althusser's critique. Heidegger says, "Every humanism is either grounded in a metaphysics or is itself made to be the ground of one."¹⁶ And he also goes into the problem of the essence of man. He also says, interestingly, almost (and without wanting to) explaining Althusser's meaning of *theoretical* anti-humanism, that the opposition to humanism "does not mean that such thinking aligns itself against the human and advocates the inhuman, that it promotes the inhumane and deprecates the dignity of man."¹⁷ Of course, this must be the case. And he adds, "Humanism is opposed because it does not set the *humanitas* of man high enough."¹⁸ Very well. We can take this again as a sign of the need to go from a discourse on the essence of man to one about the human condition, which is what Sartre's existentialism, in particular, with its reversal of the essence/existence paradigm,

---

13   Ibid., 227.
14   Martin Heidegger, "Letter on Humanism," in *Basic Writings*, ed. D.F. Krell (New York: Harper and Row, 1977), 198.
15   Ibid., 199.
16   Ibid., 202.
17   Ibid., 210.
18   Ibid.

accomplishes. Obviously, there is a huge difference between Heidegger and Althusser. For Althusser, we have a "real humanism" whose object is not "an abstract speculative "one, but "a real object."[19] For Heidegger, there is the idea that "Man is not the lord of beings."[20] I agree with both positions, and I think that they might reaffirm a humanism of some sort if cleansed of any essentialist attributes. To me, humanism is ultimately the thinking that the human animal has its specificity, its singularity, whereby a worldview is formed, for better or worse. With this also comes a responsibility, if you will, and we are on the terrain of ethics once again. So, humanism does not entail any notion of the superiority of the human form of life over other forms of life, but only an acknowledgement of its singularity, and there are many other singularities. However, history, politics, and ethics are human made. This remains true whether we think of ourselves as humanist, anti-humanist, post-humanist, and so on. What Sartre's philosophy still offers us is the paradox of freedom, in the sense that *we are condemned to be free*,[21] one of the best conceptualizations of freedom to my mind, and the political and ethical responsibility that comes with that. So, I think that any philosophy is bound to be a humanism of some sort; not a humancentrism, or anthropocentrism; but the limited and humble expression of our lifeform, among many other forms of life, yet with the capacity, to make an implicit reference to the 'early' Marx, of speaking universally. It is not really a question of speaking *for* the other, but rather of speaking *as if* we were the other, as indeed we are.

BG asks: Another very important, philosophical, moment in your *Spectacular Capitalism* is the distinction between the thing itself [i.e., capitalism/socialism] and the realm of the spectacle. You ask, "What is the difference between the thing itself and its spectacular form,"[22] for instance, the difference between real capitalism and spectacular capitalism.[23] Like in other places in your work, including *The Communism of Love*, I think there is here a Kantian philosophical framework. But you also use Marx, an interesting

---

19   Althusser, op. cit., 242.
20   Heidegger, op. cit., 221.
21   Jean-Paul Sartre, *Existentialism and Human Emotions*, trans. Bernard Frechtman (New York: Kensington Publishing Corp., 1958), 23.
22   Gilman-Opalsky, *Spectacular Capitalism*, op. cit., 18.
23   Ibid., 19.

quote from *The German Ideology*, and then you say, "We must cut through all of the ideological narration to the core meanings in order to find the things themselves."[24] I believe that this distinction – and philosophy is the science of distinctions – is perhaps the most important element in your book, one whereby the critique of ideology becomes the major task of the practice of theory. Can you tell us more about the importance of this distinction for you?

RGO answers: The connection to Kant is very important, not only in terms of the thing-in-itself, but in terms of Kant's political theory, which philosophers have not attended to as well. There is his most famous essay, "What is Enlightenment?" in which Kant argues for a kind of politics from below, where what he calls "the public use of reason" is essentially a near-totally free civic responsibility of public criticism. Kant is very clear to include everyday people in his conceptualization of politics when he specifies all taxpayers as "men of learning" on the subject of paying taxes, and he says that even though police officers can command obedience from everyday people, that people cannot be forbidden from criticizing laws and police.[25] He insists upon this freedom and ethical obligations of everyday people as a counterpower against despotic rule, but unlike Debord, Kant thinks only of textual (i.e., published articles) or oral (i.e., public speeches) argument. Those are the only modalities of the public use of reason that Kant advocates. His theory does not allow for strikes, insurrections, contentious forms of civil disobedience, or disruptive performative politics, because he maintains that competent citizens will know when is the appropriate time for public criticism, and that such a time must never conflict with the formal obligations of work or one's office.[26] The passive and compliant side is what Kant calls private use of reason, where a good citizen would keep her criticisms to herself (i.e., private).

I think it is very fair to say that Debord's basic theory of revolutionary praxis is essentially a radicalization of the public use of reason. Debord wants to abolish the spectacle, and wants to do so by a kind of illegalist and insurrectionary Kantian politics, although moving Kant in more

---

24   Ibid.
25   Immanuel Kant, "What is Enlightenment?" in *Kant's Political Writings*, trans. H.B. Nisbet (Cambridge, UK: Cambridge University Press, 1999), 55-56.
26   Ibid., 56.

disruptive directions, and against the law, also marks a break with Kant. Kant would have to reject Debord and Debord would have to reject Kant. At the end of *The Society of the Spectacle,* Debord writes that "a critique capable of surpassing the spectacle must know how to bide its time."[27] In "What is Enlightenment?" Kant says that while revolution may be fast, "a true reform in ways of thinking" takes time.[28] Both are talking about major social and political transformations by way of critique.

Debord writes, "Self-emancipation in our time is emancipation from the material bases of an inverted truth. This 'historic mission to establish truth in the world' can be carried out neither by the isolated individual nor by atomized and manipulated masses, but – only and always – by that class which is able to effect the dissolution of all classes, subjecting all power to the disalienating form of a realized democracy... It cannot be carried out... until dialogue has taken up arms to impose its own conditions upon the world."[29] Notice that Kant's theory is a bit more individualist, because he speaks of the "man of learning" and imagines a courageous soldier, clergyman, etc., while Debord directly disqualifies "isolated individuals." Moreover, another radicalization of Kant is in Debord's final line about the dialogue that takes up arms. What does dialogue take up arms against? Debord's answer, "an inverted truth." In the final analysis, then, Debord, much like Kant, wants a politics of epiphany, realization, and exposé. Debord's Situationist idea aims, in large part, at helping us see things as they really are. We should see how the spectacle of democracy is not democracy, how it is only an absurd spectacle of democracy, for example, to declare the ones with the fewest votes the winners. Deeper than that, only a spectacle of democracy declares as democratic the demos choosing one or another version of capitalist imperialism. Instead of this, Debord wants what he calls "realized democracy," which comes about only in the face of a powerful exposé and breakdown of the spectacle of democracy. People too often gloss over Debord's interest in "realized democracy," a term that appears in the final thesis of his book. However, we should not gloss over that, and we must note what he means by it. He juxtaposes "realized democracy" to "reformist compromises," and the former belongs for him to revolutionary praxis.[30]

---

27 Debord, *The Society of the Spectacle* (New York: Zone Books, 1999), thesis 220.
28 Kant, op. cit., 55 and 59-60.
29 Debord, op. cit., thesis 221.
30 Debord, op. cit., thesis 220.

We may connect Debord with Kant in several ways, and of course, you rightly note the difference between the thing-in-itself and its spectacular form. When we speak to people even today, roughly thirty-five years after the end of the Cold War, so many still talk about a spectacle form of communism, a spectacle form of socialism, a spectacle form of capitalism. All of these spectacles need to be exposed, abolished, and ultimately replaced with their actual historical, philosophical, and political meanings. When you and I think about communism together in this book, we are not thinking about its spectacle form. We are not thinking about huge government bureaucracy, Stalin, Mao, heads of state, rationing food or healthcare, long lines in Moscow to purchase blue jeans or peanut butter. In short, neither of us mean by the word and idea communism to refer to the ideological instrument of Cold War capitalists. For communists like us, it is perhaps even shocking that such a Cold War weapon is still operational in common discourse. After 9/11, a lot of us thought we were finally seeing the old villain of the bad communist replaced by the new villain of the terrorist. Alas, we have returned to the trusty old communist enemy rather quickly.

However, we do not use the word and idea communism – or communist – as if it were an insult or a simple synonym for an evil that was thought to have been exorcised by Ronal Reagan. When we speak of socialism, we similarly begin with its etymological and conceptual content, and then move on from there to the study of socialist philosophy and socialist literature, not with some ideological vilification inherited from the Red Scare.

The same goes for capitalism. It is not hard to find all manner of ideological discussion about capitalism where the word is deployed as a synonym for democracy or freedom. Angela Y. Davis wrote about this well in her *Abolition Democracy*.[31] According to its spectacle form, to be a capitalist means being free and democratic. That is not what actually existing capitalism is or does in the world. Its tendencies go in the opposite direction. We can study this in many places, from Kellee S. Tsai's study of China, *Capitalism without Democracy*, to global macroeconomic data, published each

---

31 Angela Y. Davis, *Abolition Democracy: Beyond Empires, Prisons, and Torture* (New York: Seven Stories Press, 2005).

year in UNDPs, by OXFAM, the EPI, and many other places.[32] In short, actual capitalism is very different from its spectacle form. According to its spectacle form, the ones who work the hardest get the biggest rewards. Meanwhile, according the EPI, the ones who work the longest hours doing the most exhausting forms of labor can often barely make ends meet and are far from receiving the biggest rewards. That is one way we can see the difference between real capitalism and spectacular capitalism.

Noam Chomsky has written much about "Really Existing Capitalism" or "REC." Chomsky defines "really existing capitalism" in order to distinguish "what really exists and what is called 'capitalism'... The term 'capitalism' is vague enough to cover many possibilities... It's worth bearing in mind the scale of the departures of 'really existing capitalism' from official 'free-market capitalism.' To mention only a few examples, in the past 20 years, the share of profits of the 200 largest enterprises has risen sharply, carrying forward the oligopolistic character of the US economy... The government insurance policy, which provides big banks with enormous advantages, has been roughly estimated by economists and the business press to be perhaps on the order of as much as $80 billion a year."[33] Chomsky is not a communist, Marxist, nor is he a revolutionary when it comes to politics, but these facts have never stopped him from helping his readers better understand what is really going on. Many important terms and concepts continue to circulate uncritically, without stopping to think about their actual meaning. How can people everywhere make so much conversation about freedom, democracy, capitalism, socialism, communism, etc., if it is so hard for any of the interlocutors to stop and offer a good definition of those terms?

I try the experiment often in my classes. Students talk about freedom and democracy for weeks, and then I stop them and ask them to define freedom. It is not so easy to do. The difficulty is not that my students are incapable of defining the terms. The problem is that we understand sentences full of terms like freedom, democracy, socialism, (and many others) only because we rely on and reproduce a highly ideological discourse. When you

---

32 See Kellee S. Tsai, *Capitalism without Democracy: The Private Sector in Contemporary China* (Ithaca and London: Cornell University Press, 2007). I cite several UNDP and EPI reports in *Spectacular Capitalism* for mainstream macroeconomic measures of democracy.
33 Noam Chomsky, "Can Civilization Survive 'Really Existing Capitalism'?" Truthout, October 1, 2014, https://chomsky.info/20141001/.

say "communism" people everywhere still think first about the Soviet Union, and the simple image they have of that – and particularly of Stalin. I am not an apologist for the Soviet Union. Any serious reading of my work makes that crystal clear. I am more interested in defending the concept of communism from its spectacle form, from deliberate vilification, and I want to criticize the capitalism that takes cover behind its own spectacle.

You are right to observe all this as the most important element of *Spectacular Capitalism*, in addition to the book's confrontation with the question of praxis. The radical critique of ideology is so crucial because it helps us grasp the actually existing reality, the world as it is, not as it appears through a particular *Weltanschauung*. It is in this way, precisely, that I claim Debord makes his key contribution to Marxism. Marx was also concerned about the ways that ideological interpretation could confuse or obscure the structure of reality, but he felt this was a good enough reason to avoid getting lost in the superstructures of the world like so many wayward Hegelians. Whereas today, materialists really must focus on the superstructures, because of the ways that the ideological clutter of spectacles conceal the actual world. We have to deal with that in order to carry out the still-necessary analyses and tasks of materialism. In his *Theses on Feuerbach* Marx famously said we could not change the world by merely interpreting it, but how much of the world is, at least insofar as we know it, the knowledge of a particular interpretation?

RGO asks: I will confess a certain discomfort with utilizing the philosophies of Heidegger and Schmitt for communist theorization. In *Earthly Plenitudes* you say that you "do not think that Heidegger's philosophy can be described as National Socialist in character."[34] Against Emmanuel Faye's claim that Heidegger taught his students Hitlerism, you write that "anyone who reads Heidegger seriously realizes how mistaken these charges are."[35] I am inclined to trust that you are right about that. I never read Hitlerism in Heidegger. Moreover, we can see from *Humanity and the Enemy* how fruitful it was for you to theorize from Schmitt's claim that humanity has no enemy. At the same time, of course, we know that Schmitt joined the Nazi Party in 1933 and supported the burning of books written by Jewish authors. As to

---

34 Bruno Gullì, *Earthly Plenitudes: A Study on Sovereignty and Labor* (Philadelphia: Temple University Press, 2010), 57.
35 Ibid.

Heidegger, for many years before the *Black Notebooks* were published in English, I read him in the directions of my own interests, particularly with regard to poetry and technology, if not so much with regard to being or *Dasein*. (To my thinking, it is even possible that poetry is intrinsically anti-fascist.) Therefore, I felt a certain pain at the prospect of abandoning Heidegger's work. While you grapple with Heidegger in Chapter 2 of *Earthly Plenitudes*, I am nonetheless left wondering about your decision to develop communist philosophy out of the works of men who did not reject the fascism of their time, something that other philosophers of their generation had the courage to do. As a communist philosopher myself, and as one who identifies the German Communist Party as the only serious rival to the Nazi Party in the institutional politics of the late Weimar Republic, I claim that communism (more definitively than poetry) is absolutely incompatible with fascism. Communism demands an incommensurate and antithetical logic, even deriving some of its core content from this total incompatibility. I *think* I want to suggest that your philosophical work can be carried out without Heidegger (or Schmitt), and that the anti-Semitism and Nazi affiliations of such philosophers are enough to warrant a complete break. I think you disagree. But, is it possible to deploy a philosopher like Heidegger for communist theory without establishing a certain compatibility between a Nazi philosopher and Marxist philosophy? I do not want to fall prey to a gross reduction here… But I perceive a political danger in this too, inasmuch as our class enemies on the right always associate Marxism with Nazism, as can be seen (among other places) in a recent slip by Bill Hemmer on Fox News, on August 8, 2021 when he stupidly claimed that Marx wrote *Mein Kampf*.[36]

BG answers: This is an interesting and complex question, and I agree with some of your points, including the idea that communism is "absolutely incompatible with fascism." Yet, I don't think that my use of the work of Martin Heidegger and, more recently Carl Schmitt, contradicts that claim. In general, my utilization of their work is part of my eclectic approach. However, more to the point, I think that it is important to know how one arrives at any given source, any thinker and work. I started engaging, in a very critical way, the work of Carl Schmitt (let me begin with him) when I began studying and writing on the question of sovereignty. I believe that it is impossible to speak about sovereignty without engaging his work, or

---

36 https://www.youtube.com/watch?v=3WNQz1Ln36U.

that of Thomas Hobbes, for that matter. Although I am critical of Schmitt, just as I am of Hobbes, I believe that both of them are very important and, in fact, great thinkers. As you point out, my engaging Schmitt's work proved fruitful in my discussion of the concept of the enemy, and in that context, I mainly dealt with his book *The Concept of the Political*. In relation to my study of the concept of sovereignty, it was his *Political Theology* that I found very important, and in *Earthly Plenitudes*, I read Schmitt against another Catholic thinker, Jacques Maritain, finding myself in agreement with the latter. I have returned to Schmitt over and over again, and I even teach him in my political philosophy class as a sequel to my session on Hobbes before moving on to other authors that allow me to engage in a deconstruction and theoretical deactivation of the sovereignty paradigm. Of course, I am aware of Schmitt's affiliation with the Nazi Party. Yet, this doesn't take away the lucidity of his analysis of the political, and there are arguments in his work, such as the critique of liberalism, with which one can even agree. My engagement of Heidegger's work is older. I have encountered his work not because I was looking for some reactionary, let alone Nazi, philosopher to read, but rather by way of reading Sartre and other thinkers that pointed to Heidegger as an important source to deal with. Additionally, that came about because of my general interest in the history of philosophy, phenomenology, existentialism, and so on, which goes back to when I was very young. Then, when I did my Master's in philosophy at San Francisco State University in the late 1980's and early 1990's, I wrote my thesis on Heidegger's interpretation of Nietzsche. I have utilized Heidegger's work in all of the four books I have written so far, and I imagine I will continue to do so, as I keep finding it inspirational.

Yet, I have at the same time always been critical of his thought, not because of any National Socialist tendency within it, of which I see no trace – and I consider Emmanuel Faye's claim completely false – but for other philosophical reasons. I haven't read the *Black Notebooks*, published, as you say, much later. Perhaps one day I will do so. However, I doubt that will change my appreciation of Heidegger's philosophical work. Of course, his joining the Nazi Party, his infamous rectoral address at Freiburg in 1933, and a few statements in support of the Nazi movement in *What Is Metaphysics?*, are horrible things. Yet, to break with Heidegger's thought on that account would be to participate in the *cancel culture* so popular nowadays, which is ultimately an expression of *ressentiment*, to refer to

Nietzsche's utilization of the concept. The same holds true for one's relation to the work of Carl Schmitt, I believe. So, I am not presenting a defense of Heidegger, certainly not of his shortsighted, to use a euphemism, political choices or his racial and cultural prejudice. But I defend our ability to read and appreciate the work of one of the greatest thinkers of the twentieth century. I do think that there is a certain compatibility between Heidegger's thought and Marxist philosophy. But I don't think of Heidegger as a *Nazi philosopher*; otherwise, I wouldn't read him.

Furthermore, I don't think there is a Nazi philosophy. There is a Nazi ideology, but that's different. In any case, in his work, Heidegger does not theorize a Nazi worldview or the Nazi state. In his lectures on Nietzsche of the late 1930's, for instance, he attacks the biologism typical of Nazi ideology. The fact that, as you put it, "our class enemies on the right always associate Marxism with Nazism" – an expression of their stupidity – shouldn't put us on the defensive and make us shrink at the philosophical level. This may be simplistic, but the difference between Nazism and Marxism, fascism and communism, is the difference between particularistic interests and universal aspirations. This is certainly an aspect of what distinguishes them, thereby distinguishing ideology from philosophy. But I want to say a word about poetry as well. I like your notion that poetry is possibly "intrinsically anti-fascist." I don't know if this is true. I hope it is. However, here we find the same problem we saw above. I believe that it would be very difficult to call *The Pisan Cantos* a work of fascist poetry. Yet we know of Ezra Pound's collaboration with Mussolini's regime. And we know he paid dearly for it. There are many other examples of this type. So, my thinking is that it is of course essential to make the proper distinctions – after all, philosophy is the science of distinctions; however, at the same time, it is also important to think without the constraints of ideology and try to see and hear what *justice* and *truth* demand.

BG asks: I would like to hear more about your critical, yet ultimately sympathetic, treatment of Jean Baudrillard. I have to say that I myself have dealt with some aspects of his theory in a perhaps unfair way. I'm thinking of my section on his book *The Mirror of Production* in my *Labor of Fire*. One thing that strikes me in your treatment of Baudrillard is your highlighting his positive moments, such as his critique of productivity and production. Yet, you also repeat that there are many other elements in his theory that can't simply be accepted, and your chapter title on him, "Selectively Forgetting Baudrillard," makes that clear. Indeed, you say that "if we read Baudrillard critically, his work can make us more critical, more analytical, less gullible, and less manipulable."[37] What I find particularly important in your critique of Baudrillard is the question of "fetishization of production."[38] This comes in a paragraph in which you say that Baudrillard, with his "position against all positions,"[39] "attacks any romanticization of the proletarian subject position, arguing that this leads to reification of capitalist production as an independent variable."[40] Again, I have never been convinced by Baudrillard's views in general, but I think this is very important and he may be right here. Obviously, the fetishization of production is not an argument against production as such, but rather against the logic of productivity, and thus capitalist production. Perhaps Baudrillard's idea that "[t]here is no longer a revolutionary subject" (from *The Mirror of Production*; quoted by you,) might at first strike us as too strong or even completely wrong.[41] However, one can ask the question as to whether any *subject* can be revolutionary (given that a subject always finds itself in a position of subjection), or whether perhaps the revolutionary impetus should rather be against the making of any subject whatsoever, or for its dissolution. Can you comment on this?

RGO answers: Sylvère Lotringer, who was a close friend of Baudrillard, reviewed that chapter of *Spectacular Capitalism* before the book's publication. Lotringer did not like the chapter because, he said, it was too critical of Baudrillard. Therefore, I find it interesting that you are able to see the way the chapter offers a deep appreciation of Baudrillard, which I was surprised that Lotringer did not see. I had always wanted to appreciate, albeit critically, Baudrillard with a close and serious attention many other philosophers would not give him. Although, looking back, it is possible that my exchange with Lotringer is part of the reason why I finally and more sharply clarified what I liked in Baudrillard's work. Keep in mind that Lotringer was almost single-handedly responsible for introducing

---

37 Gilman-Opalsky, *Spectacular Capitalism*, op. cit., 58.
38 Ibid., 39.
39 Ibid., 41.
40 Ibid., 39.
41 Ibid.

Baudrillard to English-reading scholars and activists by way of his Semiotext(e) Foreign Agents series, and that many of the Baudrillard books Lotringer helped to publish were full of introductions and interviews by Lotringer himself. Lotringer was not only a close friend of Baudrillard, but also perhaps the greatest champion of his work.

Lotringer felt it was too easy to criticize Baudrillard and that the time had come for us to evaluate Baudrillard's contributions to theory and to the understanding of present-day high-tech capitalist culture and society. I deeply agree with this. Reading Baudrillard is a bit like reading Nietzsche in that it is an experience full of encounters with more or less insight about society and culture. You occasionally get these moving little epiphanies that take hold of you and help you see and think about something you could not see and think about without that little aphorism or fragment of text. Lotringer told me that he preferred Franco "Bifo" Berardi's approach to Baudrillard, because Berardi claims Baudrillard's indispensable importance for understanding the impasses of ideology and difficulty of all political programs, no matter how radical or revolutionary. We may find this in many places in Berardi's work, but importantly towards the end of his *The Soul at Work*.[42] Both Berardi and Lotringer were also close friends of Félix Guattari who did not like Baudrillard. Berardi and Lotringer disagreed with Guattari on the importance of Baudrillard, and I think we still have a lot to learn from reading Baudrillard today.

In terms of theoretical insight, reading Baudrillard is not so different from the experience of reading Debord or Guattari, although of course, I criticize Baudrillard and substantiate a clear preference for Debord in *Spectacular Capitalism*. I would not attack Baudrillard in any categorical way. That seems to me an odd thing to do, although people like Douglas Kellner and Christopher Norris have come very close to doing that.

It may nonetheless appear as a curiosity that I would start a book on Debord with a chapter on Baudrillard. However, Baudrillard was, early on, very much a part of the French Situationist milieu, as can be seen in his early writing for the journal *Utopie*, articles recently republished in a single volume.[43] The *Utopie* group formed in 1966 around Henri Lefeb-

---

42 Franco "Bifo" Berardi, *The Soul at Work: From Alienation to Autonomy*, trans. Francesca Cadel and Giuseppina Mecchia (Los Angeles: Semiotext(e), 2009).

43 Jean Baudrillard, *Utopia Deferred: Writings from* Utopie *(1967-1978)*, trans. Stuart Kendall (Los Angeles: Semiotext(e), 2006).

vre, its central figure. The group was committed to an ultra-Left critique of architecture, urbanism, and everyday life. It was not until the 1980s that Baudrillard followed the direction of a total abandonment of politics. Therefore, I start with Baudrillard to mark paths for radical politics. Both Baudrillard and Debord were swimming in the same waters of French ultra-Left critical theory, but Baudrillard ultimately found politics dissuasive, and as could be seen in *Simulacra and Simulation*, he moved closer to an anti-political nihilism. One could argue that he became more Nietzschean, and thus, less of a leftist, less of a Marxist. Whereas Debord studied many of the same developments in capitalist society and culture, yet refused to abandon the concept of revolution. He wanted to confront the failures and the deferred utopia of revolutionary action without giving up a commitment to the absolute necessity of revolution. That is a crucial distinction, and for me, it is the right position.

In *Spectacular Capitalism*, I try to make it clear that a critical reading of Baudrillard must be selective in the way that one might make a critical reading of Nietzsche. A systemic critique of a thinker who does not systematize anything somewhat misses the point. It would be like telling Jackson Pollack that he does not color between the lines. However, what is the other side of this? Any attempt to make a critical (and political) reading of Baudrillard is immediately open to the charge of being "too simplistic." One can claim that Baudrillard's writing is too elusive for criticism, or like Marx's historical materialism, it always dodges the deathblows. My critique of Baudrillard does not want to be a deathblow. It aims to shift the ground back to some of the normative commitments of the ultra-Leftist and open Marxian traditions he came out of (which were clearer in his earlier works, like *The Mirror of Production, Symbolic Exchange and Death,* and *For a Political Economy of the Sign*). Baudrillard's critique of high-tech capitalism remains second-to-none, and to read him today, it almost appears prophetic. Berardi appreciates this especially.

In Lotringer and Kraus's Introduction to the *Hatred of Capitalism* book, Lotringer tells the story of Baudrillard's response to when he told Baudrillard the proposed name of that volume.[44] Baudrillard did not like the title, *Hatred of Capitalism* because, Lotringer says, it sounded

---

44 *Hatred of Capitalism: A Semiotext(e) Reader*, edited by Chris Kraus and Sylvère Lotringer (Los Angeles: Semiotext(e), 2001).

"old-fashioned" to him.[45] That gets to the heart of my first problem with Baudrillard, because even if we do not resuscitate the old ways of hating capitalism, the hatred of capitalism itself remains of central importance and should not make us bristle as if it were old-fashioned or outdated. Beyond this, in the abandonment of the political that characterized Baudrillard from the 1980s until his death, one could find recurring mockery of the political subject position. Thus, environmentalists, feminists, and other activists appeared to Baudrillard as misguided, sometimes a little cute, but always futile. To tell a French tale, whereas Camus took Sisyphus as a hero, Baudrillard may see him as a dunce. I want to reject precisely those aspects of Baudrillard because I think what we need more than theory are the active efforts of new abolitionists. Nonetheless, Baudrillard can aid and abet abolitionists, even if that was not his intention. He did give us a library full of powerful insights into capitalism that continues to cast light on what is happening.

Finally, to clarify one point in your question: While it is true that the words and ideas *subject* and *subjection* are connected, what I mean to invoke is the subject position of the ones who activate the direct questioning of the condition of their subjection. With regard to Zapatismo, we could speak of the indigenous subject position, and in Black Lives Matter, there is the subject position of those who question their ongoing subjection to white supremacy, racial profiling, and police brutality. I agree with you that the logic of revolution is ultimately abolitionist with regard to the making of any subject whatsoever, but real movement against subjection is rooted in the experience of subjection. Slave revolts make sense only in the context of slavery. We do not want slave revolts insofar as we do not want slavery, but as long as there is slavery, slave revolt is its indispensable other side. The revolt wants to abolish slavery, and that revolutionary desire for emancipation is shaped by the experience of its opposite, just as opposition to sexism and imperialism may be grounded in the experience of being subjected to both. Dangerous logics would not be so dangerous if they were merely logics hiding in the heads of capitalists, racists, sexists, etc. However, bad ideas really do organize human life because real programs, institutions, culture, and society materialize their logics variously in the world. A Marxist concern about subject positions capable of making history is not *for the sake* of making the subject, but for the sake of making history, or of making a new world.

---

45   Ibid., 15.

What we are after is the movement of subjects that seeks to abolish the conditions of their own subjection. Therefore, however tied to subjection, we still have to think about subject positions, collective action, and human agency, and it is precisely for that reason that I prefer Debord to Baudrillard.

RGO asks: Any student of your work will notice that you draw on Chinese philosophy in some crucial passages. Of particular interest are your connections with Laozi and Daoist philosophy in *Singularities at the Threshold*. There, for example, you say – following Daoist philosophy – that "the singular has no character of its own. It takes as its own the character of the common."[46] This is an important point for you because finding the common in singularity is your way of overcoming the dichotomous view of the individual versus the collective. I think that, originally out of India, Buddhism also overcomes that dichotomy (and many other dichotomies common in Western philosophy). Therefore, I want to ask you about the importance of Eastern religious thought and philosophy to your own work. This is, of course, not common within our milieu especially, and any serious discussion about your philosophy – I believe – should inquire about what we can learn from these traditions that we cannot find in Marx, Schmitt, Heidegger, critical theory, other forms of Marxism, etc.? Can you help us to understand this a bit more?

BG answers: My interest in Chinese philosophy, especially the Daoist tradition of Laozi and Zhuangzi, dates back to my university years in Italy when I studied and graduated in Chinese Language and Literature from the University of Venice. I particularly studied ancient Chinese, though I wrote my thesis on the *Honglou Meng*, translated into English as *The Dream of the Red Chamber*, an 18th century novel where the three main philosophical traditions of China: Confucianism, Daoism, and (imported) Buddhism, are brought together in a complex and synthetic fashion. I continued reading Laozi and Zhuangzi, as well as other Chinese thinkers, and I regularly teach Laozi, Confucius, and Buddha in my ancient philosophy classes. Usually, in the West, engagement with Daoism (or other Chinese philosophies) is limited to the context of writing within the field of sinology or comparative philosophy. This only accentuates a divide between East and West that must

---

46 Bruno Gullì, *Singularities at the Threshold: The Ontology of Unrest* (Lanham, MD: Lexington Books, 2020), 84.

be resolved. In fact, that type of engagement should be part of a global or cosmopolitan attitude defining any serious attempt at philosophical thinking, and it should become an integral part of the curriculum at any college and university. So, incorporating Daoist philosophy in my work – a thing I have particularly done in my latest book, as you notice – seems only natural to me. Perhaps I can also say that Daoism's versatility – and that is in keeping with its very substance and meaning – is such that it can enter into a fruitful dialogue with many other philosophies and traditions; with Marxism, for instance. As I mention in *Singularities at the Threshold*, there is an Italian philosopher, Giangiorgio Pasqualotto, who draws a parallel between Daoism and Gramsci, in particular between the Daoist theory and practice of the action of nonaction and Gramsci's concept of the war of position.[47] In any case, the possible ways to relate Daoism to communist and certainly anarchist thought are many. Let alone the many points of encounter between Daoism and Heidegger's thought. Obviously, implicit references to Daoism are today present in popular culture. Virtually anyone knows the meaning of *Qi*, vital energy, or *yin* and *yang*. Yet, this is not enough to bridge the gap among cultures, steeped in the unhealthy paradigm of sovereignty, nationalism, and continentalism. But we need to move towards a cosmopolitanism of contamination or, as Giacomo Marramao says, a universalism of difference.[48] So, what we can learn from utilizing Daoism or other non-Western philosophies is a way to exit a Western-centric model and consider the complexity of the world we share in a concrete way.

And I come to the passage from *Singularities at the Threshold* you quote above, "the singular has no character of its own. It takes as its own the character of the common." I think that your interpretation of this is correct. You say that this is my way of "overcoming the dichotomous view of the individual versus the collective." But it is also a way of addressing the Daoist philosophy of immanence and of interpreting the ineffable meaning of the Dao, the *Way*. The twofold structure of mystery and manifestation constituting Daoist immanence is of course similar to other immanent philosophies, for instance, the philosophy of Spinoza: *natura naturans* and *natura naturata*. The singular is the expression of the common; the common is contracted and expressed in the singular.

---

47   Ibid., 13.
48   Giacomo Marramao, *The Passage West: Philosophy after the End of the Nation State*, trans. Matteo Mandarini (London and New York: Verso, 2012).

Much of what I have said above about Daoism can be also applied to Buddhism, as you notice, especially the Zen (in Chinese, Chan) school, which is actually very close to Daoism. In both, we find the idea of the interconnectedness of all things in a cosmic and social sense, and so both are in line with a theory of trans-dividuality.[49] But I want to say a few more words about this. The fact that Chinese and other philosophies are usually not included and reviewed in works originating in the West is the result of what Sandro Mezzadra and Brett Neilson call *the pattern of the world* emerging from a "division of the world into different macroregions or areas."[50] This effectively marks the "rise of area studies," playing "a crucial role in a new *production* of the world."[51] Mezzadra and Neilson describe the "ontological moment of production connected with tracing borders." They say, "To be produced as the Rest (and to be constructed and excluded as its other), the non-Western world already had to be included in the West itself, in the hyperbolical moment in which both the West and the Rest (as well as the world itself) are produced."[52] We see here the logic of inclusion and exclusion in its particular mode of having something included as excluded. Continental blocs can be seen as "stubborn civilizational constructs" in a similar way in which nation-states are.[53] So, any activity or action that defies this *new pattern of the world*, from migration to labor struggles to all forms of resistance to domination, oppression, and exploitation, including writing as a form of resistance and revolt, can be seen as operating in the direction of the production of insurgent ontologies.

RGO asks: One of the most important achievements of *Singularities at the Threshold* is the way that you undermine the supposed divide between the individual and the collective (i.e., the one and the many), a divide which remains essential to both left-wing and right-wing political thought. On the left, the critique of neoliberalism is often a critique of individualism,

---

49 The term "trans-dividuality" is a variation on Gilbert Simondon's "transindividuality." I explain the reason for this modification in *Singularities at the Threshold* (2020). Essentially, the idea is that what we usually take to be an individual is in reality an assemblage (or gathering) of many dividuals and that the individual as such doesn't exist.
50 Sandro Mezzadra and Brett Neilson, *Border as Method, or the Multiplication of Labor* (Durham and London: Duke University Press, 2013), 38.
51 Ibid., 42.
52 Ibid., 35.
53 Ibid., 53.

or of the individual as the location of human freedoms and rights. On the right, all forms of thinking beyond the individual are often simply rejected as collectivist betrayals of individual freedoms and rights. Cutting off the legs of this paradigm, you argue that we must not choose between the one and the many in any such way. You think through singularities as nodal points of humanity, *distinguishable as nodal points*, and therefore, never autonomous from others, from the common. You write: "The common life is then asserted in an anti-individualistic and trans-dividual fashion. Singularities are not individuals in control of their own right, but assemblages of potency and confidence."[54] Singular human powers and aspirations are intimately connected to – even generated and defined by – trans-dividual human assemblages.

I find a similar effort to deal with singularity in existentialism. Sartre was accused by Marxists in the 1940s of focusing too much on the individual, of forgetting human solidarity, of essentially shifting the focus back to the one and his or her isolated individual interests. He responded to those criticisms in "The Humanism of Existentialism," and later, of course, became a committed Marxist for decades until his death. But I think Sartre never fully escaped the solipsistic danger of starting with the individual. Many of the fashionable existentialists of the 50s and 60s took the invitation to think about the meaning of their own lives and just stayed there. I think that you finally overcome this problem of Sartre wanting to move from individual to collective in the concept of singularity. Because in your theory, the one and the many are present from the start. Can you explain how you relate to existentialism on the question of the one and the many, or perhaps more broadly, how you relate to Sartre (especially vis-à-vis Heidegger) in your ontological theory?

BG answers: I agree with you about the persistence of the danger of solipsism in Sartre, and that is perhaps true of all existentialism. In Sartre, the danger of solipsism is certainly very evident in *Nausea*, a novel I read many times as a teenager, a great work of philosophy and literature, and my introduction to Sartre. However, *Nausea* is best understood as describing an experiment, and, given Sartre's philosophical connection to René Descartes, it is perhaps not too far-fetched to say that it is a similar experiment to that of the *Meditations*, where the building of methodic doubt happens

---

54 Gullì, *Singularities at the Threshold*, op. cit., 80.

in a totally solipsistic fashion. In Sartre, that danger is mitigated, in a very important way, by his two later concepts of *situation* and *singular universal*. In his plays, for instance, it is always the choice of the individual that will determine the outcome of a situation. But it is not a sovereign choice. Rather, the choice itself is based on Sartre's paradox of freedom and determined by the series of all previous determinations. Sartre's philosophy is often described as voluntarist. However, notwithstanding the importance he ascribes to the will, one's choice is still conditioned by the situation one finds themselves in to begin with. We are condemned to be free and we can't choose not to choose. In other words, there is *no exit* from freedom.

Here, the philosophical legacy is not Descartes's philosophy, but the thought of Blaise Pascal, the wager. To my mind, there is no better conceptualization of the complication that freedom is *in* and *for* the human condition than the one we find in Sartre. So, by choosing (or choosing not to choose), I am not simply affirming myself as an individual; rather, I surpass my individuality and move onto the ontologically deeper plane of the singular. This is a dangerous and cursed territory, where my existence approximates my eventual and ultimate essence. This is shown very well by Sartre in his biographical approach, based on existential psychoanalysis, to writers such as Jean Genet and Gustave Flaubert. It is here that we encounter the concept of the singular universal, which, once again, goes very much beyond the limits of individuality. So, Sartre never settles for the isolated individual. In fact, the individual is never isolated; or rather, the individual as such never *is*. For instance, in his short, and claustrophobic, story "The Room," we realize that what seems to be a tragic and *no-exit* isolation is really part of a larger reality determining the specificity, if not the singularity, of the situation at hand. So, the one and the many are always co-present. And I think that Sartre's main ontological figure is not that of the individual ("barely an individual," to quote from Sartre's epigraph to *Nausea* drawn from a play by Louis-Ferdinand Céline, not included in the English translation), but rather that of the singular. When Sartre connects the singular to the universal, he is not connecting two opposite concepts. Indeed, the singular has no opposite insofar as the plural and the common are constitutive of the singular, not opposed to it.

Singularities, as you note, are not particulars (opposed to universals) but assemblages. Yet, the concept of singular universal has its merits, too. Perhaps the main issue here is to understand the very universality of the singular universal, and I will say more about the problem of universality, or the universal, when I answer your next question. For now, I can say that this universality in Sartre closely relates to Kant's version of universality in his formulation of the categorical imperative. That formulation says that we have to act in such a way that we always will that the maxim (the reason or drive) of our actions can become a universal law. In Sartre's existential ontology, "at every moment I'm obliged to perform exemplary acts. For every man, everything happens as if all mankind had its eyes fixed on him and were guiding itself by what he does."[55] Sartre says this speaking of Abraham and his choice to sacrifice Isaac – though the sacrifice is in the end called off by God – and he refers to Kierkegaard's masterful discussion of this in *Fear and Trembling*. The singular is universal insofar as it establishes a paradigmatic example. But we can say that this is inherent in the very concept of the singular. The singular is a *this* like no other, and yet any other is equally a *this*. What I mean to say is that the singular cannot be particular, but it is always universal. Perhaps we could say that the singular expresses the common and, at the same time, announces the universal.

You ask how I relate to existentialism on the question of the one and the many. To answer this, it might be good to look a bit further at Sartre's essay on existentialism. Sartre's philosophy remains within the paradigm of subjectivity, which I reject, and arrives at a world of (Hegelian) intersubjectivity, which I think should be replaced by the concept and reality of trans-dividuality. Yet, Sartre's subjectivity is "not a strictly individual subjectivity."[56] He says that this is so because "one discovers in the *cogito* not only himself, but others as well."[57] And the relationship between the self and the other, the subject and the object, the subject that becomes an object and the object that becomes a subject through the gaze, is crucial in *Being and Nothingness*. We certainly have here a problematization of the relation between the one and the many. We find the concept of the other. But all happens within the Hegelian model of recognition; thus, intersubjectivity. As Sartre says, "The other is indispensable to my own existence, as well as to my knowledge about myself."[58] This is true, but it is not, let's say, the whole truth. Indeed, the

---

55   Sartre, op. cit., 20.
56   Ibid., 37.
57   Ibid.
58   Ibid., 38.

other – and I myself am the other, another, many others – plays a much more important ontological role in the production of what I (perhaps) am. So, it is not simply a question of this neatly defined intersubjective situation: the self and the other; the other and the self. It is much more complex, and perhaps 'messier' than that. Sartre comes close to this when he says that "a man is nothing else than a series of undertakings… the sum, the organization, the ensemble of the relationships which make up these undertakings."[59] Here we see something closer to the ideas of assemblage and the gathering of dividuals. The fact that existence, as standing out, precedes essence – the tenet of Sartre's existentialism – doesn't mean that an isolated and sovereign individual chooses and acts any way he wants, and thus makes himself. Sartre stresses that to choose is to invent, and it is here that for Sartre, in a quasi-Nietzschean fashion, art and ethics come together: "we have creation and invention in both cases."[60] But to invent is to find out, and one finds out, discovers, by searching. This search is an act of erring, in the sense of wandering, and of gathering, in wandering, whatever one can. This is another way of describing the existential anguish or anxiety that necessarily accompanies the contingency of invention, creation, and choice, starting from the nothing that, according to Sartre, the human being is to begin with. My singularity, rather than subjectivity, is not the result of a sovereign act and a sovereign choice. Rather it is the immanent reflection (similar to the "internal resonance" of Gilbert Simondon) of an unfinished, and unfinishable, process of individuation. It is perhaps only in this sense that I can relate to existentialism as the rejection of any pre-established essence or principle.

RGO asks: In *Humanity and the Enemy*, you identify a logic of universality in the end of exploitation and oppression as follows: "I think it is very easy to show that if it might be 'good for' X to oppress and exploit Y, the end of oppression and exploitation is not simply good for Y, but it is a universal good… Thus, the end of oppression and exploitation is to be held as a good in itself, as a universal good."[61] I deeply appreciate the courage with which

---

59 Ibid., 33.
60 Ibid., 43.
61 Bruno Gullì, *Humanity and the Enemy: How Ethics Can Rid Politics of Violence* (New York: Palgrave MacMillan, 2014), 73.

you speak of universals, especially as we are both philosophers who study and appreciate postmodern trajectories of philosophy and French and Italian critical theory. You speak of "universal good" not only with regard to oppression and exploitation but also with regard to dignity and singularity elsewhere. Philosophically and politically, what is the importance of insisting upon universalities such as these? What are some of the present and pressing dangers of refusing such universalities?

BG answers: The passage you quote in your question is from Chapter 2 of *Humanity and the Enemy*, "The Ethical Obligation to Disobey and Resist," which presents a reading of Martin Luther King's "Letter from a Birmingham Jail" and Sophocles's *Antigone*. That comes after a discussion of Kant's ethical theory at the end of Chapter 1 of *Humanity and the Enemy* – a chapter which also includes a discussion of Thomas Hobbes's and Carl Schmitt's theories of sovereignty. In Kant, King, and Sophocles, the question of universality is fundamental. For instance, as I say in *Humanity and the Enemy* speaking of Martin Luther King's "Letter," we are dealing with "a sort of *grammar* of the ethical," which is by definition universal.[62]

But let me start with your final question: What are the dangers of rejecting the concept of the universal and universalities? Obviously, the concept of the universal is suspect to many, and the concept of humanity is a case in point, so I will go back to it. However, I want to say that this suspicion, which has its reasons, is ultimately unfounded, or, at least, that having a critical approach to the question of universals should not end in a total rejection of them. One reason whereby we can be critical of the universal is that it does lead to forms of essentialism; for instance, a universal human nature. However, one should not fall into the opposite and paradoxical mistake of anti-essentialist essentialisms, that is, of essentializing anti-essentialist positions, as it often happens, for instance, with the politics of identity. Furthermore, while there is no human nature, and I agree with Sartre (and of course many others) on this, there is a human condition, and that is universal as well as common.

I want to say something about the question of the universal and the common. As I mention above, the common is expressed in and by the singular. Both the common and the singular are strong ontological concepts. Perhaps the same does not hold true of the universal. For instance,

---

62   Ibid., 51.

for John Duns Scotus, the concept of being is the most common, not the most universal (for, it seems to me, the universal cannot have degrees of more or less) and it is contracted and thus expressed in any thisness, haecceity, or singularity. But any singularity, as the most concrete expression of the common, also contracts within itself many other commonalities (in addition to the concept of being), and thus is, to use the expression by Jean-Luc Nancy, a *singular plural*.[63] This is different from Sartre's singular universal, which is still based on the ontology of the singular but becomes paradigmatic, and thus formal, in its universality, leaving the terrain of ontology proper. Perhaps we can say that it acquires an ethical (in the Kantian sense) certainly logical, and even epistemological value. Without going deep into the question of realism versus nominalism, I think it is safe to maintain the reality of a universal concept as a being of reason (*ens rationis,*) as Thomas Aquinas, John Duns Scotus and other moderate realists say. In this sense, the reality of the universal is different from the ontological reality of the singular (always constituted by pluralities) and the common. The universal is a form, not in Plato's sense, namely, not as actually existing (as a *really real* entity) in a separate sphere or world, and also not found *in rerum natura* (in the nature of things). It is rather an example and a paradigm. Numbers, for instance, are universals. As such, the universal has its usefulness, if used with caution.

We see such usefulness in Kant's ethical theory. Let's consider Kant's formulation of the categorical imperative: "Act only according to the maxim whereby you can at the same time will that it should become a universal law."[64] This is quite something, for it presents an existential trajectory, perhaps a schematism that seems at first sight to go from the concrete to the abstract, from the particular to the universal. However, the direction is perhaps the opposite; perhaps one starts from the abstract and universal (the maxim) in order to act, to enact one's own concrete and particular action, whereby announcing a universal law. My action is always concrete and particular, but my motives may (and, for Kant, should) be in the order of the universal, and thus abstract. It is in this sense that, as I have said above, there is something epistemological about this. We are speaking

---

63 Jean-Luc Nancy, *Being Singular Plural*, trans. Robert D. Richardson and Anne E. O'Byrne (Stanford, CA: Stanford University Press, 2000).
64 Immanuel Kant, *Grounding for the Metaphysics of Morals*, trans. James W. Ellington (Indianapolis: Hackett, 1981), 30.

about universal values, which – and that's the real danger – can also be, as they often are, ideologically easily manipulated and instrumentalized. It seems to me that here one does not arrive at universal values, but one starts from them, from a mindset, or mental disposition.

Let's consider the concept of equality. At the level of the concrete, of the singular and common, there is no equality to begin with. At that level, equality cannot be a point of departure, as is often wrongly held, but a point of arrival. Structures and institutions must be built for equality, or fairness, to obtain. However, one does not arrive, in the same way as one does with the concrete, at the universal concept of equality, which, to be sure, does not exist, and cannot exist, as such in the real world. That universal is only a mental disposition (and an aspiration) within the realm of the abstract. Yet, without such a disposition (and even desire, if you will), how can anything be brought about that might improve the human condition, promote social justice, help resolve conflict and avoid war, intervene with degrees of wisdom and efficacy in the many increasingly grave environmental issues, and so on? The question, of course, is that of the type of mental disposition we are talking about. Prejudice, for instance, is also a mental disposition. So, to go back to your question about my statement in *Humanity and the Enemy* on the universal good, I'd like to say that the way to understand this is by educating ourselves. This is what education is for. I don't need to experience a particular form of injustice in order to know that injustice is wrong. I think that realities like those of racism, genderism, ableism, hatred, and so on, before being forms of aberration at the political, social, and cultural level, are wrong from the logical and epistemological point of view. I don't think that anyone could ever make a compelling argument about the adequacy of a supremacist theory, of oppression, domination, exploitation, and so on. So, an important part of our revolutionary task, particularly as intellectuals and educators, is to show the emptiness and illogicality of positions that end up yielding disfigured and pitiful forms of the singular – a singular detached from the common and subservient to whatever particularistic and ideological interests we might think of.

The question ultimately has to do with the properties of thinking. I know many people might object, "Who are you to say what's the proper and improper way to think?" I would reply, "Look, it's not me; rather, it is those properties themselves pointing out the way," and I would dismiss their objection as uninteresting, ridiculous, and irrelevant. We often hear the platitude that everybody is entitled to their opinion, and I think this is one of the greatest stupidities people keep repeating. Of course, if I want to say that 2 + 2 equals 5, I'm 'free' to say that, but it would be nonsensical and wrong. 'I have the right to think, say, or do whatever I want' is something that obviously must be corrected. As Spinoza nicely puts it in Chapter 4 of *Political Treatise*, "If, for example, I say that I have the right to do whatever I like with this table, I am hardly likely to mean that I have the right to make this table eat grass."[65] The fact is that truth (reality or perfection for Spinoza,) however problematic this might be, is not a matter of entitlement. So, very often opposite positions, or opinions, about what *seems to be* the same issue are not equally valid. Take the issue of abortion. It is not the case that opinions are split between those who are in favor of or against it, pro-choice or – whatever that means – pro-life. In reality, the former address women's right to have an abortion, to determine their life, without imposing anything on anyone; the latter want to impose their view on all women and all society. The same logical problem (before being a political one) happens with similar issues, such as same-sex relationships, and so on. Obviously, the right to engage in same-sex relationships doesn't imply the idea that everyone has to do so; however, the denial of that right means the imposition of a narrow-minded and impoverished view about love, human relationships, and so on, on everybody – to the point, as is still true in many parts of the world, that some sexual activities and life-styles are criminalized.

Thus, the real issue is that of imposing or not imposing one's worldviews (which are often very narrow-minded and backwards) on others. It is a question of freedom, not in the liberal sense, but in the sense formulated by Niccolò Machiavelli in one of his greatest passages in both *The Prince* and *The Discourses on Livy*. Machiavelli says that what distinguishes the elite from the people is that "the elite have a desire to dominate, while the people only have a desire not to be dominated" and are consequently closer to freedom.[66] I might add that they are also closer to the universal and common.

RGO asks: You make your crucial distinction between "productive" and "living" labor in *Labor of Fire*. This is the distinction between what we do

---

65 Baruch Spinoza, *Political Treatise*, in *Complete Works*, trans. Samuel Shirley (Indianapolis and Cambridge, Hackett Publishing Company, 2002), 697.
66 Niccolò Machiavelli, *The Prince and the Discourses* (New York: Random House, 1950), 122.

for money, on the one hand, and what we do as meaning-making beings, on the other. In our capitalist societies, the only labor that is recognized as such is productive labor, which is another way to say that capitalist work is more about *having* than *being*. However, you speak of that labor which is *neither-productive-nor-unproductive* in order to emancipate labor from the capitalist mode of production. Within that context, I am interested in the status of writing, or more specifically, *writing theory*. Inasmuch as a writer *becomes* a writer by writing, she is involved in a living labor regardless of whether or not she is paid to write (and if she is a philosopher, she is not paid to write). This aligns with Marx's ontological critique of capitalist labor from 1844. It seems to me that philosophy and the writing of theory are undertaken only insofar as capital allows them, which is to say that theoretical/philosophical research is mainly done by professors or by those who can satisfy their necessities by other means. I want to know if writing (and we may add reading) theory and philosophy (in short, our common terrain) is a rare luxury? Who may be a writer, a theorist? What are the uses of theory?

BG answers: Let me begin with the concepts of time and space. Both time and space, in our daily lives, are occupied by the logic of capital, they are sequestered and nullified by it, or rather, they are put to productive use or derided as unproductive. This is why the neutral mode of labor as neither-productive-nor-unproductive yields important revolutionary results at the theoretical and, hopefully, practical level. Writing (indeed, reading *and* writing, *and* thinking) is like dynamite in this context. Writing (but again, the same goes for reading and thinking) opens up new spaces and new times, different spaces and different times. Michel Foucault calls these different spaces and different times heterotopias and heterochronias. Interestingly, one example he provides for both modalities is the cemetery, where one can see the "loss of life" and the "quasi eternity in which [an individual] dissolves and fades away."[67] There must here be an exit, just like in the case of the mirror, where "I discover myself absent at the place where I am."[68] Above, I spoke about alienation. However, here we have a different situation. Here, it is no longer a question of alienation, but

---

67   Michel Foucault, "Different Spaces." In *Essential Works of Foucault, 1954-1984: Volume 2: Aesthetics, Method, and Epistemology*, trans. Robert Hurley and Others (New York: The New Press, 1998), 182.
68   Ibid., 179.

rather one in which, precisely, the condition (and danger) of alienation is neutralized. "I discover myself absent at the place where I am," Foucault continues, "since I see myself over there."[69] And perhaps I really am over there, in the mirror, the quasi eternity, and the loss of life. I dissolve and fade away, and the possibility of doing anything other than that which is dictated by capital becomes apparent. The life I lose is the one in which I experienced, as Marx says, "the loss of [my] own self."[70] Now, I lose myself in thinking, reading, or writing. A different time and a different space, yet not one of alienation or solipsism (to connect to a later question); rather, it is one of recomposition, play, and neutrality.

Perhaps it is the closest I can get to the ontological (anarchic) agitation of doing and making, gathering and bringing forth, outside the capture of capital or any other idiotic system of oppression and domination, servitude and control. Is this "a rare luxury," as you ask? My answer would have to be, yes and no. Anyone can be a writer or theorist. We know from history of people who wrote and theorized in conditions that may not be ideal from the viewpoint of comfort – the comfort we may find, for instance, in the academy and that very often leads to very mediocre works, often done for reasons external to the essence of writing, such as getting tenure, promotion, and so on. But when there is a genuine impulse, indeed a need, for writing and theorizing, the situation is different. The name of Antonio Gramsci comes to mind, who wrote his *Prison Notebooks* in a fascist prison. But there are many others who produced important works from prison, during revolutionary struggles and wars, or in other perhaps not ideal situations. So, the question is finding or not finding access to the heterotopian and heterochronian dimension, an access denied to many. The reasons for this denial are of course various, but they fundamentally revolve around the fact that time itself is taken away from people, space is taken away, and so are potentialities (capabilities). We enter a mode of servitude, of which the logic of debt is a clear illustration. In servitude, it is easy to give up one's desires and aspirations, at least for a time. However, as Frédéric Lordon has, I think, convincingly shown, servitude is never voluntary, but always passionate.[71]

---

69 Ibid.
70 Karl Marx, "Economic and Philosophical Manuscripts," in *Selected Writings*, trans. Lawrence H. Simon (Indianapolis: Hackett, 1994), 62.
71 See Frédéric Lordon, *Willing Slaves of Capital: Spinoza and Marx on Desire*, trans. Gabriel Ash (London and New York: Verso, 2014).

Fear is one of the fundamental human passions. It must be confronted and overcome in order to regain access to another time and another space. But perhaps, as Hegel says, this has to be a special type of fear, "not of this or that particular thing or just at odd moments," but rather "the fear of death." It must be experienced as "the absolute melting-away of everything stable."[72] It is here that things break down, a crisis occurs, and critical thinking begins. Here writing can begin, not for the sake of fame, money, or success, for that's not authentic writing, but a phenomenon of the spectacle (in the modern, capitalist sense of the word highlighted by Guy Debord). Writing is not a spectacle; it is not seeing, or understanding; rather, just like philosophy (or, better, thinking), it starts from *not* seeing and *not* understanding. Writing is always a kind of creative, artistic work; it is a process through which one can get a glimpse of the singular and common – a constant individuating process.

This is interesting because you ask about "the uses of theory," and the etymology of the word 'theory' goes back, precisely, to our ability to see, to look at, and so on. However, this has always to be understood as an effort, a constant effort. And furthermore, it has to do with the senses and is thus esthetic in its essential character. So, what are the uses of theory? Perhaps the ability to see what's on the other side, in the mirror, at the threshold. I reject the separation between theory and praxis. So, I don't see theory as a solely mental exercise. Theory, as many in the field of critical theory have said, is *embodied*, however problematic this term might be. But here I'd like to refer to a wonderful passage by Marx in the *Manuscripts of 1844*, a work you also mention in your question. There, Marx speaks of *the emancipation of the senses*. For Marx, the emancipation of the senses is the direct result of the overcoming of private property, thus of the servitude of exchange value, of oppression and exploitation. He says that the senses "become *theoreticians* immediately in their *praxis*."[73] Perhaps there is now a different seeing, different time and space, different dwelling and inhabiting – an essential difference, a singularity, which is neither-productive-nor-unproductive, but living and explosive.

---

72   Georg Wilhelm Friedrich Hegel, *Phenomenology of Spirit*, trans. A.V. Miller (Oxford University Press, 1977), 117.
73   Marx, "Economic and Philosophical Manuscripts," op. cit., 74.

BG asks: Your book *Precarious Communism* is "a particular autonomist manifesto,"[74] is "a communist détournement."[75] I particularly like your use of "détournement as a philosophical methodology."[76] In a sense, this goes back to the question about the difference between ideology and philosophy, but even within the philosophical orientation itself, it does open up a new path of inquiry, a new twofold movement of destruction and construction. Thus, you distinguish "détournement as a philosophical methodology" from other methodologies, notably, those of "immanent critique" and "deconstruction."[77] You say that differently from the specific aims and tasks of immanent critique and deconstruction, "Détournement is interested in making texts speak against and beyond themselves, so that they say what must (or could and should) be said."[78] In a sense, I hope, this is what we are doing with our own respective work. Indeed, what must be said now?

RGO answers: I like the method of détournement because much of what we need philosophically, politically, artistically, is already out there in some form or another, but we must redirect or hijack and re-route it to address new situations. Détournement does not pretend to create anything from scratch. It recognizes and accounts for available materials and goes from there. It is a method that asks what we can do in the situation we face. Admittedly, there is something opportunistic and perhaps even desperate about détournement, which is what Debord and the Situationists comprehended. Not all opportunism is a kind to condemn. Rosa Luxemburg condemned the opportunism of Eduard Bernstein. In "Reform or Revolution," she attacked "the opportunist method" of Bernstein's evolutionary socialism.[79] Because Bernstein was trading Marx's concept of revolution for the concept of evolution, where socialists would try to make capitalism more socialistic over time, she felt that his idea was an abandonment of revolution and an unprincipled betrayal of Marx masquerading as Marxism. I

---

74   Richard Gilman-Opalsky, *Precarious Communism: Manifest Mutations, Manifesto Detourned* (New York: Minor Compositions, 2014), 1.
75   Ibid., 3.
76   Ibid., 6.
77   Ibid., 7.
78   Ibid., 10.
79   Rosa Luxemburg, "Reform or Revolution" in *Socialism or Barbarism: Selected Writings* (London and New York: Pluto Press, 2010), 50-51.

think she was right to condemn opportunism in that case. However, there is another opportunism that recognizes the real desperation of the situation and says that we should look for opportunities to get out a certain point of view or analysis, to seize our moments when we can. This is what détournement relies on, and it is what Debord and the Situationist International proposed in the 1957 "Report on the Construction of Situations," but it was not a reformist opportunism.[80] The whole idea for Debord at the time was precisely not to give up on revolution, but to find other ways to get it going, to seize opportunities to get out the revolutionary point of view, to spurn on or defend revolutionary activity.

Now, *Precarious Communism* detours *The Communist Manifesto*, and it is a détournement of a kindred kind. My idea was to acknowledge that much of what we need is already there inside of that single short text, but that we must make it speak beyond itself, to extend or revise certain ideas so that we can account for some of the major historical and political shifts of the last 170 years. The key term there is "some of the major" shifts, because I obviously could not set out to deal with everything of significance since the 1848 manifesto. I wanted my détournement to be similar in scope and length to the original manifesto, admitting of course that I could not do anything better than – or even close to – such a brilliant text. This point is important because I was by no means trying to improve the manifesto, just to think with it and beyond it in some ways that may be helpful to those of us who want to think about a twenty-first century communism. If the book has a virtue, I hope it is precisely that it offers a small contribution to those of us thinking about what communism means today.

I agree with you that what we are doing in this book is also a peculiar kind of détournement. We are trying to turn our own thinking, which added together makes up more than 40 years of thinking (about 20 or so years of your thinking plus about 20 or so of mine), and each of us has thought very separately until now. This is the maiden voyage of our co-thinking and co-authoring theory, but we are not trying to write entirely from scratch. At the same time, with détournement, one does create something new, something that was not already there. If a culture jamming activist climbs up a billboard scaffolding and detourns the advertisement to make

---

80 See Guy Debord, "Report on the Construction of Situations" in *Situationist International Anthology*, trans. Ken Knabb (Berkeley: Bureau of Public Secrets, 2006), 25-46.

it say something against itself, the detourned message is a new one. It is using materials at hand, yes, but détournement generates a new message. We try to say what needs to be said.

Now, to your central question of what needs to be said right now. I think we should turn our attentions and our work more resolutely to white supremacy, gender politics, ecology, and the evolving form and content of global social movements. I do acknowledge, Bruno, that you and I have both always attended to these issues. Indeed, the final paragraph of *Precarious Communism* draws special attention to racial profiling and police brutality; the book was published in 2014, the year of Michael Brown's murder in Ferguson, MO, and the first major phase of the Black Lives Matter movement. I would also add that I always write as a feminist. Nonetheless, I think both of us have dealt with these issues a bit more in the sidecars of our journey, addressing them along the way, and not with the kind of centralization one finds in the work of Angela Y. Davis, Noel Ignatiev, or Ruth Wilson Gilmore. Davis, for example, defines every concept, even the basic meaning of democracy, in an encounter with racism. For Davis, to think about democracy is to think about the abolition of slavery and Black peoples' struggles from that historical point on, following the lead of W. E. B. Du Bois in *Black Reconstruction*.[81] I am reluctant to speak for both of us, but you and I do nothing quite like that. We arrive at such questions from very different starting points, for example, from German and French philosophy, Continental critical theory, and of course, always grounded variously in Marx and Marxism.

Davis, Ignatiev, and Gilmore are also Marxists, but they always begin by thinking about the position of the impoverished, imprisoned, and marginalized, and for them, philosophy is often in the sidecar.[82] I think we

---

81 See Angela Y. Davis, *Abolition Democracy: Beyond Empire, Prisons, and Torture* (New York: Seven Stories Press, 2005), 91.

82 This characterization is a bit tricky, and not intended as a rigid categorization. Gilmore does not so openly and consistently identify as Marxist as do Davis and Ignatiev, although Marxism is also Gilmore's basic milieu. Moreover, Davis is indeed a full-fledged philosopher, although her writing tends to be more in the world of radical politics and activism. I am only trying to highlight that there is a very different center of gravity and thematic attention there. Reading those authors is an experience of learning about historical and present struggles, with a keenness to maintain theoretical sophistication, whereas reading us is more an experience of reading philosophy that is keen to stay connected with historical and present struggles.

need to centralize some of these most pressing controversies a bit more sharply in our work. Some of that we will do in this book now. We should go further in that direction, I think.

Let me make the point more concrete. One of the most pressing issues of our time is race and racism, brought about by resurgent and recently emboldened white supremacy in the US and elsewhere. Other pressing issues pertain to gender politics, which have developed in marked ways since your first book in 2005. Today, we are in a world of declared pronouns and I have openly transgender and nonbinary students in almost every class I teach. Young people have a conceptual language that was not previously available so widely, and this proliferating conceptual language about transgender possibilities has answered questions for many people about why they have been so miserable in their bodies, in their gendered being-in-the-world. It seems obvious that if we are going to talk about ontology and social and political transformation, we cannot only lightly touch on such issues in passing. I think that will be a mistake. It is tempting to say that, as philosophers, we need more time to think. That is true to a certain extent, but as communists, we must enter the fray.

We can choose to take the side of those who want to become something else, who want the world to become something else, or we can defend the world as it is against, for example, transgender and nonbinary gender challenges. I think the latter defensive position is on the wrong side of the issue, and our ontological work should deal with this (more on this later). Ecology is yet another ontological issue, especially as we confront the fact that certain forms of life are unsustainable. Ecology will ultimately require human beings to learn new forms of life. Kohei Saito has made this argument most powerfully.[83] Finally, as is always important to my epistemology, I claim there is an intellect and philosophical activity at work in global uprisings and social movements. We must remain ready to receive their wisdom, not to try to teach them, but to be faithful students of the latest struggles.

BG asks: The last question here is about anarchism, particularly since you have an excursus on it in *Precarious Communism*. I very much like what you say about this issue here, and it is a position that I completely share. You

---

[83] Kohei Saito, *Marx in the Anthropocene: Towards the Idea of Degrowth Communism* (Cambridge, UK: Cambridge University Press, 2023).

say, "From Bakunin and Malatesta to the present, anarchists have always been communists who have seen how much repression and destruction of humanity have been wrought by governments."[84] In the next paragraph, you add, "Today, we must understand that a communist who distrusts and rejects state power as destructive and repressive is very much an anarchist, just as every good anarchist is also much of a Marxist."[85] It couldn't have been said better. Again, this is something that I myself often say. And I truly appreciate your losing patience with this attitude, which is ultimately a form of ideological stupidity, when you say, "If you want the anarchists to renounce Marxism and if you want the communists to renounce anarchism, get over it! *We are too precarious for all of that*" (emphasis added).[86] Very well said, and this is a result of your critique of ideology, and ideological communism in particular, and of your highlighting the transformational power of precarious, philosophical communism. Perhaps that ideological stupidity and fallacy, just like many similar others, will be left behind and abandoned as we move forward to the path of thinking. Can you share your thoughts on this?

RGO answers: I am really enjoying your interest in the question of anarchism (which recurs several times below), especially since it gets peripheral attention in my books. However, you are right to observe an anarchist sensibility in my work. I am not sure how much more I can add here, as the question of anarchism gets more in-depth attention in subsequent chapters of our book.

Anarchism contains – to my mind – some of the richest streams of thought and histories of action from which to find and develop a critique of power. It is a deep well of inspiration. In Marxism, I find the most penetrating study of capitalism, the best answers to the question: what is capital? There are many other things to fish out of both streams of course, including different approaches to revolution, collective action, spirituality, technology, and many other things. However, returning to the problems of power and capital, it seems to me simply obvious that, at the present juncture in time, we should be both worried about vertical and centralized forms of institutional power, and that we need the depth and breadth of

---

84 Gilman-Opalsky, *Precarious Communism*, op. cit., 121-122.
85 Ibid., 122.
86 Ibid.

the best political economy. This may not have been so obvious to anarchists and communists in 1871, but it should be now, and what it means is that we need to help both these streams pool together and gather their forces as kindred undercurrents.

Let me make this point differently. One of the things that should make the best communists today more precarious is learning from the experiences and failures of some of our less precarious (more confident) communist forebears. We cannot count on anything today. If we assess the resources at our disposal, how can anyone justify discounting a whole trajectory of anti-capitalist revolutionary theory and history? Doing so would be a remarkable feat of ideological stupidity. The differences between Bakunin and Marx in the light of the debates of the First International do not make much difference today. I am surprised and discouraged when anarchists renounce Marxism and communists renounce anarchism. It still happens, in some circles, as if it really were 1871. We are not so close to winning anything that we should split up the only people in a relatively small room who see so much eye-to-eye.

Yes, I think the critique of ideology demands that we overcome this self-important and self-righteous debilitating dichotomy. If we are the least bit philosophical in our approach, if we have any philosophy left inside of us, we should think about what is happening in the world, about what we need to do, and about how to do it. If we are philosophical, we should be open to thinking out of bounds, against the ideological tendencies of our own movements, which have proven that they are not beyond reaction. There are and have been many reactionaries in our midst. Unfortunately, reactionaries are not the private property of fascism and capitalism. In politics, they belong to the field of ideology.

Nonetheless, I still believe in thinking. Like Simone Weil who, in *Oppression and Liberty* was full of despair and cynical realism, I still believe in thinking.[87] She described humanity as "a party of ignorant travelers in a motor-car launched at full speed and driverless across broken country" only wondering *when* "the smash-up will occur."[88] I think we have good reason to be a bit more hopeful than Weil when all she saw on the horizon was the inevitability of fascism, imperialism, and servitude. I think we can

---

87 Simone Weil, *Oppression and Liberty*, trans. Arthur Wills and John Petrie (London and New York: Routledge Press, 1958).
88 Ibid., 114.

see some other things now, but we should remember that even Weil still held to thinking as the best way to identify our ideals, which, like a North Star, could help us to move as near to them as possible. This was, for Weil, the practicality of Utopianism. We have no choice. We simply must move forward on the path of thinking, against ideological reaction, and while I am not advocating crass opportunism, the fact is that we revolutionaries are far too precarious to deny ourselves any useful insights. The multifarious streams of diverse revolutionary history and writing are teeming with useful insights. We must take our insights wherever we find them, we must go and get them out of bounds, and against the anarchist and Marxist police who want to tell us where to walk and how to speak.

BG asks: Here, I want to go to the end of your book *Specters of Revolt: On the Intellect of Insurrection and Philosophy from Below*. First of all, the phrase "the intellect of insurrection" is very intriguing. Usually, people immersed in insurrection and revolt might primarily think of bodies, rather than of the intellect. Of course, I very much like your phrasing, and I know what you mean. Indeed, you say that "revolt is an expression of reason,"[89] and you speak of "an understanding of the philosophical content of revolt... of revolt as philosophical work."[90] This is simply beautiful, and it is very important. So, could you elaborate a bit on this? The other question is about something you say on the last page of your book – something which captures the main idea of the book itself. You say, "In between every revolt we are haunted by the specter of its possibility."[91] Some readers might take this as a sign of a metaphysical (in the negative sense of the word) distance. I remember posting one of your remarks on reason and revolt on Facebook, and I got some comments such as, "Revolt is only in the present; there is no before or after revolt," "There is no reason in revolt; it's only instinct," and so on and so forth. Yet, you are saying something different. Of course, revolt happens now. And yet, its spectral (perhaps transcendental?) presence seems to be as important as its actual occurrence. What you call *anterivolta*, instead of *antebellum*, throws light on the existential precariousness you highlight in *Precarious Communism* and on the constant possibility of change.

---

89 Richard Gilman-Opalsky, *Specters of Revolt: On the Intellect of Insurrection and Philosophy from Below* (London: Repeater Books, 2016), 224.
90 Ibid., 224-225.
91 Ibid., 261.

In the introduction to *Earthly Plenitudes*, I make a similar point through a close (though cursory) reading of a few pages of Ken Saro-Wiwa's great novel *Sozaboy*. You may want to look at that as you answer this question. At the outset of Saro-Wiwa's novel, as a horrifying civil war is about to start, we find ourselves in a time of suspension, in a spectral transition. That's the *antebellum*. However, the same is true of *anterivolta* as long as conditions of exploitation, oppression and injustice remain. I imagine that these are the conditions that constitute "the intellect of insurrection," and, if I may, *the general intellect of insurrection and revolt.*

RGO answers: While I am interested in the complex concept of *Geist*, and especially in its neglected ghostly and spiritual dimensions, I by no means want to retain or revive a Cartesian juxtaposition of the body to the intellect or mind. To speak of the body is also to speak of the intellect. Human intellect is embodied in various ways, not only in the gray matter of the brain itself, but in the collective action of bodies in the world. The ghost of *Geist* is very important for approaching a hauntology of human psychology. What are the specters that haunt our understandings of the world, of history, of ourselves? On the tripartite structure of *Geist*, one could say that the mind is the intellectual faculty, the spirit is the sensibility and emotional comportment of the thinking being and the ghost is what troubles or unsettles the whole intellectual-spiritual apparatus. I think a good understanding of *Geist* leaves none of that out.

I have never wanted to reduce or convert the bodily activities of revolt into something like a transcript. Revolt does not say a single cohesive thing, and much of what it says would be lost in transcribing revolt into a legible text. One cannot say that the revolt communicates this or that single point of view. Nonetheless, I do want to confront and refute the common idea that revolt is nothing more than an irrational emotional tantrum, that it is senseless violence without any clear purposes. That is a longstanding and widespread caricature of revolt, with a well-documented history, and it has to be overturned. When I claim that "revolt is an expression of reason," when I write about its "philosophical content," I do so in order to articulate the most radical antithesis to that common bad reading, to present a total inversion of the idea that revolt is irrational violence. Revolt is never an irrational senseless violence. Revolt is full of the most pressing insights of its time, and often, it takes the form that it takes because it expresses a disaffection otherwise ignored. People in a state of revolt are saying many different things, doing many different things, yet one of the most basic overarching messages of revolt is that something long hidden has to be seen, something has to be heard, something has to be done, something urgent, something *right now*. Beyond that, the discursive content is unwieldly and sometimes contradictory. Still, we cannot go on thinking that if it does not look like an essay or a newspaper article, if it is not dressed up to speak calmly on a television screen, radio show, or in an academic conference of experts, then it must be nothing more than inchoate stupidity. I first learned this lesson from feminist epistemology, from writers like Linda Alcoff, Elizabeth Potter and others.[92]

We should confront the fact that "hysteria," a certain kind of emotional frenzied thinking, was diagnosed a nervous disease of women as recently as in the 19th century. That is a gendered disqualification of reason. The idea of hysteria comes from the Greek *hystera*, which refers to the womb, woman's abdomen, or uterus. For some time, people believed that some dysfunction of the uterus caused hysteria, which led to diagnoses of a woman's excitement, anger, or even joy as aberrant behavior, an indication of sickness. Thus, a woman enraged at her abuser is called "hysterical," a woman's fierce opposition to sexism is a sign of hysteria, and accordingly, the woman is advised to calm down and speak kindly with reason. According to this, only when calm and accepting does she move from hysteria to reason. We must reject all of that.

Sometimes, the truth only comes out in an explosive way, mobilized by anger. Sometimes, that is the only time you may hear the truth in a repressive, patriarchal, white supremacist society. Often, an outburst expression carries the truth, while what appears calm and reasonable only conceals the truth.

James C. Scott studied this phenomenon very well in *Domination and the Arts of Resistance: Hidden Transcripts*.[93] Feminist epistemology demonstrates that women who give birth actually possess real knowledge on childbirth. What a surprise! A simple and perhaps even obvious insight, but one that's been locked out of a medical establishment that preferred

---

[92] See Linda Alcoff and Elizabeth Potter, *Feminist Epistemologies* (New York and London: Routledge, 1993).

[93] James C. Scott, *Domination and the Arts of Resistance: Hidden Transcripts* (New Haven and London: Yale University Press, 1990).

to categorize all the experiential knowledge of women as "old wives' tales." Today, you may have a doula or a midwife who does more – indeed, *knows more* – than the OBGYN who knows more about how to use the hospital equipment to bring the baby out in time to meet a friend for golf. That is one reason why I refuse to view revolt as "hysteria." It expresses many truths, and often they are the most important truths to express precisely because they have been silenced, locked out, and invisible for so long. Revolt is not a text, but it is philosophy. Those who think all philosophy is merely text have forgotten about Socrates, who wrote nothing.

Regarding your question about being haunted by the specter of revolt when revolt is not happening: This is an extension of Deleuze and Guattari's point in "May '68 Did Not Take Place."[94] Historians like to frame events with start and stop dates. Historians like to say that the revolt started on such and such a date, and ended on another date. I do not think that works. After the murder of Michael Brown in Ferguson, MO, and Freddie Gray in Baltimore, MD, there were some years of Black Lives Matter revolt. It appeared to end for a time after that, for years in fact, until it resumed in the George Floyd Rebellion of 2020. The George Floyd rebellion tells us that #BLM did not end. One could argue, as I do in the book, that there is a long history of Black revolt in the US, stretching back to slave rebellions, and that, in periods of relative quiet, the specter of revolt still haunts. Why do I say that? Well, racism, white supremacy, are not over. White supremacy keeps on going, which guarantees that opposition to it will keep on going too. If Black revolt, or earlier, the gatherings of Occupy Wall Street, seem to settle down and fade away, I would look to the persistence of growing inequality, debt, and racism. The pervasive persistence of these things tell us that even when the revolt is not happening, it has unfinished business, and will come back to pick up where it previously left off. To be clear, I am not talking here about a repetition, but about a certain continuity we can trace.

There is always the time before revolt, too. Police kill roughly a thousand people every year in the US alone.[95] There is no major revolt like the George Floyd rebellion in every single case. There are times when what is truly shocking is the absence of revolt. However, if the world is still

---

[94] Gilles Deleuze and Félix Guattari, "May '68 Did Not Take Place" in *Hatred of Capitalism: A Semiotext(e) Reader* (Los Angeles: Semiotext(e), 2001).

[95] See, for example, https://mappingpoliceviolence.org/.

upside down, full of realities we have to abolish, then periods of relative calm are times before revolt. People rise up. It is only a question of when and in what ways and places. I stick enough to a dialectical understanding of history to insist that this is true. History bears it out. Likewise, there is a period after revolt too, and perhaps paradoxically, the period after revolt is, at the same time, a period before revolt. Something has happened, but because it is not finished, it will continue. There is no rigid differentiation between "before" and "after" revolt because both temporalities indicate a low period of contentious uprising, inevitably interrupted at some point on the horizon. Unless we are at the end of history, an utterly absurd proposition, this continuity is certain. Therefore, yes, when we are not experiencing periods of open revolt, we are always in the state of *anterivolta*, at least for as long as exploitation, oppression, and injustice persist. History is still happening, which we see best in times of revolt.

I fully agree that instinct is part of revolt. However, I do not understand why anyone would say that instinct is inconsistent with intellect, that if one follows their instinct they abandon their intellect. If one's instinct is to run from the cops, why should that mean there is no intellect in the decision? It simply does not follow. This was already true in the LA Riots of 1992, after the acquittal of the officers involved in the beating of Rodney King. The riots were an instinctive response to the injustice of the acquittals. Footage of the beating had been widely shown on television by that time, just as more recently, there was footage of George Floyd with Derek Chauvin's knee on his neck all over the internet. The revolt is a dignified instinct against such injustice, but is it not also an intellect at work? Does it have nothing to say, nothing to teach us, does it offer no real analysis of what is going on? Of course it does! I think we must appreciate this. Why should we pretend that instinct is dumb? We have more to learn from the revolt than from those scholars who want to analyze it. It is itself already an analysis, and does not require translation and textual publication to say what it has to say. The revolt is, as you also say, *"the general intellect of insurrection and revolt."*

We can speak of instinct, but I will not deny living thinking things like revolts, which have so much to teach us about the justice and reality of the world, their intellects. A lot is at stake in this. We must not concede to our enemies who think of riots and revolts as irrational violence devoid of intellect. They are wrong, and we should ask, "Why is it so important to people in power that we think of revolt that way?"

52 COMMUNIST ONTOLOGIES

BG asks: Following on the previous question, you do say that *"Specters of Revolt* aims to think through how systems of oppression are always haunted by revolt, how revolt is the oppositional (and historical and liberatory) theory and practice of transformative aspirations."[96] Although I used (in parenthesis) the word "transcendental" above (as it seems to me that there is a Kantian moment throughout your work), it is obvious that for you this *specter* is historical (perhaps transhistorical). You make the examples of Spartacus, John Brown, the Zapatista revolt, and Occupy. Then you speak of "the dignity of the oppressed."[97] One of the main concepts in my book *Earthly Plenitudes* is the *dignity of individuation*. Indeed, what is this dignity when dignity itself is denied and trampled upon? How can this dignity remain as an indestructible ontological moment, as "a ghost-like power," as you say, and a potentiality?[98]

RGO answers: In our exchanges, you rightly identify several Kantian moments in my work. It is true, as mentioned in other contexts, that much of what I am doing is a kind of radicalization of Kant. There are several dimensions of that, but with regard to what I call "the dignity of the oppressed," one could say that there is a Kantian humanism at work. Kant was a humanist and cosmopolitan, and he wanted to expand – not diminish – the dignity and commonality of the human person. In his "Theory and Practice" and "Perpetual Peace" essays, Kant argued for hospitality, against war, for the common sense and capabilities of human beings for private and public reasoning; his moral idea of the human as an end-in-itself counters the indignity of any form of life where humans become a means to ends.[99] As a Marxist, what often appears to me most pressing is the conversion of the human person into a means to an end for capital. Here, I think we are kindred spirits, and I appreciate that you too are deeply concerned with human dignity, not only in *Earthly Plenitudes* but also very much in *Humanity and the Enemy*. It is useful to go back to the etymological thirteenth century core of the word dignity, which meant a state of being worthy. To be dignified is to be made to feel that you are

---

96 Gilman-Opalsky, *Specters of Revolt*, op. cit., 13.
97 Ibid., 15.
98 Ibid., 16.
99 Find both essays in Immanuel Kant, *Political Writings*, trans. H.B. Nisbet (Cambridge: Cambridge University Press, 1991).

worthy, but worthy of what? Money does not confer dignity, nor does any prize of commodities. Dignity is a sense of worth closer to the concept of honor, which includes a feeling of being appreciated befitting a healthy sense of self. If one takes a salary, yet there is no indication of any interest in or appreciation of one's work, the salary does not confer dignity. Robberies of human dignity can only go on for so long before the emergence of indignation.

Let us return to the LA Riots of 1992, to the case of Rodney King. That was long before the time when everyone and anyone could record cops beating up or killing Black people. Indeed, many think of the Rodney King case as the very first instance of a sort of viral video, footage taken by an amateur with a consumer video camera. I would ask readers to muster the courage to go back and watch this footage again (or for the first time). Look it up online. It is very hard to watch. What you see is a sustained beating with overwhelming excessive force, the gratuitous violence of a large circle of cops bludgeoning King who was already posing no threat to any of them. When Black people in the US saw this footage, they knew what made the event extraordinary was that it was captured on video, not that it happened. We have to remember that in the early 90s it was close to impossible for everyday people to simply record things like this. Many Black people expected that, because of the clear abuse and incredible violence (which is still shocking to watch over thirty years later), the cops would be held accountable this time. That is not what happened. We have to ask, what message did the acquittal of those cops send to Black people in the US? The message was hard to miss. Cops could encircle a Black person, beat them nearly to death with grotesque violence, and doing so was more or less OK. Try to imagine the sense of robbed worth and dignity denied in the face of that acquittal. It is hard to imagine the realization that catching it all on tape was not even enough. The conclusion said that Black life was not worth much, if anything at all. That is an American story of dignity and indignity from thirty years ago.

You ask how dignity remains as an indestructible ontological moment. I believe that dignity asserts itself in the revolt in 1992 in this example. Dignity was not in the law, not in the response of the state, nor in the LAPD. Dignity was in the uprising. We must be clear that the revolt was fundamentally about being-in-the-world. The LA Riots respond to the acquittals that say King's dignity is worth nothing, and the riots reject that conclusion. With all due fury (arguably even more fury was warranted), they reject the ontological state of indignity. The revolt declares, "We are not worthless!" The revolt screams for a different being-in-the-world, screams that we cannot accept this form of life. Therefore, the revolt is an ontological moment that asserts a possible and desirable being-in-the-world against an actually existing being-in-the-world. It is perhaps an instinct too, and yet, for everything else that it may be, it is an ontological argument.

From our perspective, as philosophers, we can recognize some part of this argument as Kantian. There is the human person and there is the question of dignity, and then there is that humanist and cosmopolitan sensibility that says that even those unlike us are of equal moral worth. We may bring in Kant this way or sideways as we wish, but from the perspective of the revolt, Kant is irrelevant. Philosophy from below has no need for Kant.

BG asks: In your book *The Communism of Love,* in the chapter on Plato's *Symposium,* there are many wonderful moments. First of all, you note the fact that "love is a tumultuous power"[100] and "an active aspiration for the not-yet."[101] Without going into the details of your reading of Plato's dialogue here, I'd like to remark on your statement that, in the context of the *Symposium,* in Aristophanes's view, love appears as "essentially an ontological problem,"[102] and, with some important qualifications, you seem to agree with that. This is of course complicated by your discussion of the relationship between love and desire. But I very much like your "personal and anecdotal articulation of a rival vision," when you speak of your relationship with your children.[103] It seems to me that this might relate back to what I call *the love of others,* which seems to be part of the "nonteleological notion of becoming" you mention.[104]

RGO answers: I am grateful for some comments on my reading of Plato's *Symposium,* as that part of the book has received little attention, yet is one of my favorites. I suspect that people interested in the titular big idea of the communism of love may skip over a chapter on Plato and Socrates.

---

100 Richard Gilman-Opalsky, *The Communism of Love: An Inquiry into the Poverty of Exchange Value* (Oakland, CA: AK Press, 2020), 63.
101 Ibid., 64.
102 Ibid., 70.
103 Ibid., 78.
104 Ibid., 79.

Yes, I totally agree with the ontological dimension of Aristophanes's view on love. I also appreciate that Aristophanes endorses a concept of love as an activity of healing, of health and well-being, and that his speech offers a counterpoint to some of the dominant and narrow heterosexist discourses of love that still function. However, my agreement does not go much further than that. There are deep problems with his argument about love as a process of becoming whole, and they are problems that continue to plague discussions of love today. There are also problems with Aristophanes's discourse on sexuality, not terribly surprising in an ancient text from a very different present.

The main problem in Aristophanes's speech is the tale of Zeus cutting every human into two so that each person is compelled to search for their missing half to become whole.[105] I refer to this as the "completion theory" of love, according to which each one seeks the other who completes them. I find this deeply problematic, and it remains among the most prevalent bad ideas today. To say to your beloved, "you complete me" retains a romantic power. However, it is a wrong and dangerous idea. The expectation that one other person should complete you is not a fair expectation to hang on a beloved. Moreover, it is absurd to expect human wholeness from a single relation of two. Indeed, the notion of wholeness is itself a problem. Wholeness, or completion, presumes a finished project. Whereas, it may not be a virtue or goal to be finished with becoming.

A parental relationship with children serves to illustrate serious problems with Aristophanes's view. I love my children but I will not take them as my missing halves or thirds or fourths, or what have you. I want them to become something they are not yet as children, but I understand that a whole set of active relations – *and not some single missing half* – should participate in that becoming. I want them to experience love relations beyond those of the family, and even possibly, to understand and support the fact that their becoming may require their separating from beloved others. That last part is crucial, the notion that separation from the family, or from a relationship or friendship can be a major passage in a history of becoming, even without finding some other half. This underlines my point that the concept of a whole person is a problem. When I speak about a "nonteleological notion of becoming," I mean to say that we have to

---

105 See Plato's *Symposium*, trans. Avi Sharon (Newburyport, MA: Focus Philosophical Library, 1998), 38.

participate in the becoming of our beloved without knowing, specifying, or insisting upon, a particular destination.

At the time of this writing, my older son does not want much from me at all. I would like to play a greater role in his becoming than he would allow. It is painful, but I must appreciate two things in this experience: First, his becoming is not bound to the ways that I have participated in it up until now. Second, I do not know what he will become and I cannot decide the question. That love cannot decide this question is one of love's many limitations, although it is ultimately a good thing that love cannot decide the question. A human life calls for a certain degree of openness and autonomy, a field of contingency, of possibility, and that includes failure, sickness, and death. We cannot exclude these possibilities from the start, but can actively love the other nonetheless.

BG asks: I'd like to go to the introduction of *The Communism of Love* for a moment. When you present your main arguments, there is a point when, once again, I detect your affinity with Kant's thought, which I remarked on previously. You say that "love is a practice that socializes a unique polyamory beyond the structure of romantic relationship." You specify that this is "not about having multiple partners, and is not primarily sexual or romantic, but is instead the polyamory of a communist affection for others," or what you also call "a form of communist relationality."[106] You also say, somewhat apologetically, that this "communist tendency of love" is a form of *universality*.[107] This is wonderful. And it is here that I see your relationship, not only to Rosa Luxemburg, a relationship you make explicit and elaborate on later in the text, but to Immanuel Kant as well. In particular, I'm thinking of Kant's notion of practical, or universal, love, based for Kant on moral duty – or, to update and perhaps betray Kant, on empathy, if you will – as against 'pathological' love, based on sympathy. Yours is obviously a radical take on that, but I think it's very close to it. Do you see this relationship of affinity, and would you care to elaborate on it?

RGO answers: Polyamory is yet another casualty of a narrow private notion of love. When people think of polyamory, as with any other love relation, they tend to think of multiple sexual partners. The fact that

---

106 Gilman-Opalsky, *The Communism of Love*, op. cit., 4.
107 Ibid., 5.

this is so is another indication of the poverty of exchange relations. For example, why do we not think about love for others more broadly in a social sense? It is because of the conceptual privatization of love, a privatization I seek to oppose.

I am always a bit nervous to speak of universality, not only because of my education in French critical theory and postmodern philosophy, but also because universality has a long history as the purview of Eurocentrism and imperialist thinking. Even if we must speak of universality, then, we have good reasons for caution. Nonetheless, I want to risk the daring and propose that the aspiration of love is both irreducibly communist and universal. I think the proposal is worth bearing out, to see how far it goes. If it stops short in various ways, that too is worth understanding.

It is easy to say that I prefer Rosa Luxemburg to Immanuel Kant, but I am comfortable with the relation to Kant, which we have discussed already. For now, I will only add that I have often said that what we need to do in philosophy is variously radicalize Kant beyond Kant. Such radicalizations are indeed betrayals of Kant, who was consciously aware of and openly committed to a reformist slow improvement led by rational arguments. Though he favored the public use of reason as an emancipatory force, Kant retained a crucial place for the private use of reason, which required him to favor free speech over things like strikes, law-breaking revolt, and other disruptive actions. He warned against the dangers of revolution, insisting instead on the necessity of a very slow "true reform in ways of thinking."[108] Kant beyond Kant may indeed be a radical take. Is it still Kantian? Does that question even matter? I am happy to let a Kantian decide.

---

108 Immanuel Kant, "And Answer to the Question: 'What is Enlightenment?'" in *Political Writings*, trans. H.B. Nisbet (Cambridge, UK: Cambridge University Press, 1991), 55.

CHAPTER 2

WORKS (DOING AND UNDOING)

Richard Gilman-Opalsky (RGO) asks: Productive labor is a category of political economy, whereas the productive power of labor is a category of ontology.[1] This means that capitalist political economy wants labor to serve it, which we can juxtapose to an alternative power of labor to produce being-in-the-world. The former is exploitative, the domain of surplus labor and exchange value, whereas the latter is the domain of "revolt against capital."[2] The latter is the connection between doing and becoming. However, I wonder if this distinction is too categorical, too dichotomous. Some years ago (2014) I attended a Digital Labor conference at The New School where one hot topic of discussion was "playbor." The idea of "playbor" is a kind of détournement inside of capitalism, which allows workers to make productive labor more playful, less exploitative. What do you think of such efforts at joyful work, or productive labor that people are happy to identify with? Is that, in your opinion, just a more insidious evolution of productive labor meant to deceive workers into thinking we are not exploited? Related to this, what about the compatibility of a living labor that is integrated into capitalist political economy? There is the old dangerous saying: "Find something you love to do, then find someone willing to pay you to do it." Of course, that rarely happens (hence the danger of the lesson). But what do you think about the fact that some people may be *doing* what they want to *be*, and yet, the work that makes them a musician,

---

1   Bruno Gullì, *Labor of Fire: The Ontology of Labor between Economy and Culture* (Philadelphia: Temple University Press, 2005), 69.
2   Ibid.

a professor, a surgeon, a scientist, a nightclub owner, an artist, etc., is work they get paid for, and is not in fact a "revolt against capital?" What is going on there where people claim to be free and to identify with their work, which seems to produce both surplus labor *and* joyful existence?

Bruno Gullì (BG) answers: Let me start here by answering one of the questions you ask above, namely, whether joyful work might be "a more insidious evolution of productive labor meant to deceive workers into thinking we are not exploited." My answer is "yes," absolutely. What comes to mind is Frédéric Lordon's notion of *joyful obedience*, which is the result of the false dichotomy of coercion and consent. Indeed, Lordon says that "consent does not exist."[3] He also says, "Those who consent are no freer than anyone else, and are no less 'yielding' than the enslaved; only, they have been made to yield differently and thus experience their determination joyfully. There is no consent, in the same way that there is no voluntary servitude. There are only *happy subjections*" (emphasis added).[4] Throughout his book, Lordon argues that there is only passionate servitude. Coercion and consent are for him, from the standpoint of Spinoza's thought, names given to the different determinations of sadness and joy. What appears as consent is the result of what he calls co-linearization, which is precisely a very insidious and powerful process of normalization.

The fact that we may happen to love what we do for a living does not necessarily imply that we are happy to identify with it insofar as it is a form of productive labor. Ultimately, this goes back to the question of the commodity form and of labor as a commodity: use value and exchange value; useful (or concrete) labor and abstract labor. I may love the useful labor I perform, but that doesn't mean that I have to embrace and defend its abstract character. In fact, I may (as I should) remain aware of the degree of exploitation involved by it and maintain a critical and defiant stance vis-à-vis it. Consider the work we do in the university, especially teaching political philosophy or similar subjects. Of course, we love what we do, but we also know that today the university, even a 'public' university, is a place of great institutionalization, oppression, exploitation, and so on. The logic of debt is pervasive within it. Students are seen as customers, faculty are

---

3   Lordon, op. cit., 55.
4   Ibid., 91.

seen as dispensable workforce, and many of them, the 'adjuncts,' the contingent faculty, who at some institutions become the majority, work and live under appalling conditions. What is there to love about this, what to be joyful about? We would probably teach, certainly practice philosophy, even without these deplorable and diminishing conditions of exploitation and domination. To be sure, unless we are adjuncts, we are given decent, even good, salaries in return, as well as good benefits, and so on. However, this should not make us oblivious to the underlying reality of the whole situation; the fact, for instance, that education itself is sold as a commodity and that we are, from at least one point of view, mere producers of exchange value and participants in the logic of productivity, the logic of capital. There is nothing joyful about this.

So, it is essential to distinguish – and philosophy is the science of distinctions – between the love we have for our activity and the sadness, even the anger, we feel about the conditions under which this activity is forcefully subsumed. The main point is not to give in to (capitulate) and fall within the mode of happy subjections. Yes, we are subjected, and even subjugated, by institutional forces that with the aid of capital, the state, and the law, are able to subsume all work and all life under their interests, purview, and power. However, the point is to be able to maintain a distance, a sense of clarity, and an aspiration for radical and revolutionary change. In my view, it is better and healthier to experience the sadness of (and anger at) subjection rather than fall into the illusion that because I love what I do all is well and good. No, all is not well and good. The situation is terrible at all levels of our work and life experience. It is much more terrible for some (indeed, for many: migrants, seasonal workers, children forced to labor, the precariat in general, and so on) than for others. In fact, those who are lucky enough to love what they do (such as ourselves when we teach) are privileged with respect to others whose prospects are bleak and often tragic, not because of any fault of their own, but rather due to the horrifying conditions of indifference and cruelty of our societies. So, I would rule out the idea of joyful work under the conditions of exchange value and capital. The fundamental question is not whether our work is joyful or not. The fundamental question is, why work? With a universal basic income, work would lose its compulsory character. But for that to happen a radical reshaping of our societies is needed – a *"genuine* resolution," as Marx says.⁵ Under capitalist conditions of production, work, which "is not voluntary, but coerced, *forced labor*... is not the satisfaction of a need but only a *means to satisfy other needs".*⁶ It is difficult to find any joy in such a situation.

As for the concept of "playbor," as far as I can see, the implication is not necessarily that work becomes more playful and less exploitative. Rather, the implication is that, as Trebor Scholz says, "the social factory is cloaked by an ideology of play."⁷ I haven't given much thought to the concept of playbor, and I don't think I would use it myself. But I can certainly relate it to that of the user – a concept I utilize in my latest book, *Singularities at the Threshold*. There, I say that the user is neither simply a producer nor a traditional consumer, but a figure of disindividuation.⁸ If there is any play, any playful moment, in the incessant activity (incessant labor or doing) of the user, that must be sought in the capacity, indeed the injunction, to *adapt to whatever*. The user will be an artist, an operator, an entrepreneur of the self, to use Maurizio Lazzarato's expression.⁹ It (the user) will be a doer, a worker, and yes, in a sense, a player. But that doesn't mean that what the user does is playful or joyful. It will perhaps be, if I may indulge a bit with language, *appful* – a word that, by the way, is already in use in at least one context. Completely encircled by the network of Apps, the user has no choice, no exit from capture, subjection, and subjugation, until a line of flight is hopefully and eventually found, which may very well be cooperative and collective organizing.

In any case, freedom is not found in identification, but rather in the refusal to identify with anything, in disguising oneself and camouflaging, in simulating and dissimulating. This is of course also part of the game, of playing, and it does entail a lot of work: physical, mental, and emotional. This happens at the threshold of alienation and disindividuation, and it is a movement whereby one does not necessarily find oneself, but shadows projected in the tension between what-is and what-could-be.

---

5   Marx, "Economic and Philosophical Manuscripts," op. cit., 71.
6   6 Ibid., 62.
7   Trebor Scholz, *Uberworked and Underpaid: How Workers Are Disrupting the Digital Economy* (Cambridge, UK: Polity Press, 2016), 87.
8   Gullì, *Singularities at the Threshold*, op. cit., 55.
9   Maurizio Lazzarato, *The Making of the Indebted Man: An Essay on the Neoliberal Condition*, trans. Joshua David Jordan (Los Angeles: Semiotext(e), 2012).

RGO asks: You and Marx both speak about the difference between the space and time when one is working and when one is not. There is that famous line of Marx's from 1844 where he says that one is not at home while at work, and not at work while at home. You cite Marx's claim that capitalist political economy does not consider the worker even as human during the time that the worker is at work.[10] Today, it seems to me that this divide between home and work has been razed to the ground. Long before COVID-19, capital had been trying to colonize all space and time away from the workplace, invading homes, and seizing human energy *at all times*, perhaps with the sole exception of sleep times when cellular devices are charging. Recent developments of this colonization of life by work were taken up well by Jonathan Crary in *24/7*, Franco Berardi in *The Soul at Work*, Peter Fleming in *Resisting Work*, as well as in many other studies by authors from Byung-Chul Han to Maurizio Lazzarato. However, in the wake of pandemic life, I think it may be possible to say that the home has finally been converted into a workspace, that every home is a little factory of "productive labor." I am therefore interested in your thoughts on the space and time available today for what you call living labor. Living labor requires space and time too. In 2005, you observed some of these developments, but still maintained that living labor can contest capitalist political economy, that "there still remains, there must remain, a space for rebellion and revolt."[11] As we approach twenty years since you wrote that, I wonder if you can comment on what has changed.

BG answers: Let me start by saying that of course productive labor is a form of living labor. It is living labor distorted by the logic of capital, and, if I may put it this way, it is living labor on its way to the scaffold. Unproductive labor is also a form of living labor. The argument in *Labor of Fire* is that living labor, in its ontological neutrality, is, as Marx says, "not productive."[12] To stress the character of its ontological neutrality, I called it *neither-productive-nor-unproductive*. I should also say that when I use the word 'neutrality' I don't mean to refer to some abstract category; rather, the ontological neutrality of living labor is equal to its ontological power,

---

10   10 Gullì, *Labor of Fire*, op. cit., 18.
11   11 Ibid., 20.
12   Karl Marx, *Grundrisse: Foundations of the Critique of Political Economy*, trans. Martin Nicolaus (New York: Vintage Books, 1973). 308.

ontological potency, and as such is absolutely real and concrete. It is the *fire* that shapes everything. So, productive labor, the labor that produces and increases capital, cannot exhaust the potency of living labor, especially when living labor is understood – as it should be – as any human activity or doing, ontologically prior to its descent into the forms of productivity and unproductivity. These are indeed spurious forms, which only serve the interests and logic of capital, but which may be at odds – as they often are – with the reality and commonality of daily life. Thus, without whatever capital likes to call unproductive labor, life could not flourish or even be sustained and reproduced.

At the same time, what for capital is productive often amounts to a series of useless or even harmful human activities and enterprises, without which life would be much better on our planet. So, as a theoretical exercise – which might however have positive political and practical consequences – let's bracket out the forms of productive and unproductive labor and see what living labor might be able to do. In *Labor of Fire,* I use the category of creative labor as an alternative to productive labor and its unproductive counterpart. I have to say that today I am not very happy with this choice, especially given that the idea of creativity has been completely subsumed within the same logic of capital, and the notion that we may be doing some creative work only engenders a lot of ideological confusion which, once again, serves well the logic and interests of capital. This goes back to your previous question about the dangers of believing that one engages in some kind of joyful and playful work when in reality one is exploited even more, and is also more effectively subjected and subjugated. So, instead of creative labor we can simply speak of useful, or concrete, labor. This can still remain as a space for rebellion and revolt. Even today in the 24/7 economy we do engage in useful and concrete activities that defy the productive/unproductive split demanded by capital. These are instances of unsubsumed living labor. Although they happen at the threshold of the productive/unproductive split, they are neither-productive-nor-unproductive, but useful. In order to appreciate this, we must move towards a *minor ontology* of labor and doing. This ontology is minor because it operates at the interstices of the territories occupied by capital, within the precarious and vacillating borders of daily life.

I don't mean to sound too optimistic, but I think that living labor – as useful and concrete, rather than productive or unproductive – has a great role to play in the transformative process of our daily life. Perhaps an emerging figure today – outside the producer/consumer distinction – is that of *the user*, a perhaps awkward and confused actor that might be superseded by something different in the future. Yet, the user, in its precarity and contingency, deals with the useful, and perhaps only coincidentally (yet necessarily) touches on the terrain of productivity, in which it may as well drown. The user deals with use values, though constantly under siege by the assault of the logic of exchange value and surplus value. *Life put to work,* as an article by Cristina Morini and Andrea Fumagalli say, and they stress the importance of caring and relational labor.[13] But caring and relational labor still has within itself a degree of potency, the power to do things, able to disrupt and subvert the demands of productivity and capital.

I agree with you when you say that the divide between home and work has disappeared. This calls into question both concepts, home and work. For a long time, for women in particular, for what is called "women's work," the divide was already nonexistent. Much is made today of the fact that, especially with the pandemic, many people work from home. However, this is not necessarily a terrible thing. Actually, for many people, it can be a privilege or an advantage, for a variety of reasons. Marx's rightly famous and wonderful statement should not be taken too literally. Indeed, the closed home can be a dispositif of capture. Perhaps there has never been a home, but a constant search for it. Being confined to a home is not necessarily a good thing. Nor is the separation between home and work always and necessarily healthy. In fact, if the home becomes a place where one does things and from which one connects to the world outside, it might be a different situation. Marx's statement that one is not at home while at work has to do with alienation and exploitation, regardless of whether work happens in the factory, the office, or the home itself (housework). In other words, I may physically be at home, and yet not really being there. And this not necessarily because I work from home, digitally or otherwise. The fact that digital economy has changed everything is an undeniable fact.

However, contrary to some theorists' constant and recent indictment of it, I believe that digital technology has positive potentials (like all technology) and the real issue has to do with the political and practical use of it. Perhaps we need to find a new orientation today. Perhaps now the

---

13   Cristina Morini and Andrea Fumagalli, "Life Put to Work: Towards a Life Theory of Value," *ephemera: theory & politics in organization,* Volume 10 (3/4), 2010 (234-252).

(virtual) home can potentially be found everywhere, anywhere. What's more disturbing is the disappearance of the divide between life and work. This is the meaning of the expression *life put to work*, which I mention above. This situation is described well by the writers you mention in your question. Franco Berardi, for instance, in *The Soul at Work*, says that the cognitive faculties of high-tech workers "are in fact put to work."[14] Of course, for this to happen, the totality of the workers' existence (in its physical and emotional aspects) must be equally put to work. Perhaps sleep as *a radical interruption*, as Jonathan Crary says in *24/7*, can offer an exit, a line of flight – provided that we are still able to sleep and dream.[15] So, the situation is dire today as we confront a growing global homelessness, at the real and metaphorical levels, a descent into the permanent territory of catastrophes, the constant injunction to work in order to pay back debts that never end, and the total loss or theft of time – of the future, but also of the past, of memories.

Yet, living labor, even in our age of digital technology – or perhaps even more so today *because of* digital technology – still remains as the only way out of a nightmarish situation. This is a labor that, because of automation, can exit the logic of productivity of capital, return to its minor ontology of the useful and concrete, be equal to *disposable time*, as Marx calls it in the *Grundrisse*, and thus be able to build a new home and create *real wealth*.[16]

RGO asks: Productive labor, i.e., labor for profit, faces certain existential threats in the face of global pandemics and ecological crises. What I mean is that we can see how continuing to reproduce productive labor as we know it can make us sick and intensify the ecological crisis. In other words, we can see how productive labor can kill us. Do you think that certain crises of human and ecological health and well-being might finally show to the capitalist world, at a certain point, the poverty and danger of capitalist labor? We may be convinced of a causal relationship between capitalism and extinction, but what do you think might precipitate a general loss of faith in (if not an abandonment of) the capitalist concept of labor?

---

14   Franco Berardi, *The Soul at Work: From Alienation to Autonomy*, trans. Francesca Cadel and Giuseppina Mecchia (Los Angeles: Semiotext(e), 2009), 96.
15   Jonathan Crary, *24/7: Late Capitalism and the End of Sleep* (London: Verso, 2014).
16   Marx, *Grundrisse*, op. cit., 708.

BG answers: As I write this, we hear about the devastation throughout Pakistan due to what everybody now correctly describes as a climatic, not natural, disaster. This, together with the various health crises due to pandemics, wars, famines, and so on, should clearly show to everybody the poverty and danger of productive labor, of exchange value and capitalism. But will that suffice for an effective change at the economic, social, cultural, and existential level? Probably, it will not – at least, not in the short run. When we speak about the revolution today, we should be aware that we are speaking about preparation for a possible revolution. This preparation happens at the level of education, culture, and consciousness (perhaps an undeservedly obsolete concept and word). I have a lot of hope in the younger and youngest generations, in their intelligence and sensitivity. It seems to me that it is increasingly the case that, even without particularly strong or defined ideological leanings – and perhaps in a freer fashion because of this – young people are aware that it is possible to live differently and desirable to do so. Perhaps this is an unintended consequence of the conditions of precarity and contingency brought about by biocapitalism in its senseless pursuit of new modalities of value extraction on the one hand and of a thorough and capillary surveillance and control of entire populations on the other. Precarity and contingency in themselves are not necessarily revolutionary, but they may become the groundwork for revolutionary thinking and action – where revolutionary action is not of course the seizing of power or the smashing of anything, but the movement of a refusal, a rupture, and the building of something different and new – the engaging of a new type of constituent power, based on care and caring. Indeed, what's essential is to accomplish a shift from widespread carelessness to love (the communism of love, as you say in your latest book), attention, and care. The revolution must be first of all against one's own self and subjectivity, against the notion of the sovereign and independent individual.

The issue is the end of the logic of productivity, not of production as such. I believe that the basic assumption should be that this remains an obvious and real possibility. Perhaps today the most interesting way to look at this is through the concept of postcapitalism. I believe that's the most compelling argument that can be made. As Mark Fisher says, postcapitalism "develops *from* capitalism and moves *beyond* capitalism."[17] He also says, "It's not just opposed to capitalism – it is what *will* happen when capitalism has ended."[18] The essential trait of whatever might be beyond capitalism is precisely the absence of the logic of productivity, that is to say, of exchange value, surplus value, and capital. Without this, one is still within capitalism. So, the question is not about whether digital technology or automation is good or bad, as some might wonder. I would here simply say that digital technology can be very useful. The post-work futures outlined by Nick Srnicek and Alex Williams, are not times and places in which people don't do anything; they rather signify the end, or the having ended, of the logic of value and productivity, of exploitation, oppression, and domination.[19]

Of course, we are not there yet, and the injunction to work, forced labor, is still ruling all aspects of life. Indeed, in the 24/7 economy, this might be even more the case than it was before. In what Cristina Morini and Andrea Fumagalli call *anthropomorphic capital*, or the *economy of interiority*, we witness the subsumption, not simply of labor to capital, but of life itself, *real life*, which they call *vital subsumption*, whereby, with the institutionalization of precariousness, the new modality of work has "become structural and has permeated life as a whole."[20] Yet, this has also resulted in a decline of the ideology of work. As Morini and Fumagalli say, "work is no longer regarded as the only factor of self-recognition and subjectification."[21] They continue saying, "Without ideologies and with pragmatism, the new precarious subjects frankly wonder whether, in the current crisis, it is convenient or not to activate themselves into work." Indeed, all this, they conclude, "may trigger a new political discourse."[22] I believe that this is also due to the fundamental truth that, for all the vital subsumption, life and living labor (understood in their ontological potency, not in their biopolitical and economic reduction), exceed the powers of capital.

---

17 Mark Fisher, *Postcapitalist Desire: The Final Lectures* (London: Repeater Books, 2021), 51.
18 Ibid.
19 Nick Srnicek and Alex Williams, *Inventing the Future: Postcapitalism and a World without Work* (London: Verso, 2015).
20 Andrea Fumagalli and Cristina Morini, "Anthropomorphic Capital and Commonwealth Value," *Frontiers in Sociology*, Volume 5, Article 24, 2020 (1-13), 9.
21 Ibid., 10.
22 Ibid.

Disaster capitalism, to go back to the point in your question about human and ecological health crises, is able to turn everything to its advantage – "by paving the way for more extensive and more destructive crises" – and thus delay the necessity of the abandonment of the capitalist concept of labor, of the logic of productivity.[23] However, this cannot go on indefinitely, and the hope is that post-work and postcapitalist futures might become actual realities for future generations.

RGO asks: I especially like your claim in *Labor of Fire*: "Labor is being as sensuous human activity."[24] You claim that "the concept of the sensuous brings us into the domain of the esthetic."[25] Yet, in our capitalist societies, sensuous and esthetic activity are expected to be (or are even required to be) relegated to leisure time, to the time and space left over after the obligations of productive labor. What are some of the specific dangers of this relegation of the sensuous and esthetic, and are there any hopeful inroads (or examples) of counteracting it?

BG answers: At times, I think that perhaps I have the wrong view of labor, for I often notice that people reduce it to the strictly economic realm. Labor then becomes what we are forced to do in order to pay rent, buy groceries, and so on. Accordingly, labor is only a category of modernity and capital, and it cannot be equated with doing in general, activity, making. Yet, I choose to retain my understanding of labor for now and see it as something broader than wage labor, or in any case broader than forced and compulsory labor even if unwaged. Indeed, this is what I have always found striking about the idea of living labor as a category of ontology. Again, I might be completely wrong. It might perhaps be better to completely erase labor as a concept, abolish it as a practice. However, I don't really see anything positive and fruitful in doing so. When we write what you and I are writing now, we perform some labor. The same goes on when we teach, cook a meal for ourselves or for our friends, do the dishes, clean the apartment, write a poem, and so on. Labor is this expenditure of physical, mental, and emotional energy. It is time. Then, the question really is about the quality of time. Free,

---

23   Karl Marx and Friedrich Engels, "The Communist Manifesto," in *Selected Writings*, op. cit., 164.
24   Gullì, *Labor of Fire*, op. cit., 147.
25   Ibid., 148.

disposable time is infinitely different from stolen, captured, and stifled time. It is obvious that the abolition of productive labor (and its unproductive counterpart) is not the abolition of labor as an ontological power.

I know that this is controversial, as it may steer into the discourse of essentialism. But honestly, I think that the category of essentialism itself is a rather abused one. For one thing, as Stanley Aronowitz and William DiFazio say in *The Jobless Future*, speaking about the decline of work and the liberation of time, in a post-work situation, there are still things to be done, work to be done, and "everybody should do some of it."[26] This is not a question of looking at labor or work as an essentialist category; it is not an abstract question. It is rather a very concrete question of daily life, which touches on the concept of the useful and the concept of change. Secondly, living labor as "the living, form-giving fire," as "living time," to use Marx's wonderful wording from *Grundrisse*,[27] labor "in its *immediate being*, separated from capital, is *not productive*."[28] What is it then? Certainly, it is not *nothing*. To address your question in a more precise way, it is this labor that is "being as sensuous human activity." It is a very concrete and useful power or force. To go from Marx to Hegel, it is what "forms and shapes the thing."[29] Is this an invention of modernity and capital? I don't think so. Perhaps what changes with modernity and capital is the fact that the thing, so formed and shaped, becomes property, *private property*.

In the *Second Treatise of Government*, John Locke says that "every man has a *property* in his own *person*." He adds, "The *labour* of his body, and the work of his hands, we may say, are properly his."[30] This is still an ontological claim, though of a problematically liberal and individualistic kind. However, property, in a more specific sense, that is, property as a category of capital, the economy and the law, is the result of the mixing of this labor with nature and the common. This is called *appropriation* (but it can also be called extraction and expropriation), and there is a right attached to it. In fact, the thing, formed and shaped by me, is not *mine*, but, as Marx famously says, "confronts me as an alien power" and "belongs to *a man other*

---

26 Stanley Aronowitz and William Di Fazio. *The Jobless Future: Sci-Tech and the Dogma of Work* (Minneapolis: University of Minnesota Press, 1994), 353.
27 Marx, *Grundrisse*, op. cit., 361.
28 Ibid., 308.
29 Hegel, op. cit. 118.
30 John Locke, *Second Treatise of Government*, 19.

than the worker."[31] This appropriation has nothing of the sensuousness proper to the ontological forming and shaping. It is no longer an esthetic category. It becomes a formal and legal object, an abstraction. Human life, living labor, and the human senses are excluded from it, precisely because this appropriation is also a measure of alienation, as Marx says.

However, in what Marx sees as *genuine* communism, namely, the "*positive* overcoming of *private property* as *human self-alienation*," there is also a different type of appropriation: "the appropriation of *human* life … and the return of man … to his *human*, that is, *social* existence."[32] All this happens at the esthetic level, the level of the senses. I have mentioned this above, so I just briefly refer to that again: the *senses* "become *theoreticians* immediately in their *praxis.*"[33]

It is obvious here that the fact that under capitalism sensuous and esthetic activities are relegated to leisure time is a terrible thing. Indeed, leisure time should become the main, and perhaps only, determination of time. In fact, the opposite of leisure, or free, time is unfree, captured, or stifled time. In reality, this is no longer time at all; it is living time becoming dead time. What kind of time is that? The way forward, if there is one, is not that all labor should become artistic, which is in itself a very problematic idea, but rather that the time of doing be living and useful, rather than dead and abstract. For this to become a reality, the time and space of productive (and unproductive) labor must be eradicated. Labor – perhaps no longer simply labor, nor not-labor – goes back to its original disposition of neutrality, which is equal to its explosive and sensuous ontological potency.

BG asks: In *Specters of Revolt*, you say that "revolt can and must create new forms of itself," and then you continue saying that "it must be experimental and creative (if not outright artistic)."[34] This of course goes back to the ideas of pleasure and playfulness beyond struggle. Indeed, in this chapter (Chapter 3) you discuss "Derrida's Playful Subversions"[35] and other similar instances or experiments, such as "Deleuze and Guattari's Rhizomatic

---

31 Marx, "Economic and Philosophic Manuscripts," op. cit., 65.
32 Ibid., 71.
33 Ibid. 74.
34 Gilman-Opalsky, *Specters of Revolt*, op. cit., 114-115.
35 Ibid., 123-125.

Model."[36] At the end of your section on Deleuze and Guattari, you ask the question, "How does revolt participate in a politics of creativity, subversion, and autonomy?"[37] You mainly answer this question by going back, once again, to the concept and practice of *détournement*. In particular, I like your example of illegal graffiti, which, as you say, shows "the openness and accessibility of *détournement*."[38] In *Labor of Fire*, I have a similar reference to the practice of graffiti. But can you say more about revolt as a creative, subversive, and artistic activity?

RGO answers: Yes, I had a very positive response to the concluding sections of *Labor of Fire*, because I was not expecting your focus on artistic activity. I found it surprising and hopeful that you went in the end to examples of the power of artwork, in juxtaposition to the productive labor of capitalist political economy. Graffiti is an especially good example because of the way it emanates from a rebellion against the law, and a healthy disrespect for private property. A long time ago, I noted the distinction between political graffiti and self-centered tagging when I was living in NYC. The distinction was, for me, clarified in the more political and activist graffiti common in other countries. Most of what I saw in NYC was apolitical on its face. In Argentina, for example, there is endless graffiti in cities like La Plata, which mostly takes the form of a protest message. A more famous example comes from France in 1968, in radical *détournement* that one could see and read about in René Viénet's book.[39] However, I have revised that old view about the more or less political, because I now think that what matters most is the defiance, the creativity, the insistence of expression and reclamation. This applies to graffiti in particular.

However, if we step back from graffiti, the general perspective and its connection to revolt is easier to see. In many ways, a revolt is creative artistic activity. In a revolt, there are questions of framing, theater, imagery, and affect. A revolt is not subversive for the sake of subversion; it is an effort to interrupt the quotidian, to reject the unacceptable. The revolt breaks out in the moment when people, who have been tolerating

---

36 Ibid., 132-135.
37 Ibid. 135.
38 Ibid., 140.
39 René Viénet, *Enragés and Situationists in the Occupation Movement, France, May '68* (Brooklyn: Autonomedia, 1992).

the intolerable, allow their sense of the intolerable to decide the question. The revolt gets down to questions of desirability and possibility, where people say, for example, in the face of the Rodney King verdict or the George Floyd murder, we have to break this reality right now. The revolt expresses a desire for something else. To be sure, participants in a revolt do not say this exactly, they do not speak necessarily about breaking the quotidian, or about interrupting everyday life to make space and time for their dreams. They do not have to say anything that a philosopher may write down in a book. However, if we listen we can hear that revolt is not inchoate, it is not irrational or stupid or senseless. Revolt is not incommunicado. If you listen, and if you are willing to be a student – and not merely a teacher – you can learn from revolt. It is very important to observe how artistic activity can be broadly conceived so as to include revolt, graffiti, political theater, and other expressions of disaffection that imagine what is possible and desirable. You find similar content often in music and poetry.

Here, I especially appreciate your connection to poetry, Bruno. Poetry is crucial to our discussion. I am not a poet. I do not know how to write a poem. I cannot tell you what poem is a good poem, beyond the question of whether or not it moves me. The fact that Charles Baudelaire's *Paris Spleen* has moved and provoked me does not mean I can evaluate his poetry in any formal sense. Yet, when my father died, perhaps as it was for you with your dear brother Pino, I felt compelled to write poems. I did not know how to write a poem. However, I could not express what I wanted to say about my father in a philosophical text. Therefore, I wrote poems. Maybe they were not good poems, but they were necessary. The poetry was necessary because it seemed to me the only way to get certain feelings out fully, to process what I wanted to say, and to work through pain and regret, even if I only intended to send this poetry into a void. I did not intend to share or publish this poetry beyond the boundaries of a tiny circle of family. Even though it could have possibly resonated with the experiences of other people, it felt too intimate for the wider world, too much like a medic running to me in an emergency.

What is poetry in such a context as this? When the need is so pressing, it drives non-poets to write poems. In certain emergencies, only poetry will do. At bottom, I think we are talking about different ways of speaking, different ways of saying things that cannot be otherwise said. Poetry is a modality of speaking the unspeakable, working through pain, sorrow, and suffering, making confrontations with the sublime and the beautiful, saying what only a poem can say. Audre Lorde understood the role of poetry well. She wrote political essays too, but some things required poetry. I suggest that revolt is a kind of poetry in all of these key distinctions. Revolt is poetic in its utter necessity as a modality of speaking what only revolt can say. Revolt belongs to the category of art, and if that category will not allow revolt in, we need a better definition of art.

RGO asks: I enjoyed your discussion of academic labor in Chapter 4 of *Earthly Plenitudes*, and I agree with your statement that "the transformation of the university is not possible if society itself is not transformed."[40] Your critique of contingent labor in the university is fully convincing, but what I see in the US (and increasingly internationally) are major initiatives of "academic reorganization" and the sovereignty of trade school mentalities in liberal arts colleges and universities. I am therefore wondering if you can explain, as an educator yourself, what you regard as the highest aspirations of education within the current context of capitalist contingency. I mean, we do not have the university we want, or the one that students deserve, and yet, we do not abandon *either* the universities or the students. What are we trying to do then? What are the right aspirations in the present? In Chapter 5 of *Earthly Plenitudes*, you turn our attention to "care" and you assert that "the concept of care requires that the logic of productivity and sovereignty be dismantled."[41] I am wondering if teaching in the present is a labor of care. Is that, for example, what we do in the university during a pandemic? When the pandemic first began to disrupt our lives, I was thinking about the university as a space of refuge and care. Nevertheless, how can the labor of care happen in a place of capital and contingency, in the university as such?

BG answers: I definitely think that teaching remains a labor of care even in a place of capital and contingency such as the neoliberal and corporate university today, which is increasingly (and sadly) becoming a model for the various public institutions of higher education as well. That teaching is still a labor of care shows very well in our times of pandemic disruption,

---

40 Bruno Gullì, *Earthly Plenitudes: A Study on Sovereignty and Labor* (Philadelphia: Temple University Press, 2010), 95-96.
41 Ibid., 133.

crisis, and anxiety; in our times – it is also important to note – of the debt machine, or *debt society*, as Maurizio Lazzarato says in a chapter of *Governing by Debt* called "The American University: A Model of the Debt Society." Lazzarato calls debt an "apparatus of capture"[42] and "a new technique of power."[43] Indeed, the system of debt, which envelops not just the university but the whole of daily life, is the worst and most powerful form of organized crime – organized at the highest institutional levels. It is synonymous with capital and sovereign power, sovereign violence, destroying all that is important and dear in the fragility of the human condition. The bottom line is that all institutions of higher education should be public (or better, common) and *free*, as CUNY was when it was established in 1847 and for over a century after that. Indeed, education *as such* should be completely free; this should obviously also be the case with health care, housing, and so on. Today, we are forced to distinguish between teaching as a labor of care and having an academic job, which usually pays well (if you are a full-timer, have tenure, and so on) but gets you entangled in a series of conflicting situations, petty politics, useless administrative tasks, and injustices. Contingent faculty, the adjuncts, face a much more difficult situation of job and existential insecurity, having to juggle many positions at different institutions just to make ends meet. Yet, even in that situation, and contrary to a widespread notion according to which the quality of the work of adjuncts is not as good as that of full-time faculty for objective reasons, teaching remains a labor of care against all odds. In truth, contingent faculty simply have to work much more than their full-time counterpart, with a greater expenditure of effort and energy, and under much more stress, in order to achieve the same quality of teaching and care. This may sound like a paradox, but teaching is still care even under conditions of superexploitation and oppression.

 Teaching is essentially a transformative practice. It is in this sense that it is a labor of care. But what is care? Care is a form of power. And what is power? Usually, and reductively, we think of power in the narrow political sense: power as authority, domination, *power-over*, and so on. However, the most fundamental form of power is *power-to*, the power, or ability/capacity, to do things, at the physical, mental, and emotional level. So,

---

42 Maurizio Lazzarato, Governing by Debt, trans. Joshua David Jordan (Los Angeles: Semiotext(e), 2015), 72.
43 Ibid., 69.

for instance, caring for others, especially for those who can't take care of themselves for various reasons and to various degrees – as disability studies shows well – entails an important form (indeed, the most important form) of power. Regretfully, the pathological state of our societies doesn't allow us to truly appreciate the revolutionary import of this notion (and practice) of power nor appreciate the fact that another meaning of care (intimately connected to the one I've just mentioned) is *the time between birth and death*, as stressed by Heidegger in *Being and Time*.[44] However, when we grasp the idea of care as power and as time, we can also see that teaching (as an instrument of the mode of care) is nothing but guiding, showing the way, and leading in the etymological sense of the word.

As I often tell my students at the outset of a new semester, we are going to undertake a journey together, a journey I have already taken other times, though every time that journey is singularly different, determined by the singularity of each class composition and the way it relates to the material at hand. Teaching is not about imparting anything to anyone; otherwise, one immediately falls into ideological, dogmatic, and poor indoctrination. Rather, teaching (and learning) – the two must of course always go together – entails undergoing an experience with the *power to do* things, individually and collectively. Teaching is transformative in that it transforms not simply the individual (a problematic concept in its own right), but the relations that make up an individual, which ultimately are *transindividual*.

Now, in the idea (and process) of transformation, there is a passage from one form to another. The passage is the journey I alluded to above. It can last one semester or a whole life; and perhaps, as teaching and learning never end, life itself becomes a series of these passages (or thresholds), whose main structure and framework is given by care itself, by the need for caring. In this sense, teaching (and learning) is also what is usually called *critical thinking*, a wonderful concept, though often, and especially recently, vilified and abused. However, true thinking is always critical, if one considers the etymology of that word, coming from the Greek word for *crisis*. To see thinking as the result of a crisis means to understand that thinking starts when things don't go as smoothly as perhaps expected, when something breaks down, and the need arises for a pause, for the time

---

44   Martin Heidegger, *Being and Time*, trans. Joan Stambaugh (New York: State University of New York Press, 1996), 184.

and space of analysis and synthesis, and for undertaking the task of (or the attempt at) a reconstitution of one's perception of reality.

So, I think that what I say in *Earthly Plenitudes*, that "the transformation of the university is not possible if society itself is not transformed," is correct. The nice thing is that there is a dialectical moment here: true education (not the university) is what may help transform society. True education, once again, is care – and care is power, as we have seen. The university as such may as well disappear.

BG asks: I find the following very interesting and intriguing: "In many ways, writing is a more desperate (and less dangerous) act of insurrection." However, you say, "revolt is another kind of writing," and you add, "Perhaps revolt is the writing that matters most."[45] Then, toward the end of the book, you speak of "the philosophical content of revolt" and of "revolt as philosophical work."[46] I'd like to hear more about *writing*, which to me seems to be an expression of revolt as important as (perhaps at times more important than) any other. Isn't writing (a certain, subversive, writing) an eminent expression of the reason of revolt, and potentially as dangerous as any other act of revolt? Although you say that "Revolt is communicative action by means other than words, by means other than text," you also add that "Revolt thinks, acts, writes and speaks *against* the existing state affairs."[47] In the following and final pages of your book you repeat a few times that revolt "thinks, acts, writes, and speaks *against*..." This is fascinating, and I completely agree with it. So, can writing itself be an act of revolt? Not any writing of course, but the writing from below, from the margins and thresholds perhaps, can that be precisely the intellect of insurrection, the specter of revolt?

RGO answers: Yes, it is not surprising that we are asking each other about writing in this book. We are writers, and sometimes, situated such as we are, writing is our only way to make common cause with others elsewhere making revolt. Still, I never know how much writing matters. I sometimes think I would not write anything at all if I could not imagine or willfully suffer the delusion that people will read it and find it useful. If a writer – and especially

---

45   Gilman-Opalsky, *Specters of Revolt*, op. cit., 197.
46   Ibid., 224-225.
47   Ibid., 245.

political theorists or Marxist philosophers – knew in advance that nothing they wrote would ever be read or useful, then the writer would cease to exist as such. I would become a private poet, perhaps, writing only for myself, for my own health and well-being, but I would not write for a hopeful world of strangers. I do think that good writing shares the aspirations of a revolt. Consider the fact that good writing tries to interrupt normal thinking and life, aims to discombobulate composure, wants to make epiphanies, and participate in the production of new understandings of the world, of one's self and relation to the world. If you really think about what a revolt does, it is not the same thing for sure, but there are some clear and shared sensibilities. You want to express something with other people, and you want to challenge and change things. Writing, revolt, and other forms of artistic activity are all different ways to approach that.

For me, the highest aspiration for writing would be to aid and abet revolts and revolutionary struggles. Even if the revolt does not need my help, I would want to offer my writing in its service. It is not so different from being any other kind of artist who wants to paint or play music in the service of a cause. With a book like *Specters of Revolt*, this partly entails trying to say what the revolt says directly itself, but saying it in a communicative form that might reach people who are either convinced that revolt communicates nothing, or that they cannot grasp its message. I think a writer can help with that problem, even if they cannot solve it. Writing is usually not as dangerous as revolt, although it could become dangerous in certain circumstances. There have been political prisoners, from Socrates, Antonio Negri, and from Angela Y. Davis to Assata Shakur, Mumia Abu Jamal, and Chelsea Manning, and we know that in some situations, saying something at a particular time could be very bad news for the one who says it. Some writers are jailed, some assassinated, and books have been banned when they pose real threats from the perspective of those in the ruling class (or those in a state legislature or on the school board). Efforts to criminalize writing, such as in recent book bans and right-wing scrutiny of university curricula, could be very bad news indeed. You can be fired, canceled, doxed and targeted for vigilante violence.

Nonetheless, most writers can enjoy a certain epistemological protection. Considered as part of a network of knowledge production or argumentation, the worst we often face is a bad review or disagreement. Many writers may be disappointed that is all they can rouse, and many more cannot even rouse that much. For writers like us, one of the worst fates is to be unconvincing, and being boring is close to death. Perhaps the most obvious danger for writers like us is economic... There is not much exchange value for radical writing in our capitalist societies.

Of course, people who stand up to police and white supremacists in the streets of Kenosha or Minneapolis, who come out of Ukrainian subways to risk their lives in a shootout with Russian soldiers, are facing very different and incomparably more severe dangers. I repeatedly say in the book that revolt thinks, acts, writes, and speaks *against* this and *for* that, but I also argue that this writing from below is more effective and important than my own writing or your writing. If we writers could only be as threatening as a revolt! However, revolt is more threatening, and the way to assess this is in any measure of the counterinsurgent response of capitalist power, that is, of the state, the police, the military, the law and the criminal "justice" system. Writers scarcely meet suppression by militarized police forces.

Still, I will answer your question here with an affirmation: Yes, writing can be an act of revolt, if it shares the aims of a revolt and pursues them in its own writerly ways. You are correct to qualify that not all writing does this. Moreover, what we need more than theory, far more than *our own* writing, are the collective upheavals of thought in philosophy from below. Police forces train in crowd control and repression during periods of the absence of revolt because the specter of revolt always haunts them. Police forces are not so worried about philosophy, or theoretical or political writing. Revolutionaries want to haunt their enemies. Remember what Marx and Engels said: "A spectre is haunting Europe – the spectre of Communism. All the powers of old Europe have entered into a holy alliance to exorcise this spectre: Pope and Tsar, Metternich and Guizot, French Radicals and German police spies."[48]

Marx and Engels were happy to report of such ghosts. These ghosts made them hopeful. These ghosts, they went on to argue, proved that communism was now recognized throughout Europe as a real threat. Some specters are reassuring, including the specter of communism, Derrida's specters of Marx, and, I add, specters of revolt. If our enemies are not afraid of what we write, let us aspire to the writing that haunts them... It is perhaps too high of an expectation, but we never want our enemies to sleep too soundly.

---

48 Karl Marx and Friedrich Engels, *The Communist Manifesto: Deluxe Edition*, trans. Samuel Moore (New York and London: Penguin Books, 2011), 63.

BG asks: As I write this, I realize that its tone resembles that of a letter I could be writing to you. In fact, it occurred to me that I could title this "A Letter on *The Communism of Love*." Obviously, a letter of this type is still a philosophical reflection, but one in which the distance between the one who writes it and the one who receives it is perhaps attenuated or taken away. It is interesting that you and I have never met in person (not yet), but we have carefully read each other's books, are writing on them, constructing a dialogue in which there is also something very intimate and personal: We have spoken about your children, for instance, and about the tragic death of my younger brother. I am not saying this as some kind of rhetorical flourish or Pindaric flight; rather, this is something that directly leads to another central theme of your book, one that you yourself say is "fundamental." This is the theme of *life, a life*. You say, "This book is fundamentally about what to do with a life, what life is for."[49] This is a very important, beautiful, and profound thought. It goes straight to the heart of philosophy, the question of singularity, *thisness*, the crossroads of ontology, poetry, and the political understood as "forms of being-in-the-world with others."[50] Your sections on Jenny Marx, Rosa Luxemburg, and Alexandra Kollontai in Chapter 3 of your book, "The Love of Communists," to which I will go back, make this very clear. You say that yours is "a book of difficult subjects," and I agree.[51] They are difficult subjects because they have to do with life and death. As you say, love "is inevitable – as inevitable as death – even if the experience of love is less certain."[52]

Yet, all this must be understood according to the pointer provided by your book's subtitle, "An Inquiry into the Poverty of Exchange Value." Perhaps this is one of the great merits of your book: the ability to conjugate every day and existential questions with those pertaining more closely to the Marxian critique of political economy and capital. Thus, you say that "love constitutes a collective subject with a more threatening sensibility, a collectivity capable of a defiance and creativity that capital cannot bear."[53] And in Chapter 3, "The Love of Communists," you clearly say that

---

49 Gilman-Opalsky, *The Communism of Love*, op. cit., 17.
50 Ibid., 59.
51 Ibid., 18.
52 Ibid., 17.
53 Ibid., 14.

"love is a tendency contrary to that of the system of exchange."[54] We are talking about *communist* love, love as a practice. Is this perhaps something akin to *living labor*, the form of life antagonistic to capital? If this is so, it then also redefines and broadens the concept of living labor itself. Is love as a practice a form of labor, perhaps its eminent form? Is non-subjected and non-subjugated labor a form of love? Is this what *a life*, a singularity, could be about? I don't mean labor in a narrow sense, but *living labor* broadly construed, encompassing all human activities geared towards the creation and production of the essential and useful, the production even of subjectivity, or, as I prefer, singularity, a multiplicity of singularities, and, in fact, a world. Then, perhaps the question of *what to do with a life, what life is for* points to the necessary contingency of our existence in the sense of having to choose between the poverty of exchange value, as you say, the stupidity, in the sense of Bernard Stiegler, characterizing a disfigured form of existence and the practice of love, which, as a communist practice, also includes what I like to call *the love of others*. This is different from the notion of the love for others, loving others, which is more common, obvious, and easily understood. Rather, the love *of* others means loving their love, or, as you say in your section on Simone Weil, engaging in that type of love, that type of power, "capable of helping us to see others as they are."[55] This is not simply loving them for what they are, but, as you say, creating that "connective tissue between beings"[56] that, you remark, for Weil gets to the point of connecting us to *justice*.[57] Indeed, this love of others, which is also a function of Weil's concept of attention, which you review, is perhaps the highest form of ethics. I would be interested in hearing what you think of my interpretation of this.

RGO answers: Love as a communist practice is absolutely at work in *living labor*. A free jazz musician dedicated to every facet of the saxophone knows well that their interests and creative practice is, if not antagonistic, completely extraneous to the logic of capital. If we follow your convincing arguments about the labor that is not capitalist, and we think and speak of labor as something beautiful, non-exploitative, with other values than

---

54   Ibid., 101.
55   Ibid., 21.
56   Ibid.
57   Ibid., 22.

exchange value, then I would not resist the idea of love as a form of labor. There is already the obvious example of what people call a "labor of love," which may include the work of the saxophonist mentioned above. This captures the fact that people actually do many things not for money, mobilized by nonmonetary values. This already returns us to John Holloway's notion of "other-doing." However, there is also the fact that love is hard work, even when it is not capitalist but rather, a living labor. Love is neither soft nor easy.

I am sorry to say that my arguments about love have found their greatest evidence for me personally in the challenges of participating in my teenage son's becoming. (Perhaps, Bruno, you found something similar in your experience with your brother Pino.) Active love relations are very difficult, often exhausting, and in recent experiences with my son, I have never felt more depleted physically and emotionally by any other labor that I have ever done. We make no money in our efforts to help him, could even lose all of our money in the process, and certainly cannot have the confidence that our efforts will prevail. At times, we have no idea where it will end up, what we can do, how it will go. There is no clear unit of production, and yet, the most obvious thing to my family, beyond any question, is that this love's labor will never stop as long as we draw breath. It is a peculiar commitment not found widely throughout society, and indeed, the system reminds us daily that most of the health professionals working alongside us are only there for their pay. Most of them are good, caring people, and they sincerely want to help, but are only bound to us by an exchange relation. Let us make no mistake, then, love is not only laborious, but is perhaps the most laborious activity in a human life. This makes love sound awful, and yet, it is responsible for the best and most beautiful things in a human life.

Now, your other question is different, the question about non-subjected and non-subjugated labor as a form of love. I do not think this is true. I would say that all love is non-subjugated labor, but that *not all non-subjugated labor is love.* We may think again about our saxophonist or a painter, poet, sculptor or some other artist. People can do these non-subjugated "labors of love" all alone and often do. You go into your studio or study, you paint a canvas, write a poem, you feel very good or very sad in the process, which feels to you quite necessary. However, you are all alone. You are not lonely, perhaps, and it feels good. However, in my concept of love, the activity always implicates another person or others more broadly. In my theory, love is an activity that *involves other people*. It must extend outward and reach for a social relation against exchange relations. When I think about the living labor of a saxophonist, it may go in that direction, but it may not. One saxophonist may practice and create to affect other people through their music in a recording or live performance. A different saxophonist may only play privately alone in their room as a method for feeling good. Let me share an example. I am a drummer. Sometimes I play a live performance. Sometimes I play with other musicians. Other times, I just want to play alone to work out some feelings. In the latter instance, I would call that non-subjugated labor, but maybe not love. I can work hard behind the drums, work on a technique for hours, and even break a sweat. I emerge feeling good. Is that an act of love? Perhaps it is a form of self-love. My theory accounts for that, but it is not the central point.

Simone Weil's concept of attention to others, along with the insights of Emmanuel Levinas, call upon lovers to attend to the frailties of others. This is exactly the difference that makes a difference for me here. An artist who paints alone may be doing a kind of living labor. The key, which I always emphasize, is the externalization of love in a social sense and setting. Erich Fromm got this part right, and I want to preserve it in my theory. Many other theorists of love continue to miss that, and they write about love as a private and even asocial affair.

Having said that, I agree that *a life*, or a singularity, could be about living labor broadly construed and possibly even should be, if we are not too afraid of that troubling notion of "ought." Humans must do things. Humans must make things. This is the concept of *homo faber* that is so often associated with Marx. The question is, what will they do and make? Indeed, the question of what we will do, what we will make, is the question of what to do with a life, *what a life is for*.

Unsurprisingly, I agree entirely that the love of others is a crucial aspect of any communist form of life worthy of our aspirations. I would also agree to return to the idea of love as a connective tissue between beings, although maybe we should say that other forms of living labor that are perhaps not so easily characterized as love – like painting or drumming alone – may also be such a connective tissue. Perhaps it is not so obvious how that is the case, but I can imagine that painting or drumming alone may prepare one affectively for being-in-the-world with others.

CHAPTER 3

HUMAN BEING AND BECOMING

Bruno Gullì (BG) asks: Addressing the question of the false antipathy between the national and transnational public spheres, you say, in the general introduction to *Unbounded Publics*, "I argue that there has been and can be a different kind of public sphere, a *transgressive public sphere*, which inhabits the two frameworks to complementarily."[1] As you say, there has always been, and there always is, a multiplicity of transgressive public spheres – as evidenced by social movements, acts of civil disobedience, uprisings, and so on – and you speak of this as "nonbourgeois public spheres."[2] Traditionally, you say, for instance in Habermas, social movements are not seen as instances and expressions of public spheres. You then show with compelling clarity that not only are they indeed constitutive of the public spheres but that, essentially, they express the real meaning of nonbourgeois and transgressive public sphere. For instance, in a very interesting passage in your book, speaking of the paradigmatic case of the Zapatistas, you say that "it is often the marginalized social position of nonbourgeois groups that makes a transnational construction favorable, necessary, or both."[3] It is precisely what you call the "double occupancy" of national and transnational moments that, in the case of the Zapatistas as well as many other movements, you say, gives public spheres their transgressive dimension and quality.[4] This is very important because it conceptually as well as practically prepares the ground for the fascinating logic of the neither/nor of transgression. You spell this out in relation to the Zapatistas when you

---

1   Richard Gilman-Opalsky, *Unbonded Publics: Transgressive Public Spheres, Zapatismo, and Political Theory* (Lanham, MD: Lexington Books, 2008), xii.
2   Ibid., xiv; 87-88; 90-91; 102.
3   Ibid., 88.
4   Ibid., xiii.

say, still in the general introduction, that "while the Zapatistas retained a particular nationalist rhetoric and orientation, they managed to recast indigenous politics as transnational and cosmopolitan at the same time."[5] Personally, I like the word 'transboundary' that you use to describe the character of the transgressive public spheres (*spheres*, you say, in the plural, and I like this, too).

I wonder if, in this respect, you could address the concepts of the boundary (or border), the limit, and the threshold. In other words, what takes place in the 'trans-' of the transboundary and transgressive? Is the national character of identities and struggles kept intact, or is it already contaminated? If the former is the case, how can there then be a passage into something completely different? If the latter is the case, what is the ontological plane of this contamination? I imagine it is the sphere, or plane, of the neither/nor. But could you explain that for us?

There is, as Étienne Balibar says of the border, a moment of vacillation on the plane of the neither/nor, or perhaps it is entirely (and not entirely) a space (and a place) of vacillation. Is it possible that the public, entirely lacking in ontological status, has no place, no role to play here? Is it possible that with transgression, the way you understand it, we finally enter the sphere of ontology, a new ontology of the political, which has no use for the category of the public (whether of the national or transnational type), but that it has instead exploded the restraints of that category to produce something qualitatively (and completely, and yet incompletely) different?

Richard Gilman-Opalsky (RGO) answers: Capital has, so far, reliably managed to be more transboundary than its opponents. We often struggle to find footing for confrontations. However, what is a boundary? From the seventeenth century, the noun "boundary" comes from the root "bound," so we are thinking about restriction, limitation, or being "tied up." Boundaries indicate limits. Marking the limit is a dividing line of some kind, which tells you that if you go beyond the line you will exceed the boundary. In the "trans" of the transboundary, we always find some possibility beyond the limit. With the transboundary, whether you get there in a movement beyond the nation's limit, beyond limitations of gender, restrictions of ideology, you know that you are challenging something established, that you are breaking a convention.

---

5   Ibid., xv.

Yes, the national character of political identity is always already contaminated. When the Muslim or Jew or proletarian or environmental or feminist activist identifies with a diasporic group, one finds an identification with something that prevents a strict or "pure" nationalism. One knows, for example, that they are making common cause with other environmental or feminist activists elsewhere. The ontological dimension of this contamination is of crucial importance, because it reminds us that no one is only one thing. A person may be a woman, a Buddhist, a lesbian, a German, and feminist all at the same time. This implicates expansive intersections, as is commonly discussed today under the heading "intersectionality," but it also implicates certain transgressions.

I agree with Balibar that, at the border, at that point where one can go either way, there is a moment of vacillation on the plane of neither/nor. This neither/nor is contained in the question, "What if we do not choose one of the immediately available and well-worn paths?" This neither/nor also – like transgression – indicates a questioning and a rejection, assuming of course that one does not simply delay the choice of this path or that. I would say there is more than mere negation in this. It is not just refusing this path or that, for there is also a positive dimension about the possibility of doing something else. You can perhaps go a third way, "toward a future that is *not yet*," to invoke a phrase of Emmanuel Levinas from *Totality and Infinity*.[6]

Now, I should clarify my reason for choosing to write about "the public," which you are wondering about, and even, wondering if it was the right choice. I share your concern about an emphasis on the public. I was only sure that I wanted to think about politics from below. It is worth noting that, in political science, there is a widespread and anemic view of the political, which fixates on only the affairs of public institutions of governance. Therefore, most political scientists and political theorists tend to think politics by way of the ruling political class. Of course, so much politics is the domain of the ruling class. Therefore, I have never been surprised that political science as a discipline has struggled so extraordinarily to attract impoverished people and people of color. The discipline focuses on public policy, policymakers, legislative and judicial politics, and internationally, it mostly engages comparative studies of nation-states and their policies, domestic and foreign.

---

6   Emmanuel Levinas, *Totality and Infinity: An Essay on Exteriority*, trans. Alphonso Lingis (The Hague: Martinus Nijhoff, 1979), 271.

I think we have to begin with that in mind. What the public sphere enabled me to do – and it is certainly *not the only way to do it* – was to center the political in the non-institutional activities of autonomously assembling people, and precisely, to focus on the active gatherings of everyday people outside of political-institutional power. Rather than "looking up" for the Sovereign of politics, as one might do after reading Hobbes's *Leviathan*, I wanted to look around and at ourselves in a more horizontal way, to juxtapose the politics of capital and its governments (the latter of which capital owns and controls) to a politics from below, a politics of everyday people regarded as extraneous to politics.

I retain this same juxtaposition in my later work. However, today, I prefer to think of the revolt than the public sphere, though that is probably because the revolt has reentered the stage of world history over the last 15-20 years in some striking ways. For me, the concept of the public sphere was something like a placeholder for the kind of politics that I wanted to think about and see emergent in the world. Recently, however, we do not need that placeholder, because we have seen so many rebellions and revolts from the Zapatistas to Indignados to Nuit Debout and Gilet Jaunes to the Arab Spring and Occupy and #BLM and many more powerful and disrupting examples. If we can speak of revolt instead of the public sphere, I think that is the better word and idea. However, I still want to remember the public sphere for those times in between revolts. We need to be able to think politics in between elections and revolts, and I think that the concept of the public sphere can help us to do that.

All the revolts I mentioned in passing above are also, at the same time, ontological projects, inasmuch as they are all confronting limitations of life in the existing world, and trying to think of different emancipatory pathways. We can think about life in the existing world and ask: What does it mean to live in a pandemic world where everyone is perceived as a biological threat? What does it mean to live in a world where white men with guns only need to convince a jury that they are afraid in order to murder people and be found innocent of murder? What does it mean to live in a world of financial insecurity, and white supremacy? What does it mean to live in a world where the presence of police reassure some parents that their children are safe, while other parents are terrified by that very same police presence? What does it mean to live in a world of mass incarceration, growing global inequality, in a world where capital almost totally decides what one can do and does? These are some of the questions raised by revolt, directly or indirectly, and the questions posed by revolt are fundamentally about forms of life.

So yes, we are talking about human being and becoming, that is, what could be, possible forms of life, in a city, school, family, etc. The revolt, ultimately, has no use for the category "public sphere." The revolt takes its place. Indeed, I think we should want to see revolt replace the public sphere, and ideally, we should want to see new forms of life replace the revolt. Revolt is never for its own sake. It is for the sake of something else, other than itself, and beyond the existing state of affairs.

RGO asks: Do you think there are some people who are not capable of what you call a poetic ontology, or of living labor? I mean to ask here not only about disability, but about diverse abilities and forms of labor. In *Labor of Fire*, when you speak of art and creativity, you say that "*poeisis* must become *praxis*,"[7] and you talk about "poetic doing" and the subversive work of poetry.[8] Later on, you discuss graffiti in a similar register.[9] We sometimes think about art as a special capability, as a unique power of the "right-brain." Is it possible for everyone to be an artist? Alternatively, is art only available to some of us by way of its consumption, or by way of our attentions? I ask this question in light of your idea that there is a political, moral, and ontological imperative to art.

BG answers: Perhaps we should start by demystifying the meaning of the word 'art.' Art is also skill or craft, and the Greek word for it, as Heidegger says, is *techne*. In different ways, and to various degrees, everyone is capable of doing or producing art – once we properly understand what that means; in other words, everyone is skillful in some ways, or engages in some kind of craft and *techne*. Obviously, everyone is also capable of performing living labor. But we should also demystify the concept of the artist. Dave Beech, both in *Art and Postcapitalism*[10] and in *Art and Labour*,[11]

---

7   Gullì, *Labor of Fire*, op. cit., 159.
8   Ibid., 165-173.
9   Ibid., 176.
10 Dave Beech, *Art and Postcapitalism: Aesthetic Labour, Automation and Value Production* (London: Pluto Press, 2019).
11 Dave Beech, *Art and Labour: On the Hostility to Handicraft, Aesthetic Labour and the Politics of Work in Art* (Chicago: Haymarket Books, 2021).

does that. Indeed, he does more than that. The distinction between art and handicraft and the emergence of *the myth of the artist* become, and remain, very problematic issues. I really don't know, and perhaps I don't want to know, about the "right-brain" and things like that, but I think that, more than the question as to whether everyone can be an artist, we should consider whether everyone can cross the territory of singularity, the plane of experience, and the transformative process of constant individuation whereby the potential as potential comes to the fore. A dangerous path and a frightening trajectory. Yet, this is the political, moral, and ontological imperative that can be subsumed under the name of art – even the art of writing what "ain't right to write," as a San Francisco campaign against graffiti said in the 1990's with ads on buses.

In *Dialectic of Enlightenment,* Max Horkheimer and Theodor Adorno speak of the "withering of imagination and spontaneity" in the culture industry and consumer society.[12] That was written in the mid-1940s. Today, there is perhaps a total renunciation of the imagination and spontaneity, or a transfer of them from singular and common existence to social networks, reels, advertisements, and video games. In a situation like this, attention (which should always be understood in conjunction with care) is gone. Perhaps there is still some kind of consumption, but it is not productive consumption; it is not productive of anything. It is merely consumption of the self, of time, and of attention itself. Indeed, as Horkheimer and Adorno say, "The products of the culture industry are such that they can be alertly consumed even in a state of distraction."[13] There is then no poetic doing anymore, no passing over of *poeisis* into *praxis* and of *praxis* into *poeisis*. Yet, the culprit of all this is not digital technology, as some people may think, but rather the capture and framing of spontaneity and the imagination, of living labor, by the logic of productivity and debt. The point is then to recuperate this lost spontaneity, to fire up the power of the imagination.

Subversion is of course still possible, and it is the only way out of the sadness and danger we experience today. In order for this to happen, we don't have to go back to the idea of art as an afterthought and a special activity, as something detached from daily life, and as a further inroad into

---

12   Max Horkheimer and Theodor Adorno, *Dialectic of the Enlightenment: Philosophical Fragments*, trans. Edmund Jephcott (Stanford University Press, 2002), 100.
13   Ibid.

the culture industry, business, and entrepreneurial logic. Rather, we need to contrast and subvert the logic of productivity and focus on what Marx calls – I repeat once again – *the emancipation of the senses*. It is thus that poetic ontology will show its potency, transfigure and transform reality.

RGO asks: No engagement with your work could be complete without considering questions of disability, or of differential ability. You think about disability and differential ability throughout your work, and with important attention in Chapter 5 of *Earthly Plenitudes*. I want to ask you a difficult question about the limitations of becoming in the face of disability and social exclusion. This question is perhaps as difficult to ask as it is to answer.

Like you, I critically appreciate Martha Nussbaum's and Amartya Sen's capabilities approach. Contrary to Nussbaum's emphasis on "productive contributions," I think you rightly suggest that people with disabilities should not be evaluated according to the extent to which they "might more fully join the mechanism and machinery of capital."[14] While I agree, I observe that this is the same argument you make for anyone, for people with or without disabilities or any other impairments. You do not want my children to be measured in that way, nor do you want your own work (or mine) to be measured in that way. But I want to ask you about the *specific* being-in-the-world of people with disabilities. How does a communist ontology confront real limitations of becoming in the diversity of human being-in-the-world? To what extent, for example, does caring for someone with severe mental disabilities involve a concrete confrontation with impossibilities of being and becoming *that are not imposed by capital*? Do we concede the possibility that some cannot become what they would like to be (or even *ought to* be)? Do we concede that desirable possibilities may be impossible for some people even in a transformed future world ungoverned by the logic of capital? Or, should we not concede these points at all?

BG answers: I don't know if I can answer these important and, as you say, difficult questions in any meaningful way, or if I can answer them at all. However, I will try. I love the fact that the key word here is 'becoming.' You ask about the limitations of becoming and about possibilities and impossibilities. All this, as you implicitly point out, goes beyond the existence

---

14   Gullì, *Earthly Plenitudes*, op. cit., 149.

and persistence of the logic of capital. To get this, we should go back to the idea of power I spoke about above – power as the ability to do things; not power in a narrow political sense, but power in its ontological sense. There are things that we can do and things that we cannot do. This is true at the level of the species and at the individual level. Humans can't fly, for instance, no matter how deft they are. But they can do many other things. As an individual, I may perhaps not be able to draw or sing, or at least not be good at it. Perhaps I will not become a painter or a singer. This may count as a limitation for me. Yet, I can do many other things.

You also ask about desire, and that, too, should be seen in its real, concrete, and ontological sense. Desire must be grounded and determined; it must be based on the concrete, if radical, imagination, not on fantasy; otherwise, it is no longer desire, but wishful thinking. Obviously, there are many obstacles to desire and becoming brought about by the logic of capital or by other equally nefarious and abusive ideological and repressive systems, such as patriarchy, supremacism, racism, sexism, and so on. These obstacles may, and indeed must, be deactivated and dismantled. So, when Amartya Sen speaks of poverty as capability deprivation in *Development as Freedom*, that's a good example of problems that need to be solved, obstacles that must be removed.[15] In any case, beyond Sen's and Martha Nussbaum's interesting capabilities approach, the philosophy of communism has always been about the full development of human potentialities. Liberal philosophies also seek the full development of the individual, but they consider individuals in their isolation and separateness. The superiority of communism is that it looks at the individual as a social being and thus within a framework of superindividuality or transindividuality.

Furthermore, the overcoming of those limitations of becoming that are the result of socio-economic, political and cultural conditions requires a total reshaping and transformation of society, namely, of the mechanisms and dynamics that make those conditions possible in the first place. This is indeed what the project of the revolution is about. However, "even in a transformed future world ungoverned by the logic of capital," as you put it very well in your question, some "desirable possibilities may be impossible for some people." I think that, yes, we have to concede this.

The truth is that human potentialities can be limited or impaired in

---

15 Amartya Sen, *Development as Freedom* (New York: Anchor Books, 1999).

at least two ways. One way is when conditions of limitations of becoming are human-made, as I have just said above. The other way has to do with some natural conditions that arise spontaneously (for instance, at the genetic level) or because of an accident or trauma at any point in a person's life, including at the very moment of birth. In this case, which is typically that of severe disabilities, some possibilities, considered desirable in general, may remain impossible for some people. However, it is perhaps precisely the general and abstract way to look at the desirable that constitutes a problem. When viewed in its generality and abstractness, the desirable loses its meaning – no longer connected to concrete desire – and becomes a mere, and perhaps counterproductive, normative formality and indeed a code of normalization. To make a concrete example, if I am not able to walk because of some irreversible condition of impairment, I wonder whether walking would be desirable for me. The point is that desire (and thus the desirable) is concrete and singular, not general and abstract. Yet, when something that is desirable in general becomes singularly impossible, there is actually a lot to be done in terms of care. And it is here, as well as in similar situations, that the importance of the dimension of superindividuality or transindividuality becomes fully apparent.

I believe that a communist world would make it possible for a concrete and singular desire to flourish, for becoming to unfold within the full and utmost limits of the finitude of each existent, of its finite potential. Contrary to trivializing accounts and widespread misconceptions, the communist project is that of a world that values difference as difference, singularity, and the contingency of desire. And I would like to end the answer to this difficult question with a quote by Nicholas of Cusa from *De docta ignorantia*, "There is present in all things a natural desire to exist in the best manner in which the condition of each thing's nature permits this."[16] It is often the pathological state of our societies that tampers with that.

BG asks: I particularly like Chapter 1, "Becoming-Ghost" in your book, *Specters of Revolt*. I find it fascinating. First of all, I'd like you to say more about the presence and the absence of ghosts.[17] You say that the formal situation is "real and normal," while the latter is "paranormal" (a word that

---

16 Quoted in Johannes Hoff, *The Analogical Turn: Rethinking Modernity with Nicholas of Cusa* (Grand Rapids, Michigan: Wm. B. Eerdmans Publishing Co., 2013), xix.
17 Gilman-Opalsky, *Specters of Revolt*, op. cit., 29; 32.

you put in scare quotes.) But what I find especially interesting is the analysis of "ghost" and "*Geist*" and the use of the work of Guattari throughout this chapter. I like the way you highlight the importance of "ghosts" at the everyday, personal, and existential level: "Each person comes with some ghosts."[18] Then you move to the social and political dimension, that is, to "*our* ghosts."[19] You take this very seriously and ask the question, "What do we do with these ghosts? Or, what can these ghosts do?"[20] Soon we find the *ghost of communism*.[21] So, in what sense is communism a ghost? In line with Marx and Engels' famous statement in The Communist Manifesto, you say that "communism aspires to threaten the constituted present *in an existential way*, and inasmuch as communism threatens to abolish or transform the existing world, the world is haunted by it" (italics added).[22] Can you say more about the "*existential way*" in which the specter of communism threatens the constituted present? Is this perhaps a total ontological remake of the world and of existence? On the next page, you speak of "dignity and love," and of course your latest book is precisely on the question of love, the communism of love.[23] Is it perhaps the case that what is haunting us, our disfigured existence, is the insuppressible potency of dignity and love?

RGO answers: People tend to think of the "paranormal" as a domain of ghosts, the supernatural, mystical, etc. I define ghosts as active agents of haunting, but haunting need not be paranormal. Most people are haunted by something from their past, many cities are haunted by war, and states are haunted by imperialism, genocide, and other tortures. Germany may forever be haunted by the ghosts of its Nazi past, and undoubtedly, the recent revanchist attack on Ukraine will surely haunt Russia for a long time

---

18   Ibid., 37.
19   Ibid., 38.
20   Ibid., 48.
21   Ibid., 53.
22   Ibid., 54.
23   Ibid., 55.

to come.[24] Everyone everywhere, every state and every person, is haunted by something. When we think about ghosts according to such a hauntology, there is nothing paranormal about them. Such ghosts are common, part of our everyday lives, normal. What is outside normal experience – and therefore more worthy of the name paranormal – would be a person or state that is haunted by nothing from their past, who has no ghosts at all. The total absence of ghosts may even be suspicious, since it suggests the absence of any considerate reckoning with the past.

From Hegel's *Phenomenology of Spirit* to the present day, philosophy has been obsessed with "*Geist*," the German word for spirit and mind. It also means ghost, although philosophy usually forgets this third term. I have tried to think about the spectral dimension of *Geist*. Marx and Engels understood the spectral status of communism, in that they saw how fearful capitalists and governments were of revolt in the nineteenth century. Communism was the specter haunting Europe in 1848. After the end of the Cold War, however, communism seemed to be ghost-busted, and Jacques Derrida went on to consider *Specters of Marx*.[25] Derrida's proposal was that, even if the specter of communism is gone, the specter of Marx should continue to haunt, and that it undoubtedly will. I went on in a kind of sequence to think about the specter of revolt. To answer your question more directly, communism has somewhat surprisingly returned as an active ghost, proving that even the first in the series of famous specters still haunts. As long as the logic of capital organizes so much of life on Earth and so much of world affairs (the logic of capital's

---

24　When I speak of Putin's revanchist attack, I should clarify that this does not imply any kind of Hollywood proclamation that "I stand with Zelenskyy." I do not accept the premise that one must choose to take sides with one or another head of state, with one or another government, in any international conflict. I prefer to look at conflicts from the perspective of the affected populations, specifically from the bottom up. Inside every civil society too, we will find deplorable things, fascistic tendencies, and reactionaries of all kinds. We have to insist on condemning whatever deserves condemnation, and reject the false choices presented in ideological wars of position waged by nation-states. This means that one can condemn revanchist or imperialist militarism, taking sides with neither Putin nor Zelenskyy, but instead with courageous anti-war activists inside of Russia as well as anti-fascist insurgents in Ukraine.

25　Jacques Derrida, *Specters of Marx: The State of the Debt, the Work of Mourning and the New International*, trans. Peggy Kamuf (New York and London: Routledge, 1994).

organization of life and affairs is capitalism), as long as the rule of capital endangers our planet (and all of its animal life), there will always be a communist specter.

As we mention many times in this book, Marx called communism the real movement to abolish the present state of things, and the present state of things is not so good that we will be done with the specter of communism. Therefore, the specter of communism may reassure communists like us, although it guarantees nothing. We are stuck with a precarious communism. However, when I wrote about the communist aspiration to overthrow the present *in an existential sense*, I meant to grasp the ontological side of communism, as you also do in your work. Communists look at a world organized by the logic of capital and ask, "Can we exist differently? Can there be other forms of life? Is this what it means to be?"

Let us consider where we are today. When you visit friends and family in California or Italy, money and time decide your ability to do so, and concerns over money colonize our concerns over time. People like you and me who want to question a world governed by capital are so dis-incentivized from doing so that there are precious few who can actually pay rent and raise families doing the work of thinking and writing. We are few, and we have little mobility to choose where to live. Then, we look at a wide world of impoverished people, overlapping predominantly with BIPOC sectors of society, suffering disproportionately from ongoing racism, classism, imperialism, and colonization. You and I read Bernard Stiegler. We know from Stiegler and others that a world organized by capital creates incredible anxiety, exacerbates suicide, and generalizes competition and panic over cooperation and well-being. If I want to see other people, friends beyond the spheres of family and work, I have to figure out how to manage it. Not only how will I reclaim time from money to create the space for friendship, but do we even know how to be with others anymore? One has to worry if friendship is becoming a lost art.

Long before Stiegler, Roland Barthes wrote about much of this in his powerful book *How to Live Together*. There, he writes about "idiorrhythmy," which means that we each have our own idiosyncratic particular rhythms of life, and we try to live together while really wanting to remain apart.[26] Beyond the psychosocial and economic dimensions of racism and classism,

---

26   Roland Barthes, *How to Live Together: Novelistic Simulations of Some Everyday Spaces*, trans. Kate Briggs (New York: Columbia University Press, 2013), 8.

we inhabit a world that commodifies everything, even things like love, health, education, care of the most vulnerable, drinking water, air, and fields of green grass. It is daunting to consider. We may read Silvia Federici and think about "the commons" under attack by a rampant global privatization that knows no bounds. Then, there are the ecological, sexual, and other crises we face. It is impossible to think about how to change all of this and more, but we have no choice. We cannot survive the current form of life. Just because we have survived it up to now (and many millions have not survived it, of course), does not mean we can go on and expect the same in perpetuity.

Ok, to say something about existentialism. Existentialists are concerned about existence beyond a simple biological status. Jean-Paul Sartre, Maurice Merleau-Ponty, Albert Camus, and Simone De Beauvoir all argued that even if we take biological human life for granted, we must move beyond functioning organs to the question of what it means to be. In other words, existentialism marks a passage from the *fact of life* to the *meaning of life*. Nowadays, in an era of pandemics, ecological catastrophe, and renewed nuclear peril, we cannot even take the fact of life for granted. Our world, such as it is today, is haunted by the specter of many different worlds that we may variously imagine. Our active love relations reveal that human relations can actually be something other than exchange relations, and that is why I moved on from the theory of revolt to the theory of love. The irrepressible eternal return of revolt reminds us of a potency to aspire for something else, for a different life on Earth. We may find that aspiration elsewhere, such as in the aspiration to love, but it is always present in the activity of revolt.

RGO asks: In *Humanity and the Enemy*, you claim that "there are three categories of people that can be said to be more at risk [from the enemy] ... They are the categories of disability, race, and foreignness."[27] You then clarify that these categories "are all part of a broader category: poverty."[28] That broader categorization fits with the conception of class war, but one immediately notices that gender and sexuality are not categories here. What is striking about this is that you say that the "enemy/other is the one who looks different and lives and behaves differently, or so at least

---

27 Gullì, *Humanity and the Enemy*, op. cit., 78.
28 Ibid., 79.

the system perceives."[29] Gender and sexuality, and perhaps especially the transgender dimension of sexuality politics, come immediately to mind when I think of looking, living, and behaving differently, and yet you do not name them here. Can you explain the relationship of gender and sexuality to the class war you discuss in this context?

BG answers: You are right, Richard. I should have dealt with that as well because of its importance and also because I am particularly interested in the issue. Gender and sexuality are usually part of what is considered foreign, other. So, they are certainly included in one of the three categories I had in mind. But this should be spelled out, I agree. This is so especially when one considers the violence against women, gay and transgender people occurring daily everywhere in the world. Today, we live a particularly dark moment in this respect – from the movement against abortion rights in the US to the vitriolic rhetoric against lifestyles different from the 'traditional' one – traditional couple, family, and so on: all poor and laughable notions. In countries with reactionary governments, from Brazil (before the recent reelection of Lula da Silva who defeated Bolsonaro) to Hungary and, now, Italy with the new government led by a neo-fascist party (ridiculously called *Brothers of Italy*! – and paradoxically founded by a woman), the prospects of further liberation in terms of gender and sexuality seem to be eliminated and there will likely be greater attempts at oppression and repression. In many countries worldwide, homosexuality is still illegal, and in some of them it is punishable by death. Violence against transgender people, in the US and everywhere else, is as common as is appalling.

Transgender people, more than other people with a sexual orientation and sexual practices different from those dictated by the various ideologies and systems of repression and control, of sadness and misery, of indifference and cruelty, easily become *homines sacri*, in Agamben's sense, namely, people whose lives can be taken at will and for no reason whatsoever – or rather for no other reason than the one produced by societal and cultural ignorance, prejudice, and the inability to accept and appreciate difference as difference. In this case, too, a serious project of education is important, geared toward the elimination of ignorance and stupidity, a total reshaping of subjectivities, or rather their destruction, a

---

29   Ibid.

transvaluation of values, so to speak, and a new individuation, a trans-dividuation toward what *can be* different.

BG asks: At the outset of your final chapter in *Unbounded Publics*, Chapter 9, you say, or reiterate, something very important for a new political ontology. You say that "it is not the case that any group, regardless of their ideologies and objectives, can utilize transgressive public spheres. Only those committed to democratization, radical democracy, or revolutionary schemes that challenge structural inequality, social and economic injustice, and political exclusion will be well suited for transgression."[30] This is a very strong statement, and I completely agree with it. The answer as to why this would be so is already in your book. Simply put, it is the logic of inclusion that gives a group, ideology, or movement the character of transgression, and it is the logic of exclusion that denies that character to it. Accordingly, any nationalist, supremacist, or sovereigntist group, movement, or ideology is denied access to the threshold of transgression. This makes a lot of sense. Indeed, before being a political judgment, it is simply logical. Erecting barriers, establishing limits, and so on, can only lead to an impoverished autarky, not only in the economic sense, but in the social, cultural, and spiritual sense. It leads to a lonely and miserable (unhappy) consciousness of oneself, one's community, one's nation, and so on. You show that very well in this final chapter when you say that "a fundamentalist, exclusivist, antidemocratic politics is wholly incompatible with the transgressive paradigm."[31] I imagine that I can only ask you to expand on this in light of the various political situations that have taken place since the publication of your book. I mean the increased rise of nationalist and supremacist groups and movements, the terrifying multiplication of violent, racist, and sexist/genderist rhetoric all over the world, with its odious institutionalization in government forms or personification in cult leaders.

One can think of the example of Trump in the US, Bolsonaro in Brazil, and so on. On the other hand, however, we have witnessed the birth of inclusionist groups and movements (perhaps similar to the Zapatistas), such as Black Lives Matter, which, to my mind, has a universalist scope and aspiration, singularly touching on the ontology and spirit of the common.

---

30   Gilman-Opalsky, *Unbounded Publics*, op. cit., 303.
31   Ibid., 303-304.

Can you tell us how the inclusionist/exclusionist opposition can help us make sense of the political, social and cultural confusion we are living through right now?

RGO answers: Yes, absolutely. We are witnessing in the US, Brazil, Russia, Ukraine, Yemen, Gaza, and many other locations ontologies of dehumanization. It is not only in resurgences of white supremacy and chauvinistic nationalisms, but in real fears and hatred of other people as viral dangers. In *Immunodemocracy*, Donatella Di Cesare discusses global histories of viewing other people as direct and existential threats to health and wellbeing.[32] People at borders, in pandemics, in war, by way of racism, reduced to nothing more than viruses to fear. Di Cesare looks at this issue from the points of view of democracy and community. She argues that immunitarian democracy converts citizens into patients of the state, the latter of which is charged with protecting each individual from the dangers of others, thus trading community for immunity.

However, I would like to suggest that we juxtapose ontologies of dehumanization to communist ontologies, which poses a logical opposition of incommensurate positions. Before we touch communist ontology, let us think for a moment about ontologies of dehumanization. If we look at the question of dehumanization from a humanist point of view (which many readers may resist), for example, from the perspective of Raya Dunayevskaya or Maurice Merleau-Ponty, we would want to see and encourage intersecting and growing "spheres of affection."[33] Humanists do not want to ignore or soften differences, for if there were no differences humanism would be superfluous. Nonetheless, by emphasizing a common humanity beneath the differences, we may enlarge spheres of affection and multiply intersections. Such a basic humanism seems to me necessary not only for ethical reasons, but for political ones.

---

32 Donatella Di Cesare, *Immunodemocracy: Capitalist Asphyxia*, trans. David Broder (South Pasadena: Semiotext(e), 2021).

33 This term, "spheres of affection," comes from a short essay of the same name by Michael Walzer in Martha Nussbaum's *For Love of Country?* (Boston: Beacon Press, 2002). My use of it is completely different, however. Walzer's discussion of community in books like *Thick and Thin: Moral Argument at Home and Abroad* (Notre Dame: University of Notre Dame Press, 1994) is antithetical to what I want to specify in communist ontology. However, thinking about "spheres of affection" with the visual assistance of a Venn diagram, is a useful way to capture difference with overlapping commonalities.

Such a humanism is the countervailing idea to dehumanization. Human beings have no choice but to deal with – *either right now or very soon* – ecological crises, pandemics, war, racism and growing inequality, resurgent misogyny, all of which have their global iterations. Therefore, it is crucial to reject ontologies of dehumanization, which would shrink rather than grow our spheres of affection, so that we only feel solidarity or common sensibility (*Gemeinwesen*) with those who are most like us. Racists often say that they do not hate anyone, but that they especially love their own kind. We must beware self-interest that parades as self-love. We cannot rise to the most pressing challenges of our time if we delimit our own sense of being-in-the-world to the narrowest spheres of affection. The tendency to shrink our species being, to shrink our sense of being in community with others to extend only to one tiny subset of the human community is an ontology of dehumanization. Whenever we see that at work, we have to oppose it, point out its dangers. As communists, humanists, cosmopolitans, internationalists or some combination of these, we have to insist on a different ontology.

Having some idea of this ontology of dehumanization, I want to add some thoughts on the ontological dimension of transgression. Ontologically, the Zapatistas – and yes, Black Lives Matter too – do not have to obscure or abandon indigenous or Black political community in order to open themselves up to others. I completely agree that there is a transgressive dimension in these examples, which requires *both* a focus on indigenous and Black lives *and* welcoming others to the struggle. We could say the same about the uprisings referred to as the "Arab Spring." In Cairo, the uprisings of January 2011 focused on Egypt and Mubarak and, soon thereafter, Morsi; meanwhile in Tunisia, the uprisings focused on Ben Ali, etc. However, as Hamid Dabashi has discussed, there was a common refrain of "down with the regime."[34] The sentiments of the Arab Spring had wide international resonance that even found their way to Wall Street in the Occupy movement. This indicates a transgressive ontology that simultaneously specifies particular forms of oppression and modes of liberation, but also activates a universal discourse about human emancipation globally.

This transgressive ontology, which for the Zapatistas required shifting from *Indianismo* (an ethno-politics of racial resistance to liquidation) to *Indigenismo* (an open politics of indigenous rights and solidarity), likewise

---

34 Hamid Dabashi, *The Arab Spring: The End of Postcolonialism* (London: Zed Books, 2012).

required no abandonment of the indigenous subject position. This is crucial. We are talking about singularities, as you do so well in your work, and singularities are not *individuated individualities*. No, we are talking about intersecting and connected singularities, and from this transgressive ontology of specificity and collectivity, emancipatory power can multiply. This happens, for example, when others than indigenous Mayans go to Chiapas to join the struggle of the Zapatistas, not only because they are welcome and invited, but because the struggle against neoliberalism is their struggle too. Ontologies of dehumanization mistake singularity as individuality, because they do not understand the meaning of either term. I would say that your books, especially *Humanity and the Enemy* and *Singularities at the Threshold* should suffice to correct that error.

What you call the "ontology and spirit of the common," or what I propose we call communist ontology, does not mean a practice of inclusion that welcomes our enemies. I think this is a most important point. We want to oppose exclusionist tendencies, but that does not mean losing sight of the fact that we have real enemies in the world. We cannot forget that conflicts with employers, politicians, police, and governments will continue to be necessary. Obviously, inclusionists will have exclusionists to oppose. The spirit of the common cannot invite white supremacy in because white supremacists oppose communist ontology at a maximal limit. We do not declare our enemies to be friends or comrades.

The question is, as you explore so well in *Humanity and the Enemy*: What physical and human forms can enemy thought take? What we really oppose may ultimately be a way of thinking, but that way of thinking is only a real problem in the world because it organizes and mobilizes human behavior. We have to oppose human beings who bring enemy thought into the world by, for example, materializing white supremacist Zionist aspirations into an active program of war, wherever we find them. The consequence of not doing so is dire. It is not that we oppose human beings per se, not even the soldiers who may really lament their charge. We can say that the real enemy thought is something like what bell hooks called the imperialist white supremacist capitalist patriarchy; if only it were just an idea. It is not. It moves through and arranges the world by way of human embodiments that must be confronted. Imperialism is nothing without imperialists. Imperialist white supremacist capitalist patriarchy has to be opposed in whatever form it takes, and that is why we cannot give up the concept of the enemy, but should be careful about defining who or what the enemy is.

The discussion here reminds me of when Hannah Arendt observed the "banality of evil" in the case of *Eichmann in Jerusalem*.[35] Part of Arendt's point was that, if Eichmann refused to help carry out some of the plans of the ideas of Wannsee conference, the Nazis would have found an easy replacement to take up his role. This is why hanging a single fascist or standing him before a firing squad cannot solve the problem of fascism. Doing that will rid the world of one fascist, but fascism is something else. Fascism does not live only in the body of one or another fascist. We must confront and oppose fascism in *both* its material and philosophical forms. We must abolish fascism from earth. That will require getting down to its root causes. Therefore, we must never make the mistake of the most stupid governments that seem to believe, for example, that they strike a blow against terrorism by killing Osama Bin Laden, or that they defeat racism by finding a single killer cop guilty of murder. Terrorism, racism, and fascism have no problem surviving men like Bin Laden, Derek Chauvin, or Mussolini. So we do not invite Nazis and white supremacists in, but at the same time, we oppose *what they embody, not their bodies alone*.

BG asks: I particularly like your discussion of freedom and autonomy, or freedom *as* autonomy, in *Precarious Communism*, and I have remarked at length on it in *Singularities at the Threshold*. In the chapter "Freedom and Mystification, Mystification of Freedom," you speak of the freedom, or autonomy, "of everyday people, which invokes *our* mobility – not the mobility of capital – *our* ability to stretch ourselves out toward what we desire to be, to do, to become."[36] Toward the end of the book, in an excursus titled "Autonomy," you say that "the maximum of autonomy is self-governance," and you ask the question, "*Does freedom exist if one is only free to do those things one does not want to do?*" (your emphasis).[37] In my discussion of this in *Singularities at the Threshold*, I link your remark to Frédéric Lordon's themes in *Willing Slaves of Capital*. Can you say more about this and about the concept of disaffection you use in this section? You say that 'expressions of disaffection

---

35 Hannah Arendt, *Eichmann in Jerusalem: A Report on the Banality of Evil* (New York: Penguin Books, 2006).
36 Gilman-Opalsky, *Precarious Communism*, op., cit., 40.
37 Ibid., 103.

can be unpredictable, spontaneous, and dangerous, which is what makes them both effective and affective."[38] Then, you speak of singularity, saying, "Within this context, the term 'singularity' does not connote the individual person, but rather, singular expressions of disaffection and desire that may or may not link up with other such singularities in a unified way."[39] In my book, I say that you are here very close to what I call the political ontology of trans-dividuality. Can you say something about this as well?

RGO answers: First, let me say that it was an honor to read your discussion of my theory of autonomy in your book *Singularities at the Threshold*. I think *Singularities at the Threshold* is one of the most important studies of its kind, and indeed, it is far more important than *Precarious Communism*.

There is still a big problem (perhaps it is even worse today) of people speaking about freedom without bothering to say what it means. In the US, for example, freedom means nothing more than a self-centered concept of being able to do whatever one wants without any regard for other people, animals, or the natural environment. We could forgive someone for concluding that freedom is a destructive force of total indifference to others. Many people feel that if a law prevented a man like Jeff Bezos from doing whatever he likes on a rocket ship that everyone (even people without rocket ships) would see their freedom plummet towards extinction. This concept of freedom is even narrower than that of Thomas Hobbes in his chapter on "The Liberty of Subjects" in *Leviathan*. Hobbes thought that if you could move your body from place A to place B, you had total liberty, even if the decision to move your body to place B was punishable by death.[40] Bad concepts of liberty and freedom motivated me to write about ideological mystifications of "freedom." You capture the central point well in the emphasis you make in your question, focusing on the distinction between the mobility of everyday people and the mobility of capital.

As usual, I begin with a consideration of the powers of the supposedly powerless, with the abilities of everyday people to become what they desire to be, and never to look at the question from the perspective of a pharmaceutical company, imperial power, the misguided frauds of "national

---

38   Ibid., 41-42.
39   Ibid., 42.
40   See, for example, Thomas Hobbes, *Leviathan* (Cambridge, UK: Cambridge University Press, 1996), 146-149.

interest," or from any perspective of the ruling class. Human freedom is never at stake – nor is it abridged in the slightest – when the ruling class takes a setback. They want us to think that their freedom to do whatever they want is human freedom as such, when in fact the autonomy of everyday people to increase their capacities of self-governance are usually inversely and adversely related to the so-called "freedom" of the ruling class. For example, if landlords and property-owners have no regulation on what they may charge for rent, if rent is in no way controlled by anything beyond peoples' ability and willingness to pay it, then in a city like Chicago or New York, landlords and property-owners have total freedom to charge whatever they wish. Our question must be, how does their freedom to charge whatever they wish affect the autonomy of everyday people living in the city? As we know from gentrification and costs of living, not being able to live here or there shrinks autonomy in the world. In a capitalist society, autonomy often maps out over one's ability to pay for it. Not everyone can fly around on planes, go wherever they wish, do whatever they like.

We should look at human freedom within the context of a capitalist class system. That is where we are. It is important to ask, *"Does freedom exist if one is only free to do things that one does not want to do?"* In our capitalist societies, there is often a menu of options, yet just as often, the options do not coincide with real desires and needs. Someone who wants to point out your options could say, for example, "Just quit your job and get a new one" or "Do not pay the high rent." However, what is the other job? Where is the lower rent? The alternatives may be so bad that anyone who can afford something else will regard them as unacceptable. A concept of freedom that accounts for the liberties of the bourgeoisie, and gives to everyone else a rule of freedom that says to accept the unacceptable, is no worthy conception of human freedom.

I agree with your connection of my theory to Frédéric Lordon's *Willing Slaves of Capital*.[41] Lordon is not only a philosopher but also an economist who understands that capitalist political economy determines levels of autonomy very concretely, and that capitalist freedom is in the end about the relative autonomy of a small subset of the population. As Lordon puts it, the basic idea is that "some are free to use others as a means to an end, while others are free to allow themselves to be used in that

---

41   Frédéric Lordon, *Willing Slaves of Capital: Spinoza and Marx on Desire*, trans. Gabriel Ash (London and New York: Verso, 2014).

manner, has been proclaimed the very essence of freedom."[42] I completely agree. Lordon and I are both talking about a dilapidated concept of freedom that only serves the interests of capital. We must not accept a concept of freedom that only pertains to the freedoms of the ruling class.

On the question of disaffection, I would shift the focus to a different yet related matter. When people are unhappy with their lack of autonomy, with a miserable situation in which someone else has decided to call their exploitation "freedom," there is the question of what to do with that disaffection. Mostly, people try to bear it, internalize it, as they suffer from bad feelings and from inopportunity and insecurity in their material conditions of life. However, in moments of explosive upheaval, social movements, collective action, in moments of riot and revolt, for example, people let loose their disaffection in a social disruption. That is where we can find realizations of power from below, which I focus on with more sustained attention in *Specters of Revolt*.

Finally, I completely agree about singularity. *Singularities at the Threshold* is very important for the ways it provides a vocabulary and conceptual framework to speak about all this better. I fully agree that "singularity" is not an "individual," but rather a legible and cohesive expression of disaffection that marks a moment in time, expresses a very specific content, a desire or indignation, expressed precisely because it wants to find and link up with other singularities to move beyond its own limitations. Singularity does not want to be individual at all, but trans-dividual, as you say. You are right that I completely agree, although I use a different language. For both of us, however, I think this is the crucial ontological point. We are not talking about miserable individuals out there floating in a sea of happiness. We are not so sharply individuated, though capital would like us to think that we are. Indeed, expressions of our disaffection reveal this fact, the fact of the trans-dividuality of our disaffection. No one's misery is a private property.

BG asks: As you often say in *Unbounded Publics*, transgressive public spheres are by definition inclusive. Indeed, the neither/nor logic is one of inclusion, not of exclusion. The modality of exclusion is perhaps what more easily brings about a dimension of violence, or it is perhaps always an instance of violence – a violence that touches on the question of

---

42 Ibid., IX.

identity (and difference). To the contrary, in and through inclusion, particular traits, such as those of the various categories of social identity, are suspended in view of the singular and common. The neutrality, or univocity, of the neither/nor of transgression cuts through these categories (such as those of national identity), as if in a subterranean or rhizomatic movement, without eliminating them, but rather by exploding them at the threshold of their vacillating positions.

A passage that I find telling in this sense is when, speaking about nonbourgeois, or transgressive, public spheres, you write, "Nonbourgeois public spheres are often populated by people who understand their own citizenship as unstable or partial, by those who do not understand themselves and who are not understood by others as full-fledged members of society (we may think here of the marginalized positions of women, "racial" minorities, immigrants, gays and lesbians, indigenous people and people with disabilities, just to name some)."[43] This is a very powerful passage, which gives a concrete dimension to the abstract logic of the neither/nor of transgression. But as Marx says in the *Grundrisse*, it is important to start from the abstract in order to arrive at the concrete. I would like to say a few more words about this passage. It is obvious to anyone who thinks that all these instances of the nonbourgeois public sphere are transgressive in their very essence – transgressive in your sense of the word. In fact, the emancipation of women is equally an emancipation of men; the end of racial discrimination and oppression is not only in the interest of those who are discriminated and oppressed at any given historical stage of society, but also – if we take Kantian ethics as a measure, for instance, or think about people like Martin Luther King or even Frantz Fanon – of the oppressor as well. The recent and current example of Black Lives Matter shows that very well, not in the incorrect and confusing sense that "All Lives Matter" or, even worse, that "Blue Lives Matter, too," but rather, in the singular sense that Black Lives Matter – a historical and concrete, not an invented and fictional category – has in its very essence a universal and common scope and aspiration; the same goes for the plight of immigrants crossing deserts and oceans, and often dying in them, always carrying with themselves, wherever they go, the movement and potential for the creation of new transgressive public spheres, that is to say, new and *contaminated* (as a positive word) ways of upsetting false boundaries and fictional and

---

43   Gilman-Opalsky, *Unbounded Publics*, op. cit., 90.

violent borders, the 'danger' of creating new worlds, better societies, new commonalities and singularities. The struggle of LGBT+ people fighting for sexual and existential freedom is not different. Indeed, the end of what is undesirable from a sexual point of view in traditional and conservative societies (the frightening figures of the homosexual or transsexual, for instance) is also the end of an oppressive heterosexual hegemony, with its arrogance and violence, and of heteronormativity. The neither/nor logic of transgression, here too, yields a universal and common goal for the improvement of the human condition as a whole; the struggle of indigenous people, as you explain speaking of the Zapatistas, can also be immediately transgressive in character; the same can be said of the fight for dignity of people with disabilities, whose condition is not at all marginal as is often thought, but central, if one thinks of the importance of dependence, in the human condition itself.

It is in this sense that in *Earthly Plenitudes* I say that disability (regardless of the problematic nature of the word) must become the measure of a new humanity. Here too, the struggle for a good life of dignity and happiness reaches into the universal and common and is *ipso facto* transgressive. But even more specific and localized struggles for liberation acquire this universal and common meaning. The phrase "Free Palestine," for instance, is a call for general liberation and emancipation from systems of violence and oppression. All these examples can be understood, as they should, within the open framework of the neither/nor of transgression, which forms the basis of your book. Can you elaborate on some of these important issues and themes?

RGO answers: I can elaborate on some of these questions, but I start by just appreciating your own elaborations from my theory, which I find convincing and insightful.

Yes, it is probably worth saying a few things about my use of the peculiar word "nonbourgeois," and something further about transgression and gender politics. I confess that I was never happy with the term "nonbourgeois," but it specified something very important in evolving discourses about class composition. In the literature on the public sphere, you obviously find Habermas's classical study with the subtitle, "An Inquiry into a

Category of Bourgeois Society."[44] Negt and Kluge fiercely criticized this classic study from the more radical position of their book, *Public Sphere and Experience*, which juxtaposed the "proletarian public sphere" or "public spheres of production" to Habermas's analysis of the bourgeois form.[45]

When I was studying those books in relation to the Zapatistas and ecological crises, it was clear to me that we had to surpass the binary of bourgeoisie and proletariat. Of course, class analysis was still – and remains – necessary. However, there are global uprisings that are not clearly proletarian in terms of their identity, self-understanding, or substantive character. It is not so easy, for example, to say that the indigenous Mayans of Mexico are the Mexican proletariat. It was also obvious that we should not attempt to force women's struggles and LGBTQ+ struggles into the old Marxian rubric of two great hostile classes. Despite the fact that the Marxian mode of analysis remains crucial today, we have to exceed it to appreciate new formations and developments in class composition, as many other Marxists in the 60s and 70s also understood.

Therefore, I decided upon the term "nonbourgeois," which for all of its faults, is still probably better than "the precariat" in many ways. What I liked about the concept of nonbourgeois was that it included the proletariat, but also included other oppositions or challenges to what Marx called "bourgeois society," such as we see in Black Lives Matter, the Zapatistas, and so on. Therefore, I wanted to specify a range of experiences and subject positions, and thus, certain points of view, all of which were variously antagonistic to dominant perspectives in capitalist society.

This is one way that we can effectively specify the more critical dimensions of gender politics and anti-racist politics today. Some elements of LGBTQ+ politics are essentially about reproducing the gender binary and focused on queer people winning equal rights to fight in imperialist wars with heterosexual soldiers, rights to marry, raise kids, etc. I certainly want to appreciate that the victories of such a politics of inclusion represent important advances in the liberal order. That is true, and we must appreciate this because advances like same-gender marriage and the

---

44   Jürgen Habermas, *The Structural Transformation of the Public Sphere: An Inquiry into a Category of Bourgeois Society*, trans. Thomas Burger (Cambridge: The MIT Press, 1991).

45   Oskar Negt and Alexander Kluge, *Public Sphere and Experience: Toward and Analysis of the Bourgeois and Proletarian Public Sphere*, trans. Peter Labanyi, Jamie Owen Daniel, and Assenka Oksiloff (Minneapolis and London: University of Minnesota Press, 1993).

overturning of DOMA make real differences for real people in the real world. On the other hand, we have to point out that these advances are not opposed to bourgeois society as such. They accept bourgeois society, and seek equal rights within it. Of course, there are radical dimensions of queer politics and theory, which make bourgeois liberals very uncomfortable. Early transgender ideas like those expressed in Félix Guattari's essay "Becoming-Woman," or in Judith Butler's *Gender Trouble* are much more subversive and potentially revolutionary in the ways that they set the stage for abolitionist and transformative goals.[46] We could identify these more radical approaches to gender as "nonbourgeois" by pointing out how they destabilize and subvert liberal contentions. Likewise, there are liberal aspects of #BLM that focus on community-police relations, body cameras, sensitivity training, and accountability. Again, those are very good for real people in the real world too, but they are compatible with the bourgeois liberalism of mainstream Democrats like Joe Biden and Hillary Clinton. On the other hand, we have watched liberals squirm and react against the more abolitionist and radical content of #BLM, such as calls to abolish the police and prisons, etc. That abolitionist side is the nonbourgeois side of a politics that includes and exceeds conventional class analysis.

Regarding transgression, when I was first discussing my theory with Andrew Arato at The New School for Social Research, he wanted me to ground my theory of transgression in its religious and theological origins and meanings. This was an important conversation for me because the theological concept of transgression, which implies going against God's law or breaking with the commandments of religion, aligns transgression with evil. You may notice that this alignment is still at play in conservative (and often religious) reactions against gender-transgression in queer politics. For example, transgender men and women have hell to pay for their gender transgressions, because such transgression opposes God's establishment of two genders mapped over biological sex. Conservative religious thinking accepts the conflation of anatomical sex with gender, and thus finds a claim of "imperfection" against God, because transgender men and women appear to be accusing God of putting people into the wrong

---

46   See Guattari's "Becoming-Woman" in *Chaosophy: Texts and Interviews 1972-1977*, trans. David L. Sweet, Jarred Becker, and Taylor Adkins (Los Angeles: Semiotext(e), 2009) and Butler's *Gender Trouble: Feminism and the Subversion of Identity* (New York and London: Routledge, 1990).

bodies. The nonbourgeois side of queer politics insists that gender is or can be autonomous from anatomical sex, and that makes certain transgressions possible, as we are seeing in our own lifetime.

Even so, many people still dehumanize and demean transgender people, and want to make them feel ugly, disgusting, or ashamed. Now we must finally say that such transphobic and transmisic tendencies belong to an ontology of dehumanization. To use your own language above, there are some positive contaminations of woman in man, of queer in straight, and so forth. Obviously, all of this implicates how we understand our multifarious being-in-the-world. What we are talking about is ontological indeed, and I would say here that transgression in my sense of the word, which we are discussing, is a practice of communist ontology *against* ontologies of dehumanization.

BG asks: Your exposition of specters of revolt, ghost as *Geist*, and becoming-ghost also becomes a beautiful reflection on the philosophical concept of time, and it has an obvious phenomenological dimension underlying or accompanying it. Of course, those who maintain that revolt happens only in the here and now seem to have a poor understanding of the phenomenology of time. They are those who believe that the actualization of revolt is everything; thus, some believe that revolt itself will change everything forever, while others (the police, the establishment, and so on) count on this fallacy, which allows revolt to be easily crushed. Yet, this here-and-now of revolt has nothing to do with Walter Benjamin's concept of *Jetztzeit*, the "time of the now," which points to a structure that encompasses the continuum of history. Thus, your reflection on becoming, aided by the use you make of Félix Guattari's conception of "becoming-woman," complicates things (in the positive sense of complex thinking) and shows how the spectral dimension and the haunting are real – where reality includes, as it should, potentiality and the whole temporal *spectrum*, if you will, reaching back to the no-longer of the past and forward to not-yet of the future. It is all a matter of open contingency/contingencies. This becoming-other, where, as you note quoting Guattari, "becoming-woman" is "a reference 'for other types of becoming,'"[47] is really about "constructing new forms of life, new forms of being."[48]

---

47 Gilman-Opalsky, *Specters of Revolt*, op. cit., 59.
48 Ibid.

Obviously, this is also the topic of the present work, which we are doing together, an inquiry into the construction of new forms of life, an inquiry into "the politics of subversion."[49] I'd like to hear your thoughts on this.

RGO answers: The phenomenology of time. Everything has its time. Some things only happen when they happen and you only know that it is their time when they start happening. This is perhaps obvious, but it is one of the most politically frustrating dimensions of the question of revolution. People interested in revolution cannot say anything about a specific uprising until after it breaks out. Some self-congratulatory commentators will say they saw everything coming. However, there is only a little truth in that, and far more chance than they may be willing to admit. Indeed, revolt does not come from nowhere, and when it happens, you can explain it. Yet, it does not happen all of the time, even when there is an abundance of good reasons for it to happen. Therefore, there is something about the time of the happening of revolt. Perhaps this connects back with the earlier point about instinct.

I reject both sides of the equation that says, on the one side, that revolt will change everything, and on the other side, that revolt is easily defeated. I think neither position is the truth. Revolt may change its participants forever. We know, for example, in the so-called Arab Spring or in the US in Occupy Wall Street and #BLM, that the experiences of young participants transform them. Part of what happens is that young people experiment with their own powers and find community and possibility in uprisings, which makes many of them into activists with a sense of potency. At the same time, the capitalist reality is more or less exactly as it was before the revolt. The revolt does not change the reality, and it does go away and is even sometimes made to go away by the violence of counterinsurgent forces, militarized police, etc. My point, in *Specters of Revolt*, is that repression of revolt is not its obliteration. It always comes back.

Now, Guattari's "Becoming-Woman" is one of the earliest and most radical transgender theories.[50] "Becoming-Woman" is more than an essay on transgender politics or transgender becomings. Guattari was thinking about subversive forms of life, forms of life that subvert so-called "normal"

---

49 Ibid.
50 Félix Guattari, "Becoming-Woman" in *Chaosophy: Texts and Interviews 1972-1977*, trans. David L. Sweet, Jarred Becker, and Taylor Adkins (Los Angeles: Semiotext(e), 2009).

forms of life, and thereby open up new possibilities for being-in-the-world. I like what you say about open contingency in this question. Many things that appeared to be static and fixed, like gender, can become indeterminate and open. For Guattari, "becoming-woman" is more about "becoming-other" than about a gendered destination. Certainly, he includes and centers transgender possibility, but marks that as a point of entry for other types of becoming too. Ultimately, Guattari's theory is in many ways more radical than a transgender becoming-woman or a transgender becoming-man, because he is challenging the journey from one binary position to another. What about other positions beyond the binary? Gender politics is getting there today, but Guattari addressed this directly in his short text from the 1970s when he talks about "the sexed body" and the "exclusive bi-pole."[51] What is most subversive is not the arrival at a gendered destination, but the "intermediary" point in between the two poles.[52] This is about the possibility of new forms of life, new forms of being. That is what we are considering in this present work, as you say. Part of what it means is that we have to subvert false choices. It is not, when it comes to revolt, simply success or failure, and it is not, with gender, simply man or woman. The use of they/them pronouns, which generates a lot of controversy, has helped to make this "intermediary" dimension more visible. What is even more promising in current gender politics is that they/them may not ever seek to arrive at the resolution of she/her or he/his. This development introduces an undecidability, or rather, a refusal of the bi-pole. Thus, the "intermediary" becomes a new position, not simply a road one travels to arrive at a fixed position.

Our communist ontology is, in my view, aided and abetted by the more subversive developments in transgender politics today. We do not seek a "weaponized" transgender politics, but we must make our observations, arguments, and alliances. Transgender and non-binary gender horizons mark for us not a controversy so much as an emancipatory possibility. We communists who insist on the possibility of new forms of life have to embrace all kinds of transgender becomings, and not only because such becomings support what we want to say about possibility and being-in-the-world. There is also a crucial humanist dimension there, which we should not forget. Subversive becomings are enabling people to become more of what they want to be in a world generally set against

---

51   Ibid., 229.
52   Ibid.

human flourishing. Of course, we must resist any idea in identity politics that suggests anyone can become whatever they wish, because we are also Marxists who understand political economy, material conditions of reality and history, and the limitations of life in the capitalist present. Nonetheless, we cannot take the side of those who want to minimize or suppress the destabilization of fixed things, whether those destabilizing forces are in various modes of "becoming-woman" or in revolts. Here, now, is the crucial point: We do not want things as they are or have been for a very long time. We do not want things to vacillate between established poles. That defensive rigidity, or lack of imagination, would suffocate the entire ontological project. None of this means that we choose identity politics over class politics, which would be a very stupid conclusion indeed, and which would represent another "exclusive bi-pole" that we have to reject.

BG asks: In the section of *The Communism of Love* on Levinas, you say that "love is necessarily beyond *both* the lover and the beloved," almost like *meaning*, "moving beyond our being."[53] Then, you quote Levinas, who says, "To love is to fear for another, to come to the assistance of his frailty."[54] This goes back to your exposition and criticism of Weil, but it also opens up the discourse of disability and dependency. It reaches not simply into the model of intersubjectivity, but of transindividuality as well. Can you say more about this?

RGO answers: I think my theory of love has a lot to offer considerations of disability and dependency, although I have to confess that I thought more about its direct connections to disability after the book's publication. Disability only gets marginal and fleeting attention in the book. It was your work, as well as some conversation with the brilliant feminist philosopher Jennifer Scuro, that provoked me to think more about disability and the communism of love.[55]

We may approach the issue of disability through the famous motto of Karl Marx: "From each according to their ability, to each according to

---

53 Gilman-Opalsky, *The Communism of Love*, op. cit. 30.
54 Ibid.
55 See, for example, Jennifer Scuro, *Addressing Ableism: Philosophical Questions via Disability Studies* (Lanham: Lexington Books, 2018). Also see my conversation with Scuro on *The Communism of Love* and the question of disability on the Woodbine podcast: https://www.patreon.com/posts/50689501.

their needs."[56] It is a line as beautiful as it is famous, and for me it captures the heart of what I call the communism of love. It is a material fact of the human world that different people have different abilities and needs. We could perhaps speak about *differential* ability instead of about *disability* to capture the plane of diverse contingencies that make up the field of human ability. In *Critique of the Gotha Program*, Marx argues against the bourgeois concept of equality, which wrongly assumes that giving to or asking everyone for the same thing means fairness.[57] That is in fact not fair in a world of differential ability. People have different abilities, we cannot expect everyone to do the same things, and, again following Weil and Levinas, we should be attentive to such differences.

Marx also attacks the bourgeois concept of equality because of the facts of differential needs. Let us consider an example. If my colleague and I get jobs at the same time at the same university, and we both finished our PhDs in the same semester, bourgeois equality demands we start at the same salary. Liberals insist that there should be "no discrimination." According to the liberal bourgeois conception, that is how equality works. According to Marx, however, that is in fact a system of inequality. Imagine that my colleague is blind, has several kids, and one of those kids has a disability. Now imagine that this colleague's partner recently lost their job, so they are now a single-income family of five. Meanwhile, I have no disabilities, or differential abilities, and I am a single man who can afford to live in a swank downtown apartment on my new salary. Imagine now that the two of us finally catch up a few months into our first semester at the university, and I say to my friend, "Isn't this great? How are you doing?" Now, imagine my surprise when she says that she is already on the job market because the salary that may be sufficient for my bachelor lifestyle has left her entire family living on the razor's edge of precarity. She needs office technology for her blindness that the university should pay for. They are willing to pay for some of it, but not enough. She cannot supply her child with certain needs pertaining to their disability. What is enough for me is not enough for a family with different needs. This story is not an outlandish fantasy. It happens every day.

Now, a callous conservative may retort that she should not have had so many kids if she cannot afford them, even though when she had those

---

56 Karl Marx, *Critique of the Gotha Program* (New York: International Publishers, 2002), 27.
57 Ibid., 26.

children her partner also had an income. People sometimes lose their jobs without expecting to. That also happens every day. Even if the parent did make bad choices, and the child was born into poverty for those reasons, we should not punish the child for that. Being born poor is an accident of birth, not the result of a lazy fetus in the womb. Moreover, I may be a liberal professor offended by the fact that the university pays my colleague thirty to forty thousand dollars more each year, because I want her pay also for myself, and after all, we both got our PhDs from the same university at the same time and were hired at the same rank! Marx's point is that we must not look at these differences from a competitive capitalist perspective, which refuses to see differential needs. I should be happy that my colleague and her family get what they need.[58] Why should that trouble me? From Marx alone, then, I would argue that disability and dependency find a good response in communism.

I also agree, however, that my theory of the communism of love reaches beyond the model of intersubjectivity to transindividuality, and that this connects our work further. One fatal limit of intersubjectivity is that it retains the individual subject though it appreciates how that subjectivity emerges in an interactive relation with others. Intersubjectivity may be a crucial sociological insight about the individual, but transindividuality gets to the multiplicity of singularities that you write about so well. Transindividuality requires a move beyond the individual, and views each singularity as a nodal point of a social being. This move is important, but why? In the common comportment towards dependency and disability, the focus is on assisting the person with a dependency or disability. In my example of the colleague, then, we think about how to comport ourselves to the colleague as an individual with particular demands based on ability and need. This is an orientation of a charitable position, and can be read as a question of how generous those more fortunate are willing to be to the less fortunate. Communism cannot function as charity, however. Transindividuality is the more communist approach.

---

58 This is, of course, not what explains vast differentials of pay in the existing capitalist present. What I am illustrating here is a communist consideration of differential needs. In fact, however, there are vast disparities in pay for equal work and comparable worker qualifications, but those disparities are not communist as in the example imagined above. They are more often than not arbitrary, unfair, unethical, and yet, totally legal.

Transindividuality moves us towards an understanding of how the social body is composed of a manifold of singularities, and in fact, how the social body also depends upon singularity. Therefore, it flips the charitable model on its head. We would not assess the generosity of a colleague who supports an unequally larger salary for a needier colleague. Rather, we would ask how attention to differential needs and abilities is part of one's own health and well-being, part of the society becoming what it could be and should be. Transindividuality transcends the question of individuals without liquidating singularity. The idea that each singularity is a social being even goes beyond Marx's treatment of individuality in *Critique of the Gotha Program*. I would say that transindividuality is a more radical development, though consistent with the communist approach discussed above.

CHAPTER 4

COMMUNISM, COMMON, MARXIST TRAJECTORIES

Bruno Gulli (BG) asks: Your third book, *Precarious Communism*, starts with a great introduction. First of all, I want to note the continuity between this book and your previous one, *Spectacular Capitalism*. One aspect of this continuity is your going back to the difference between ideology and philosophy. I have already asked you a question about this in relation to *Spectacular Capitalism*, but it's worth dwelling on this again. You apply the philosophy/ideology distinction to your definition and description of precarious communism and what it is to be a precarious communist. In particular, you say, "What it means to be a precarious communist is to be, as much as possible, *a non-ideological communist* who is honest about the past, present and future. While ideology makes communism more confident, *precarious communism is more philosophical, less ideological*" (emphasis added).[1] This is great. On the one hand, you take all possible distance, indeed an infinite distance, from any form of dogmatism; on the other, you position yourself and your work on the plane of contingency, the certainty of past determinations, the history of the present, and the poetry of/from the future. With a reference to Anton Pannekoek, you speak of "a new orientation."[2] I think this is also the meaning of détournement, or rather what détournement makes possible. I will go back to this key concept below.

For now, I'd like to ask you to say more about this new philosophical orientation for communism – something with which I completely agree. It is indeed something of the greatest importance, even more so today, seven years after the publication of your book, as we enter the third year of

---

1 Gilman-Opalsky, *Precarious Communism*, op. cit., 5.
2 Ibid., 3.

the pandemic, as economic, ecological and existential precariousness and global social and political instability (think for instance about the current situation in various African countries) have brought the world to an unsustainable point with problems that most likely neither capitalism (even disaster capitalism) nor any ideological variety of socialism or communism will be able to solve, but only aggravate and compound. However, as you will see in one of my later questions, I am going to problematize this a little more in light of the recent concept of postcapitalism.

Richard Gilman-Opalsky (RGO) answers: I look forward to sharing my full critique of the concept of postcapitalism in its fiercest form, but since we will do that later, I will focus first on your question about the new orientation. My idea is to some extent already expressed in the passages you cite; I am fundamentally trying to retain a communist identity, disposition, and active commitments without any strident hopes or confidence in our ability – as communists – to confront and abolish the capitalist reality. Those who want to abolish capitalism, and know this is necessary, do not know how to get there. The time of dogmatic communism is over and should be. Any dogmatic revolutionary with high-level confidence about "what is to be done" is announcing their ignorance about the world, and should appear suspicious and possibly even dangerous. Confident communists who know exactly what to do belong in the dustbins of history. I argue instead for a precarious communism, which is to say, a very certain sensibility – with a good deal of confidence about at least one thing: namely, the violence, immorality, racism, and ruthless unsustainability of capitalism. Communism is a real opposition to a world governed by the logic of capital, a world ruled by money and its ruling class. We must oppose capitalism for dire existential, ethical, and ecological reasons, and that serves as an adequate grounding for communism.

Therefore, that is the basic profile of the "new orientation." Anton Pannekoek was a Left communist and an early critic of the Soviet Union, so his call for a new orientation had a different historical context. In his book, *Workers' Councils*, Pannekoek wrote, "New orientation needs time; maybe only a new generation will comprehend its full scope."[3] In that book,

---

3 See especially Part V, Chapter 3 "Towards New Freedom" in Anton Pannekoek, *Workers' Councils* (Chico, CA: AK Press, 2002). Pannekoek discusses this "new orientation" several times throughout the book.

Pannekoek was writing critically of "state capitalism" in Russia, insisting that what was happening in the Soviet Union by the 1940s was nothing close to the dreams of communists. In fact, I think that Marx's theory of history demands that we always need to be doing the work of reorienting ourselves to historical developments, a point about historiography made well by Antonio Gramsci and Georg Lukács. Therefore, it is precisely as you put it, communism is a plane of contingency.

Détournement is a part of this, because we cannot simply allow communism to mean whatever it has meant for previous generations. We must take some of its meaning, and turn it out towards different realities and new impasses. Thus, the question I wanted to address in *Precarious Communism* was essentially the question of what it means to be a communist today. If you say this word before students or their parents, and in the face of too many political scientists, most will take you to mean you want to see a big bureaucratic government seizing administrative control over the economy. If you utter the word communism to far too many anarchists, many will unwittingly agree with their right-wing enemies in assuming that you want to see human freedoms crushed in a Stalinist fashion by a repressive state. If you say the word among Marxists, at a Marxist conference, for example, there is no predictable consensus on what they think of as communism. Perhaps for all these reasons, it may be tempting to let go of the word and idea altogether. But we must not abandon what we need, and communism – however we define it – is still fundamentally an antithetical logic of life, incommensurate with and opposed to that of capitalism. It is for this reason that I think, for all the confusion and trouble, we must keep to the communist idea of an antithesis and even, a possible antidote, to the ills of the present capitalist reality.

That is the starting point for what I call "precarious communism." When we were entering the third year of COVID-19, we saw that there was no silver bullet solution to the pandemic. Not even virologists and infectious disease specialists had a confident solution. A single virus with the world's expert attention fixed on it, and for some of us – myself included – there were moments when it was dumbfounding how something so stupid could outsmart us. However, that *was* happening, and there were many times during the pandemic when we learned that we were wrong in some of our basic assumptions. Obviously, then, we should not be so sure of a communist solution that could encompass a whole range of problems in society, economy, ecology, politics, and psychology. It is impossible to be confident. Even in the face of confidence, we also witnessed the fact that many do not follow the confident recommendations of scientists and public health research. People will certainly not get their reassurances from a confident communist. Whoever would dare anything but a precarious communism today is not only failing to learn from history, but is not paying attention to what is happening now.

It is nonetheless necessary to confront the fact that capitalism remains the prevailing ideology of the world, and therefore, the problems of the world, including authoritarian resurgences in West Africa, ecological crises, global inequalities in health care, including access to life-saving vaccines, resurgent racism and white supremacy, and many other problems, are problems of the existing capitalist world. That is not hypothetical. We cannot simply assert that all these problems would disappear in a postcapitalist communist world, but what we can say is that capitalism has had a long time to address these issues, and it has not done so. It is, at the very least, absurd to blame communism or socialism or anarchism or feminism for problems that plague a world that is overwhelmingly anti-communist, anti-socialist, decisively not anarchist, and viciously patriarchal. My students often ask me, what will the anarchists do about crime? They want to suggest that if the anarchists cannot create a world without serial killers and rapists, then anarchism has nothing to offer. What they conveniently forget in the questioning is that the serial killers and rapists they are so worried about are also here in the capitalist reality. One cannot refute communism, anarchism, or any other rival and revolutionary theory simply because one can imagine problems it may not solve. If that were true, apologists for capitalism who want to reject anarchism for not solving the problem of crime would have to reject capitalism for the exact same reasons.

This is important because it stresses that not knowing how to proceed for certain (i.e., being precarious) does not mean knowing nothing at all. It is possible to be both precarious and to know some things at the same time. It is not true that precarious communists know nothing at all. My late father died by a heart condition that no doctor knew how to solve. I remember how frustrating it was in the years before he died. Often, what was most troubling was the absence of a diagnosis. The doctors never really knew what was wrong with his heart. Of course, we wanted solutions, but the first step to solving any problem is often to get a good diagnosis of

120 COMMUNIST ONTOLOGIES

that problem. You cannot hope to solve a problem you do not understand. We must understand the coronavirus to stop it. We must understand capitalism to stop it too. That is yet another reason why we still need communism. For even if communism has no confident solutions, it is indispensable in the diagnosis of capitalism and its problems.

RGO asks: I read *Humanity and the Enemy* as your communist manifesto of ethics. The enemy of humanity today is no single person or human villain, but rather capitalism. You claim – and I agree – that the "flourishing of the human condition requires the deactivation and abandonment of the system of capital" and that capitalism "disfigures and crushes human dignity."[4] Later, you put it this way: "Notably, in our modernity, the system of capital *is* the enemy of humanity."[5] Towards the end of the book, you say that the "logic of capital alienates humanity, and humanity becomes inhuman."[6] You claim as well that humanity "is the coming community: the family, friendship, and love."[7] You therefore present humanity as a hopeful antagonist to the enemy. But in juxtaposing humanity to capital in this way, are you suggesting that the system of capital is not itself distinctly human? It seems to me that capitalism is in fact uniquely human, that it is exclusively a human development, albeit one that sweeps the whole of non-human life into its exploitative field. On this point, I am partial to Jean-Paul Sartre's claim in "Freedom and Responsibility" that the "most terrible situations of war, the worst tortures do not create a non-human state of things; there is no non-human situation."[8] Sartre's argument was that the worst things human beings face are not inhuman, but distinctly human. Can you address this? Can you address the following question: What is the humanity *of the* enemy?

BG answers: I totally share your partiality to Sartre here, and I obviously don't deny that capitalism is distinctly human. To begin with, what comes to mind are the rightly famous lines from *Antigone*, "Many wonders, many

---

4 Gullì, *Humanity and the Enemy*, op. cit., 5.
5 Ibid., 32.
6 Ibid., 115.
7 Ibid.
8 Jean-Paul Sartre, "Freedom and Responsibility" in *Essays in Existentialism* (New Jersey: Citadel Press, 1965), 64.

terrors, / But none more wonderful than the human race / Or more dangerous."[9] The human, too, is capable of producing wonders as well as disastrous situations of terror. Capitalism is one of these dangerous human-made terrors. When I say that capitalism "*is* the enemy of humanity" because it "disfigures and crushes human dignity," I don't mean to imply that it is therefore *non-human*. However, I think that there is a difference between "non-human" and "inhuman"; or rather, the latter can be understood in two different ways. It can simply be seen as a synonym of the former – and there is nothing problematic with something not being human – or it can be understood *ethically* as a situation or condition in which common characteristics of what it is to be human (in this case, perhaps, humane,) such as empathy, care, and so on, are lacking. I'm well aware that this is a very slippery terrain. However, we can't forgo the discussion of this important topic on account of its difficulty. Indeed, if instead of love, care, and compassion one has hatred, abuse, and cruelty, one is still within the horizon of human possibilities (and actualities). Yet, one is justified in referring to this second set of human characteristics as inhuman, meaning not that they display aspects pertaining to some other, non-human, forms of life – for, in fact, those other forms of life don't have these aspects and traits – but rather that they show destructive and self-destructive tendencies within the human itself and fail in the difficult management of that complication within the human condition which is called freedom. These are tragic situations, for which any moralizing discourse would be fruitless and inappropriate. However, an ethical appraisal of them remains important.

So, on what account can one make the distinction between the human and inhuman in the human? How can one do that without falling into the moralizing platitudes that we hear every day when terrible situations of extreme violence occur? The first thing that comes to mind is the centrality of care in the human condition. I never tire of referring to Eva Feder Kittay's extremely important description of the human condition as one in which the fact of dependency is inescapable.[10] The need for care and caring arises from this inescapable fact. We are all dependent on one another even when there are no particular, important, or severe moments

---

9   Sophocles, *Antigone*, trans. Paul Woodruff (Indianapolis, IN: Hackett, 2001), lines 332-334.
10 Eva Feder Kittay, *Love's Labor: Essays on Women, Equality, and Dependency* (New York: Routledge, 1999).

and situations of dependency, such as in very young or very old age, traumas, disabilities, and so on. Obviously, even when faced with the need for care and caring, one can take at least two courses of action, both of which are distinctly human: one can use one's freedom and power in order to try to provide the care necessary in any given situation – and often this may not be an easy thing; it is, in fact, rather challenging; it requires effort and work – or one can respond to that with total indifference and the thoughtlessness that often leads to abuse and cruelty: the banality of evil, as Hannah Arendt famously put it.

It is undeniable that the history of capitalism – just like the history of sovereignty and modernity – is a history of violence and cruelty, of genocides and ecocide. Yet, there is also a transformative history of resistance and revolt, of difference and utopias – or perhaps heterotopias, to mention again Michel Foucault's important concept. This second type of history shows that a seemingly all-encompassing and almighty system like that of capital does not exhaust all human potential and power of action. The history of capitalism, like any other history of oppression and domination, brings out the inhuman in the human. From the standpoint of the oppressor, be it the capitalist, the slave-owner, the colonist, and so on, it is the oppressed that is dehumanized and thus becomes inhuman; the oppressed is the enemy from that point of view. From this, it follows that the oppressor is the enemy of the oppressed.

In your question, the last two quotes from *Humanity and the Enemy* come from a page where I deal with Franco Berardi's interesting reinterpretation of alienation in what he calls *Compositionism* – an interpretation that, Berardi says, is radically different from that of humanism. Accordingly, for Berardi, there is no restoration of humanity, and I don't disagree with this idea. However, he also says that "a human collectivity autonomous from capital"[11] can be founded on "the radical inhumanity of the workers' existence."[12] So, there is no restoration of some abstract idea of the human, of humanism, but there is a human collectivity potentially built on a condition of radical inhumanity. I don't see this as a necessarily antihumanist idea, but rather as a way of grasping the concrete singularity of the human. This condition of inhumanity, manufactured by capital, is very real. However, by dehumanizing the vast majority of

---

11 Berardi, op. cit., 45.
12 Ibid., 44.

human beings, the workers, the real producers of wealth, by looking at them as the enemy, capital becomes their own enemy, and in fact the enemy par excellence.

You also ask about "the humanity *of the* enemy." Typically, the enemy is dehumanized, so it loses its humanity. Of course, Carl Schmitt is correct in pointing out that the concept of humanity is constantly invoked, usurped and confiscated in order to declare the supposed enemy "an outlaw of humanity" and have a war "driven to the most extreme inhumanity."[13] Yet, the question of the humanity of the enemy enters the discourse of general ethics, biomedical ethics in particular, and, to employ this very strange and awkward expression, *the ethics of war*. For Schmitt, this is part of a spurious and wrong type of logic. For him, the friend and enemy relation is a political and technical concept, to which the question of the humanity of the enemy should not apply at all. In fact, it goes without saying that the enemy, the political enemy, retains its humanity – and in fact, as Schmitt says, humanity has no enemy; so, the enemy must be another human being. However, the concrete inhumanity experienced by the oppressed, their *radical inhumanity*, to use Berardi's phrase again, is something that defies Schmitt's abstraction and, of course, it is something very real. But this is due to the fact that the logic of the oppressor has usurped and confiscated the concept of humanity. It then ceases being a purely technical and abstract question of the political. It becomes a concrete question of political and cultural violence. The logic of dehumanization is the logic of sovereign power and sovereign violence. Essentially, it is this type of logic that *Humanity and the Enemy* wished to address.

BG asks: I want to go to the central moment of your first book, *Unbounded Publics*: the neither/nor of transgression. This concept, or movement, is introduced early on in the general introduction, and it is then developed in a special way in Part III, on transgressive public spheres.

I say concept or movement because it provides the conceptual framework for your argument, which for you becomes "a third conceptual framework,"[14] and it is at the same time the movement whereby the false dichotomy of national and transnational public sphere is overcome.

---

13   Carl Schmitt, *The Concept of the Political*, trans. George Schwab (Chicago: University of Chicago Press, 1996), 54.
14   Gilman-Opalsky, *Unbounded Publics*, op. cit., 240.

The neither/nor of transgression seems to open up a wholly new ontological plane, or it seems to be the actual transgressive movement of political theory and practice onto this new plane. It is perhaps a dialectical movement, or perhaps something that does not fully belong within dialectical logic, but it rather has the force of a transductive (and transgressive) line of flight – that is, an exit from an impasse and a situation of capture, the aporias of a narrow either/or, or a feeble and inoperative (as well as impractical) both/and, though, about this latter point, you do speak of a "double occupancy." I wonder if this movement, the way I read it, does not exit the idea or paradigm of *the public* altogether to become something different from the public, that is, *the common*. In other words, it seems to me that when you describe and develop the neither/nor logic of transgression, this very fascinating concept and framework, you are no longer speaking of the public, with its necessary (stated or hidden) relationship to the private, but of the common, with its, as necessary and complex, relationship to the singular.

Can you address this point? Could it be that the transgressive public sphere has, in fact, the character of the common, the singularly common or commonly singular? Below, I will try to connect this point to the question of the making of complex identities, as you yourself often do in your book. For instance, and by way of anticipation, you say, "The transgressive public sphere is the place where the restructuring of a transgressive political identity occurs."[15] I like this very much. But again, I would like you to address the question I have framed above and say whether this place of restructuring is not perhaps the common and these transgressive, complex identities another name for the singular, or singularities.

RGO answers: In social and political science, there is a common and sensible expectation that we should always specify a period, a place, and particular events. Otherwise, we risk speaking about the world with a generic inaccuracy. One such expectation of political discourse is that we should decide if we are thinking about problems in a national or sub-national framework, or if we are talking about transnational problems. If a student in one of my classes wants to speak about mass incarceration, human rights, or poverty in very general terms, I will always press them to specify a time, a place (or places), and to ground their discussion in a consideration

---

15   Ibid., 328.

of concrete examples. However, I cannot follow my own advice, or stick to the conventional expectation, when discussing transgression.

I developed my theory of transgression from the example of the Mexican Zapatistas who insisted on a total rejection of that old imperative to choose between the national, sub-national, or transnational. On the one hand, the Zapatistas called themselves an Army for National Liberation (EZLN). Their politics of self-determination and autonomy focused on immediate existential threats facing the indigenous Mayans of Chiapas. In that regard, this was a national liberation struggle with local and indigenous sub-national contexts. However, at the same time, the Zapatistas declared themselves in 1996 at the first *encuentro* as being "For Humanity and Against Neoliberalism." With that declaration, their 1994 rebellion took aim at NAFTA, which represented a signature phase in the Post-Cold War trajectory of capitalism. In stating that they were "for humanity," the Zapatistas sought to exceed the specific concerns they themselves faced in Chiapas. They did all of this all at once, and that is where I took my first lesson.

It is possible to think – and even to organize ourselves practically – in transgressive ways, as human beings who can confront an enemy where we live, but also with connections to global struggles in other places. It is not always necessary to choose and specify a national or transnational project. That was the lesson. In fact, when it comes to climate crisis today, to pandemic politics, and new wars of imperial power, we have to insist on *both* the context of specific crises facing particular people, and at the same time, we have to insist on seeing the global dimensions of the problem. The third conceptual framework I intended to name with the idea of transgression has actually been realized (as in the example of the Zapatistas, to name but one realization), and I felt we needed that conceptual framework. I wanted to resist running away too fast from the local and particular crises (first conceptual framework) that real people face in order to arrive with the rest of the social sciences on the new stage of globalization (second conceptual framework). I wanted to think about global issues without forgetting the struggles that matter most urgently to real people where they really live. That was one part of the story.

However, transgression is absolutely an ontological plane, as you rightly say, although I did not fully articulate this ontological side of the question in my book. You are completely correct. In Mexico, there was an opposition named *"Indianismo,"* which was an opposition to the Mexican state's miscegenation policies (these policies were called *"Indigenismo"*). For a long time, the indigenous people claimed a politics of *Indianismo*, according to which they asserted themselves as Indians against their cultural liquidation and literal assimilation. *Indianismo* was a politics of ethnicity, which asserted a resistant ethno-political identity of indigeneity, of *being-Indian*. For a long time, the opposing side was only the assimilationist *Indigenismo* politics of the state. Then, more recently, the Zapatistas introduced a third framework, "Zapatismo." Zapatismo offered a way for indigenous Mayans to resist their liquidation and assimilation, but in a new way. Zapatismo was a way to say, "Yes, we are Mayan Indians, but we also represent the subject position of other disaffected, exploited, and marginalized people of the world. Others can join us, and we can join them." This was the message of Zapatismo. You could join the Zapatistas by way of Zapatismo, regardless of your ethnic identity, language, or geographic location. This expressed a certain humanism, but not one that threatened to subvert or erase indigeneity.

The Zapatistas were therefore too liquid, as Zygmunt Bauman might say, to hold in place as a fixed Mexican phenomenon, and yet, they remained committed to changing *their world* in Mexico. This implicates a new being-in-the-world, one that has also become necessary for contesting the capitalist crisis in ecology. Transgression says that we cannot refuse thinking and being global citizens, but also that we must attend to the variegated ways global crises disproportionately affect different communities. Therefore, transgression does not mean being everywhere and nowhere in particular. Rather, transgression means that we have to find ways of being everywhere while being somewhere in particular. If this sounds too vague, many other examples could concretize the point, from the Marxian idea of proletarian revolution to the Arab Spring. We will pursue this further soon.

You wonder about a possible exit from the public to the common. Here, there is no door with an "exit" sign above it. Some part of the public contains the common, and some part of the common contains the public. However, there are some crucial differences. The public forms and dissipates in collective action. When we go to sleep – unlike citizenship, for example, which sleeps right there in the bed with us – the public dissipates until the next pooling of people's attention, active deliberation, and gathering. The public disappears in our inactivity, which is one form of privatization, a form of privatization that Jürgen Habermas studied in *The Structural Transformation of the Public Sphere*. The common, while also subject to privatization, is different. We may specify the common at the level of a logic or a valuational-norm. The common is not just a modality of gathering and thinking, for it is also a central purpose of gathering. For example, in Turkey, the public gathered to defend the common of Taksim Park in Gezi Square in 2013. The public does not gather for the sake of itself. The public may or may not be on the side of a particular politics, and may even take sides against the common. For me, the concept of common has an irreducible connection to communism, whereas the public does not.

However, can *the public* become *the common*? That is of course just another way of posing your question. Perhaps the public can give rise to the common, or maybe even vice versa. I think the concept of singularity, which is so important to you, is helpful here. Singularity emanates from the common. Singularity is a nodal point of the common, we could say. To the contrary, private is antithetical to the public, for private and public move in opposite directions. We could not say that the private interests of the individual mark a nodal point of the public sphere. No. Such a private person stands against the public. I take this from Hannah Arendt's conceptualization of private and public realms in *The Human Condition*. Privatization undermines and erode the public, as could be seen in the economic example of the privatization of public universities. The singular does not have a similar relationship to the common. Privatization is – etymologically and conceptually – very close to *privation*. Privatization is bound to property and individualist ideology. Now, back to the exit door… While we may find a path to the common from the public, we may not. What distinguishes the public is that it goes in an opposite direction from privatization. What the public shares with the common is an enemy, for privatization is also the enemy of the common. What I call a "transgressive public sphere" may aspire to the common. What is clear is that there is a complicated relationship between these concepts, which have some convergences and divergences too.

The making of complex identities I discussed in *Unbounded Publics* is usually called "intersectionality" today. "Intersectional" has greater resonance than "transgressive." However, I still prefer the word and idea "transgression." To transgress is always in relation to a norm or boundary, and transgression always implies a rejection or refusal of that norm or boundary. Intersectional does not carry the same connotation of rejection and refusal. A transgressive political identity is intersectional, but there is something else in transgression. This is because the word and idea of transgression also contains the ontological dimension of a "being-against," which I always want to capture. Transgression is against choosing a static political identity determined by geography and ideology. Transgression is against choosing one side of a binary position, or of given dichotomies, because things are not always "on" or "off" like a light switch. Transgression is therefore compatible with deconstruction, not only as defined in the philosophy of Jacques Derrida, but also as acted out in the deconstructive practices of queer politics. Transgression is against choosing to go along with what is happening in your own lifeworld, your own city or school or neighborhood. Of course, the singular may also indicate being-against. Transgressive is the being who eludes categorization in the field of fixed and narrow political identities.

BG asks: In *Unbounded Publics*, you say that "Cosmopolitanism is always transnational, but that which is transnational is not always cosmopolitan."[16] You give the example of capitalism. How about communism? Is it perhaps always transgressive? You say, in parenthesis, "remember, for example, Marx's insistence that communism could not work within a national framework, because capitalism did not work within those limited bounds."[17] What is the relationship between the false transgressive dimension of capitalism and the genuine one of communism? Does communism go beyond national borders just because capitalism also does so, or for other, perhaps more intrinsic, reasons? The twofold direction of transgression is important here. You say, "A loosening of national identities and national cultures is well underway, in part due to globalization itself, but what forms in their place remains to be seen."[18] Later, speaking of the Zapatistas, you say, "The transgression of the Zapatista public sphere, which both defends indigenous peoples where they live and raises a transnational critique of neoliberalism, is normatively at odds with any

---

16 Ibid., 152.
17 Ibid., 139.
18 Ibid., 142.

conception of unbounded capitalism – unbounded publics are thus presented as a kind of antithesis."[19]

Can you elaborate on this logic of antithesis and opposition? It seems that the idea of antagonism is included here, or is it also one in which the logic of difference, an *essential difference,* is at work? In other words, it seems to me that the transgressive character of communism entails the total displacement, supersession, deactivation, and destruction of capitalism. I imagine (that is, I am certain) we are in agreement about that. Can you elaborate on this question?

RGO answers: First, all cosmopolitanism is humanist, but not all humanism is cosmopolitan. Cosmopolitanism is a specific form of humanism, but many humanists do not feel that cosmopolitanism is either necessary or useful. Capitalism, I would argue, is an obstacle to humanism; capitalism is also not cosmopolitan in terms of any moral orientation. Capitalism may be more-or-less regulated by humanist or cosmopolitan ideas, but such regulation appears as a fetter on the logic of capital; economic regulation is imposed upon capital, not borne from it. When we consider capital as a logic that actually organizes life, we see to what extent it arranges human affairs for the interests of the private accumulation of property and wealth. That logic seeks to be free from all humanist obligation, cosmopolitan or otherwise.

Following this, one might think to place humanism and cosmopolitanism on the side of communism, but that is also problematic. This is partly because of the history of Marxism itself, which often treats (for example, with Louis Althusser and others) secular moral theory as extrinsic to socialist philosophy. One of the common claims of Marxist materialism is that communism does not need moral theories because communism emerges in the real movements of real people to abolish the existing society, and such real movements are mobilized by material conditions of life, not by moral theories. Marx got to some of the same ideas of humanism and cosmopolitanism using a different language, namely the language of internationalism. Internationalism was a deep theme, and sometimes a bludgeon against nationalist politics, that was pervasive throughout *The Communist Manifesto* and *The Critique of the Gotha Program* (Internationalism was crucial to Marx's attack on the

---

19   Ibid., 234.

German Workers' Party). Internationalism was the beating heart in the founding of The First International Workingmen's Association. Marx saw the dangers of nationalism, especially in its possible reduction of his theory to the bourgeois liberalism of the League of Peace and Freedom, so he rejected it with special ferocity.

Because of this, Marxists may say that they are internationalists, but neither humanists nor cosmopolitans. They can also be internationalists, humanists, *and* cosmopolitans. There are other possible permutations. The only term in the stream of this history and political philosophy that would require rejection is nationalism. The rejection of nationalism in the major currents of socialist philosophy going back to Marx is only one of hundreds of reasons why "national socialism" was always a contradiction in terms from a communist point of view.

Now, to your question about transgression, I think we have to answer "yes," communism must always be transgressive. Why? The reason is not so difficult to discern. Any effort of historical materialism, of class analysis, will have to confront the historical contingencies of place and time. Historical materialism simply cannot accept an ideological "leveling gaze" that would make the situation facing workers in every different country and time identical. We cannot apply a leveling gaze within the purview of Marxist theory without breaking one of its most fundamental commitments. At the same time, however, Marx insisted, in *The Communist Manifesto* (and elsewhere) that connections between historically specified struggles in one pace and international class struggle elsewhere could and should be established and developed. In *The Communist Manifesto*, Marx and Engels write: "The Communists are distinguished from the other working-class parties by this only: 1. In the national struggles of the proletarians of the different countries, they point out and bring to the front the common interests of the entire proletariat, independently of all nationality. 2. In the various stages of development which the struggle of the working class against the bourgeoisie has to pass through, they always and everywhere represent the interests of the movement as a whole."[20] Therefore, every national or sub-national struggle must strive to identify common interests in it with struggles elsewhere, must aspire to international class-consciousness and, practically, must refuse to diagnose

---

20 Karl Marx and Frederick Engels, *The Communist Manifesto*, trans. Samuel Moore (New York: International Publishers, 1948), 22.

and treat proletarian struggles as if anchored to national problems. That is fundamentally and irreducibly transgressive.

To your question about antithesis and opposition, we could think about Richard Falk's conception of "globalization-from-below" in his book, *Predatory Globalization*.[21] There, Falk accepts that there will be no "de-globalization" of political economy and culture. For Falk, this means that any antithesis to capitalist globalization cannot aim at undoing globalization altogether, to move backwards in time to some pre-industrial localism, communitarian or otherwise. No. For Falk, such "de-globalization" is not a serious goal. He argues that a more serious antithesis to capitalist globalization would be to create an alternative globalization-from-below. For him, this frames a key problem in anti-globalization politics. We should be pro-globalization of an anti-capitalist kind. Instead of what Falk calls "globalization-from-above," that is, globalization led by capitalists, neoliberals, transnational corporations, and imperialists, we need "globalization-from-below." This "globalization-from-below" emerges out of the culmination of global social movements, civil society organizations (CSOs), and linkages between popular democratic struggles led by impoverished and marginalized peoples, mainly – he insists – in the global south (because Falk also wants to address global apartheid).

Notwithstanding serious reservations about Falk's optimism regarding the possibility for globalization-from-below, we may find in his proposal an oppositional logic to that of capital. In *Predatory Globalization*, Falk calls for a globalization committed to "minimizing violence, maximizing economic well-being, realizing social and political justice, and upholding environmental quality."[22] These would be the normative world order values of "globalization-from-below." He later goes on to specify eight elements of normative democracy.[23] I think that Falk fails to appreciate the extent to which what he wants to see in an alternative globalization is categorically incompatible with capitalism. In the end, Falk comes close to wanting a kinder globalization, one a bit more aligned with Rawlsian liberalism or Piketty leftism. He seems to think, perhaps a bit like Eduard Bernstein, that the cumulative impact of globalization-from-below would guide a kind of "evolutionary socialism"

---

21 Richard Falk, *Predatory Globalization: A Critique* (Malden: Polity Press, 1999).
22 Falk, op. cit., 130.
23 Falk, op. cit., 147-149.

according to which we end up with a better globalization than the one we now have.

I will save further criticisms of Falk and simply say that I do not think we can reform global capitalism into socialism. George Lakey has studied and documented some of the more socialistic forms of capitalism in Scandinavian countries.[24] However, a certain nationalism limits the scope of the effort in those countries, and the Nordic model still contends with the antithetical forces of capitalism that threaten it daily. The Nordic model maintains, on a relatively small scale, the kindest and gentlest capitalism possible, but it is precarious because of capitalism, and reveals that the best things under capitalism are the least capitalist things.

On the other hand, Marx's internationalism was not capitalist, and neither was the Zapatista rebellion. I agree that the transgressive character of communism must entail the total destruction of capitalism. In fact, much like in Luxemburg's reply to Bernstein, I wonder if an "opposition" to capitalism that does not seek to destroy it is ultimately an opposition at all. Capitalism knows what to do with impositions and regulations. There is a very long and well-documented history of what capital does in the face of such efforts, going all the way back to Adam Smith's discussion in 1776 of "the policy of Europe" in *The Wealth of Nations*.[25] Capital resists all such policy redirection wherever possible, which we can see from Smith's time to the maquiladoras, free trade zones, economic agreements and institutions from Bretton Woods to NAFTA, CAFTA, FTAA, and all the latest pipeline projects. Capital finds workarounds and gets free from its fetters at the earliest opportunity, by way of its own policymaking, tax law, foreign bank accounts, legal theft, etc. There are times when the hands of capitalists can be tied and there are no workarounds. This is what liberals like Elizabeth Warren and Bernie Sanders call "closing loopholes." However, there is a long history of capital reopening loopholes, a history brimming with examples from the decline and repeal of Glass-Steagall to Citizens United.

All of the above is why, ultimately, I return to revolutionary theory. The real antithesis to capital cannot be a set of speed bumps, penalties, and obstacles. Communists must be abolitionists. For many years, I have wanted to bring special attention to the peculiar and widespread usage of

---

24 George Lakey, *Viking Economics* (Brooklyn and London: Melville House, 2016).
25 See Chapter X, Part II of Adam Smith, *The Wealth of Nations* (New York: Bantam Classic Books, 2003).

the concept of abolition in Marx's work, going back to his early definition of communism in *The German Ideology*. Abolition was a central idea for Marx, a fact that gets insufficient attention. In *The German Ideology* he defines communism as "the *real* movement which abolishes the present state of things."[26] The best abolitionists did not look for ways to make slavery more bearable for slaves. They regarded "better slavery" as a nonsensical notion. It is absurd and insulting. It is like calling for a "fair capitalism," as Rawls wanted to see. The abolitionists understood that slavery had to be destroyed. The same is true of capitalism.

BG asks: Another question I want to ask at this point is, once again, that of the relationship between communism and anarchism. Both in *Unbounded Publics* and in *The Communism of Love*, it seems that you feel the need to justify the possible presence of anarchist elements in your work and disambiguate your position, saying, basically, that you are not working from within the anarchist tradition. We briefly spoke about this in a Zoom meeting. But can you explain that a bit more? Isn't the question of their relation a bit dated, to say the least? Isn't it in fact the case that they have much more in common than many people may think and that communism is anarchism in the end? I was thinking of the wonderful concept of *isonomia*, recently highlighted by Kojin Karatani in his important reexamination of the origins of philosophy. Isn't perhaps *isonomia*, that is, no law, or perhaps organic law, the common character of both communism and anarchism?

RGO answers: I have focused directly and extensively on this precise question on the relationship between anarchism and Marxism, in several places throughout my work (and throughout this present book). You can find, for example, sustained attention to this question in *Specters of Revolt* (in Chapter 5 of that book: A Graveyard for Orthodoxies). It was also the focus of my 2014 article for *Left Curve* journal, "Marxism Not Statism." I have lectured on the subject in activist venues, and even to anarchist academics at Loughborough University years ago. In short, my position is largely consistent with your statement "that communism is anarchism in the end," as well as with Karatani's concept of *isonomia*.

However, the overlapping and mutually enhancing intersections of Marxism and anarchism are much easier to see if you only study them

---

26   Karl Marx, *The German Ideology* (New York: Prometheus Books, 1998), 57.

theoretically. If you hang around in anarchist circles, as I have done variously for much of my life, one of the repeatedly surprising and dumbfounding tendencies you find time and again is a deep reactionary hostility of anarchists to Marxists and vice versa. By now, that tendency of reactionary hostility should be dead and buried, which is what I meant in *Specters of Revolt* by speaking about "a graveyard for orthodoxies."[27] Unfortunately, there are too many examples of this stupid hostility for us to pretend that it does not continue to persist.

To show this, we may consider some examples. Take the old anarchist magazine Fifth Estate, which is one of the most stalwart and well-known anarchist publications in North America (it has been around for over 50 years). Fifth Estate recently released an "anti-Marx" issue.[28] I have written for Fifth Estate, where editors have told me directly that they would publish my articles after I removed all positive references to Marx.[29] This type of reaction should strike anyone as absurd, especially since, if you are indeed an anarchist, then you already have much more in common with Marxists than with almost anyone else on Earth. Nonetheless, there remains a persistent ideological reaction in certain anarchist circles, still fiercely articulated in the second half of the twentieth century – for example in Murray Bookchin's famous "Listen, Marxist!" essay – where anarchists essentially regard all Marxists and communists as big government statists, as mortal enemies to anarchists everywhere.[30] Many anarchists continue to insist that we communists want to put them into the gulag, and they ground that insistence in historical examples from the Kronstadt Rebellion to communist opposition to the CNT-FAI from 1936 to 1937 during the Spanish Revolution. There is a long history of authors and activists with names. Therefore, we are talking about real people who, for example, take wonderful books like Emma Goldman's *My Disillusionment in Russia* as evidence that communists must be the enemies of anarchists. This view should have died with Mikhail Bakunin, who himself was far more capable of appreciating Marx's theories

---

27 See *Specters of Revolt: On the Intellect of Insurrection and Philosophy from Below* (London: Repeater Books, 2016), 191-213.
28 Fifth Estate, Issue # 393, Spring 2015.
29 Personal correspondences, October 2011, January 2012.
30 The essay can be found in Murray Bookchin, *Post-Scarcity Anarchism* (Montreal and Buffalo: Black Rose Books, 1986).

(and did so extensively in his writings) than anyone associated with Fifth Estate today.

When my book, *The Communism of Love*, was recently reviewed by an anarchist, its theory was shockingly (and idiotically) aligned with Stalinism and the Soviet Union, both of which I have been relentlessly and consistently critical of since my very first published work decades ago.[31] I would even say that my critique of state capitalism and Cold War concepts of communism are defining features of my life's work up to this point.

You might think that this corpse-like zombie of an opposition was not so grotesque on the Marxist side, but it still lives there too. You can see this especially among some of our own comrades who are major figures of autonomist Marxism, and yet essentially agree with anarchists more than they seem to know. This is not only clear in the example of Michael Hardt and Antonio Negri, who make a special and especially confused effort to reject anarchism in *Empire*.[32] It is also in the writing of Cornelius Castoriadis, who claimed that anarchism leads down a "blind alley," apparently without noticing the fact that he has more in common with anarchists than with many Marxists.[33] At least Franco "Bifo" Berardi and Silvia Federici, who do not identify simply or clearly as anarchists either, know well that they are close and kindred spirits.

Now, you were wondering why I feel the need to justify the presence of anarchist elements in my work, to disambiguate my position. Let me finally say as clearly as possible that I draw on anarchist literature and history, I teach it with deep feeling and appreciation, and I believe that some of the great works of anarchist writers are among the most egregiously overlooked in the whole history of political thought. In my own estimation, there may even be no more engrossing and rousing book ever written (at least that I have read) than Emma Goldman's *Living My Life*.

The main philosophical advance that the anarchists have given us is a very sophisticated theory of power. Bakunin's idea about power invariably corrupting the good is the heart of the anarchist theory of power. The

---

31 See book review by Javier Sethness, Philosophy in Review, Vol. 41, No. 2 (2021): May.
32 See Antonio Negri and Michael Hardt, *Empire* (Cambridge, MA and London: Harvard University Press, 2001), 349.
33 See Cornelius Castoriadis, "Socialism or Barbarism" in *Political and Social Writings, Volume 1*, trans. David Ames Curtis (Minneapolis: University of Minnesota Press, 1988), 77.

idea of an irrepressibly corrupting power was at the center of J.R.R. Tolkien's *Lord of the Rings* as a power that ultimately even corrupts the least corruptible among us. In a letter to his son Christopher Tolkien in 1943, Tolkien wrote, "My political opinions lean more and more to Anarchy (philosophically understood, meaning abolition of control not whiskered men with bombs)."[34] I think that the twentieth century, and what Tolkien lived to witness in the totalitarianism of his own century (he died in 1973) vindicated what anarchists had been saying in the nineteenth century. What anarchists said in the nineteenth century made them look like fanatical ideologues to many Marxists at that time, but today, we should finally recognize the veracity of basic insights about power and hierarchy that have always distinguished anarchism. Even following the wisdom of recent social movements, for example in Argentina, we find a preference for *horizontalidad* over hierarchy, and there are good reasons for that.

This means, I think, that we should have by now basic anarchist sensibilities about the state, about any political state, and that these should be recognized and accepted as anarchist sensibilities. I share those sensibilities and am not ashamed to claim them. However, it does seem to me important still to say that I am not working from or within an anarchist tradition. Why is that important? Well, I discuss the reasons why more fully in the Introduction to *The Communism of Love*, but in short, there are two reasons. First, I do not like the word and idea "anarchism" as much as I like the word and idea "communism." Etymologically and conceptually, "anarchy" is defined negatively, in that it says what it *does not want*. What it wants is, in other words, what it does not want. "*An*" (meaning without) and "*arkhos*" (meaning leader) come together to indicate something like "without rulers." Well, I can perhaps agree to that, but communism has not only a negative content but a positive content too. The word and idea communism centralizes the concept of the commune, community, the commons, or what Marx (and I, too) call the *Gemeinwesen*. Comparing the anarchist emphasis on "absent power" to the communist emphasis on the *Gemeinwesen* largely accounts for my preference for grounding my work in a communist trajectory.

Now, any good anarchist will retort to this that such a reduction of anarchism to its etymological and conceptual meaning ignores the vast and

---

34 From a letter to Christopher Tolkien, November 29, 1943, published in *The Letters of J.R.R. Tolkien* (Boston and New York: Houghton Mifflin Harcourt, 1995).

varied positive formulations of anarchists from Peter Kropotkin's *Fields, Factories, and Workshops* to Ursula Le Guin's utopian imagination to Ron Sakolsky's exciting and subversive surrealist approaches to insisting on the impossible. However, to my thinking, the many efforts of anarchists to imagine an anarchist world are not the great gift of the anarchist tradition. I think that the greatest contribution of the anarchists has always been in the general critical theory of power, which has a wide ranges of practices. I would not wish to speak of anarchism and communism in terms of their relationship to the law, organic or otherwise. Laws implicate rules, but there are other things, such as anxiety and desire, that often govern us, and I would not speak or think of these simply as laws.

So, what accounts for the remainder of my insistence on the communist idea? It is simply that, to my understanding, the radical critique of capital and its logic is still the most central commitment of social and political theory and revolutionary struggle. The confrontation with capital and capitalism needs to stay at center stage. When we read anarchist anti-capitalism from Errico Malatesta to Charlotte Wilson, we find that what is best in its critique of capitalism was already worked out (and far more fully) by Marx. It is no accident that Charlotte Wilson began her radical education by founding the Karl Marx Club. No major thinker since Marx has devoted their entire life so fully to the study of capital. Marx gave over his life, from his twenties until his death, to the question, what is capital? What does it do? How do we confront it? I still hold to the necessity of the centralization of Marx's main questions, and I suppose that is what makes me a Marxist. However, I am also a Marxist who thinks that Marxism gets better when it is more anarchist. What I think we need in the twenty-first century, if we have learned the lessons of the twentieth, is a Marxism with deep and abiding anarchist sensibilities. That is really my conclusion in a single statement. Accordingly, it is a consistent part of my approach from the very first research.

The question of the antagonistic relation between Marxism and anarchism should never have lived this long. I wish we could finally bury that old reactionary opposition between anarchists and Marxists in a graveyard of ideology. By now, we should all be anarchist-Marxists, communist-anarchists, libertarian socialists, autonomist Marxists, anti-state communists, Marxist-humanists, Left communists, or whatever name you may want to claim in the moniker- and obstacle-ridden terrain of anti-capitalist anti-statism. Nonetheless, and as I think I have also shown, these terms and ideas are not simply synonymous even if they would ultimately head for the same destination. We cannot simply erase important etymological, conceptual, theoretical, and political differences. Therefore, I argue that we need creative integrations and evolving syntheses of anarchism and Marxism, without reductive equivocations of either one to the other.

RGO asks: You and I agree that communism is fundamentally about being-in-the-world, or possible and desirable forms of life, and we agree that Marx's focus on political economy was not meant to reassert a political economic point of view, but to criticize the limitations imposed on forms of life by capital. We agree that Marx's communism was in fact an ontological movement, that is, a real movement that creates the conditions for new forms of life. Unsurprisingly, I agree with your claim that it is "impossible to think that Marx would have seen the forced industrialization of the Soviet Union under Stalin as a correct way of proceeding on the road to socialism and communism."[35] However, a large number of communists – as well as their liberal and conservative critics – continue to insist on communism as a form of government, and not as a form of life. Can you explain the crucial importance of this distinction *in your work*?

BG answers: In addition to the one you mention in your question, I think that I make very few references to communism as a form of government in my books. Indeed, just like you, I see communism as a form of life. To insist on the former notion of communism is really not fruitful. Of course, that does not mean that it shouldn't be studied. In fact, there is much to learn from its history and practices. But that is not what the real, ontological movement – a movement towards the future – is about. First of all, communism tends towards the dissolution of government as such (that is, the distinction between those who govern and those who are governed) – the dissolution of the state, its bureaucracy, and so on. In this sense, communism shares a lot with anarchism. It is the making of heterotopias. It is not simply the overcoming of capitalist relations of production, but a total transformation and transfiguration of human existence, which, it might be argued, has historically been, and is now, deformed and disfigured. So, when in *The German Ideology* Marx and Engels say, "We call communism the *real* movement

---

35   Gullì, *Labor of Fire*, op. cit., 41.

which abolishes the present state of things," that's not simply a beautiful statement and not at all a rhetorical moment; it is rather the definition of an ontological, world-historical and political project. In your work, you also distinguish between ideological and philosophical communism. That's a very important distinction, with which I totally agree. Unfortunately, as you note in your question, many communists and their liberal and conservative critics only focus on ideological communism and on communism as a form of government. However, when the philosophical, ontological understanding of communism is unheeded, all we have is the continuity of a wrong narrative, which is ultimately false. It is false because of its past history, and it is false in relation to future programs (of the communists who think that way) and future fears (of the critics of the communist idea). It is perhaps on this account that some people who embrace the new notion of postcapitalism have *understandably* chosen to stop using the word "communism," as Mark Fisher notably did. You and I, as well as many others, have chosen to continue using it, though I have nothing against the notion of postcapitalism and actually find it very useful. Of course, it's not a matter of words, but of their true meaning.

Whether we use the word communism or not, the critical effort must be to address the deep-rooted, institutional system of violence that characterizes capital in all its forms and applications – indeed, capital in its specificity and essential difference as *a general illumination,* as a total machine of extraction and subsumption, of harmful overproduction and utter destruction.[36] Evidently, communism is also an essential difference and *a different general illumination*. It is the illumination of the singular and common on the basis of the absolute overcoming of private property. This is a form of life, not a type of government.

It is true that under capital there have been developments in science and technology that make it possible today to envision a postcapitalist world. What is less certain is that at the dawn of modernity this was the only possible historical trajectory. In *Caliban and the Witch*, Silvia Federici shows that there were alternatives to capitalist development – not utopic, but heterotopic, one might say – that were suppressed in violence and blood. Federici says, "Capitalism was the counter-revolution that destroyed the possibilities that had emerged from the anti-feudal struggle – possibilities which, if realized, might have spared us the immense destruction of lives and the natural

---

36   Marx, *Grundrisse*, op. cit., 107.

environment that has marked the advance of capitalist relations worldwide."[37] History is a matter of contingency, not necessity.

The notion that societies must transition from one stage to the other, one mode of production to the other, one essential difference to the other, is no longer very popular, and rightly so. At the thresholds of the new, of the future, there are always many concrete possibilities. It is "the critical attitude," to make a reference to Max Horkheimer, which may decide of the outcome. Horkheimer says, "The future of humanity depends on the existence today of the critical attitude."[38] If in the past there were possibilities to build a world of social justice without entering the violence of sovereignty and capital, at this stage of capitalist development, that world of social justice, that ontology of liberation, namely, communism, can only be achieved through the end of the logic of productivity, the law of surplus value, the regime of exploitation and profit. However, this is not merely an economic matter. It is political (and philosophical) in the deepest sense. Changes in forms of government could not accomplish that. Rather, what's needed is a total reshaping of social, political, and cultural – *human* – existence. This must entail a new dialogic relationship between the human and the non-human.

I'd like to conclude with Marx who says that "nature is linked to itself, for man is a part of nature."[39] Yet, this dialogue, this new ontology, also regards and includes the machine. In my work, after stressing the importance of the mode of care and a *real* attention to issues that are usually considered marginal, but are instead essential to a healthy and just society, like the issue of disability, I deal with the machinic reshaping of our ontologies in positive, if problematic, terms. The construction of communism, of a postcapitalist world of social justice, entails the vision of new and radically different forms of life.

BG asks: I'm going back to the issue of anarchism and what I was asking you just before. What I see in *Spectacular Capitalism*, perhaps because you are dealing with Debord, is a much more sympathetic view of anarchism,

---

37 Silvia Federici, *Caliban and the Witch: Women, the Body, and Primitive Accumulation* (New York: Autonomedia, 2004), 21-22.
38 Max Horkheimer, *Critical Theory: Selected Essays*, trans. Matthew J. O'Connell and Others (New York: Continuum, 1992), 242.
39 Marx, "Economic and Philosophic Manuscripts," op. cit., 63.

which I appreciate. Can you explain the difference between your varying treatments of this tradition in your different books?

The following passage is particularly important: "The common misuse and abuse of the idea of anarchism has rather clearly come from its adversaries in power attempting to imagine the world without their indispensable good graces."[40] You also say that "there is hardly a spectacle of anarchism at all."[41] While this explains the very limited space given to anarchism in your book, it does at the same time say something very positive about it. I am very sympathetic to anarchism and consider myself an anarchist in many ways and in a deep sense. In an interesting endnote, you identify Michael Hardt and Antonio Negri as "self-identifying communists… who share the company of many anarcho-communists and autonomists."[42] You even, beautifully, say that anarchism "means peaceful cooperation as antidote to ruthless competition"[43] and later you position your own work in radical politics as "a post-Marxism informed by anarchism."[44] One important moment here is when you say that "anarchism has embodied the most antagonistic *logos* to the Hobbesian conception of sovereignty."[45] So, in a sense, it seems that anarchism becomes a sort of philosophically neutral (neither/nor) key disrupting the spectacle of the various ideologies: capitalism, bureaucratic socialism, and so on; or rather, it becomes an alternative, nonsovereign paradigm to the dominant ideologies of the spectacle: "*spectacular capitalism and spectacular socialism.*"[46] Can you comment on this?

RGO answers: Given your own critical theory of sovereignty in *Earthly Plenitudes*, I see and appreciate your deep and abiding affinity with anarchism. This is especially clear if we think of anarchism as the most antagonistic *logos* to the Hobbesian concept of sovereignty. I agree that you and I are very close on the question of anarchism. I would further point out that, in your work too, there is a much more direct and sustained grounding in Marx and Marxist theory, and that you (like me) more openly articulate

---

40 Gilman-Opalsky, *Spectacular Capitalism*, op. cit., 14.
41 Ibid.
42 Ibid., endnote 6, 30.
43 Ibid., 15.
44 Ibid., 37.
45 Ibid., 13.
46 Ibid., 15.

connections with communist philosophy, socialist politics, etc. The major primary sources from which you theorize in your own work are scarcely anarchist, and you do not announce or present your work as definitively anarchist. We are similar in that, but it could have been otherwise. There are, for example, some very important major works written by anarchist theorists, yet we have both found it more fruitful to swim in other philosophical waters. I shall only speak for myself, but I suppose this means that we find those other waters deeper and better suited for our own theorization (or else we would have selected different bibliographies full of Proudhon, Goldman, Kropotkin, Bookchin, Graeber).

I am not sure if you will agree with this, but it is possible that I come closer to a declaration of anarchism than you do, even in the above-cited lines. Regardless, we both agree with anarchist sensibilities about sovereign power, capitalist statecraft, and the existing legal order. It is certainly easy to observe that we have shared anarchist sensibility on such things. I suspect that you and I may have similar reasons for producing work that is more (if you will), "anarchist-adjacent" or "anarchistic" yet not work that self-identifies with anarchism in any ideological sense.

For my part, I have found declarations of anarchism to be overly ideological, even reactionary and anti-philosophical, as in the example of *Fifth Estate* I discussed above. Moreover, I am not willing to make a categorical rejection of all state or legal action in every case simply because some anarchist principle might require me to discount or reject everything done at any level of policy or legislative politics. I think such an ideological line in the sand can have serious consequences. Now, it is true that policy and legislative politics are never my focus; it is also true that I place absolutely no faith in policy and statecraft. However, I want to be able to speak about the crucial differences between policies that are better or worse for human beings in terms of healthcare, education, workers, gun violence, pandemics, or ecology. I despise the US Democratic Party and capitalist elections, and I find Biden and Clinton morally repulsive and dangerous, but only brazen stupidity would fail to find any differences between Trumpist white supremacy and the neoliberal fanaticism of Clintonite capitalism. One thing that puts me off anarchism today is that I have witnessed persistent ideological reaction in anarchist circles to anything that appears to appreciate such differences, coupled with a willingness to equivocate everything awful to the self-same bad thing.

When I read George Lakey's *Viking Economics* or Thomas Piketty's *Capital in The Twenty-First Century*, I can certainly see that these are capitalist books, with little to offer revolutionary thinking and politics.[47] At the same time, who could possibly deny that political economy and culture in a Scandinavian country like Norway is markedly different than that in the US or UK? It would reveal an utter stupidity to say so, but an anarchist could do it and might even want to for their anarchist credibility. However, these differences make a real difference in the lives of real people. We have to look at the reality and try not to let ideology interpret everything for its own sake.

Saying this does not mean that I simply accept Lakey or Piketty uncritically. I even co-edited a book for Temple University Press entitled *Against Capital in the Twenty-First Century*, which my co-editor and I produced as a sort of rebuttal to Piketty leftism.[48] Our book openly declares a heterodox and open Marxism, which draws heavily on anarchism, and the volume even includes texts by anarchists. I personally wanted to make sure we included Fredy Perlman, Penelope Rosemont, Murray Bookchin, John Zerzan, and Raoul Vaneigem. My co-editor, John Asimakopoulos, wanted to include David Graeber, which we also did. However, our book is not an anarchist volume. Positive reviews appeared in both the journal *Anarchist Studies* as well as in *Marx and Philosophy Book Review*. We included selections by unorthodox and more conventional Marxists, including John Holloway, Raya Dunayevskaya, Cornelius Castoriadis, Selma James, Silvia Federici, Franco "Bifo" Berardi, Dave Hill, Angela Mitropoulos and others. In our introduction to that book, Asimakopoulos and I explain that we selected texts for the volume according to three criteria: First, we insisted on a deep critique of capitalism; second, a deep critique of the top-down politics of statist leftism; third, to embody and reflect the real diversity of radical thinking. We also say that, while our book is not decisively anarchist, we "draw in affirmative and constructive ways from a rich history of anarchist theory and action."[49]

---

47   George Lakey, *Viking Economics* (Brooklyn and London: Melville House, 2016) and Thomas Piketty, *Capital in the Twenty-First Century*, trans. Arthur Goldhammer (Cambridge, MA: Harvard University Press, 2014).
48   Richard Gilman-Opalsky and John Asimakopoulos, *Against Capital in the Twenty-First Century: A Reader of Radical Undercurrents* (Philadelphia: Temple University Press, 2018).
49   Ibid., 5.

As previously mentioned, Marx and Marxism remain central for me because of the centrality of capital at the heart of all of the enduring problems of the existing reality, and because I am most drawn to the etymological and conceptual content of the communist idea.

Finally, I want to say something specifically about Debord and the more sympathetic, albeit fleeting, view on anarchism you found in *Spectacular Capitalism*. Anarchists have claimed Debord as a theorist for anarchism in North America, and largely because of the good work and hard efforts of Fredy Perlman and the Black and Red group (and publisher) in Detroit. They translated Debord's *The Society of the Spectacle*, and real connections were established between North American anarchists (like Perlman, and later, other anarchist presses) and French radicalism – especially Situationist work – from the 1950s-70s. As mentioned, I never encountered Debord in any university classroom (other than in my own classes, because I put him on the syllabus). I first discovered Debord and *The Society of the Spectacle* in anarchist circles, anarchist bookshops, in pamphlet form on activist tables at activist events. The association of Debord with anarchism is actually rather strange because it has very little to do with the actual words inside of his books and articles. When you finally dive in and read Debord's books and articles, it clearly would take a rather unnatural effort of ideological reading to make them appear as decisively anarchist. Debord was dealing with Hegel, Marx, and Lukács in creative and critical ways, with the help of Lefebvre, poetry, art, activism, and cinema. Debord does not declare himself anarchist in any notably consistent or ideological way. He did not tether himself to anarchist writing or politics.

Debord was interested in rethinking revolution in light of the major impasses of capitalist society in the late twentieth century. He was interested in this not only in light of the technologies of mass culture, but especially in light of the dashed hopes of revolutionaries who invested their faith in the Algerian liberation struggle (many of whom thought communism would be somewhere on the other side of decolonization). Yes, we do find in Debord a deep critique of Marx, especially in the chapter of *The Society of the Spectacle*, "The Proletariat as Subject and Representation." However, such a critique – and many other criticisms of Marx – is not alien to Marxism. Such critique of Marxism is often and ultimately a part of Marxism.

I will not declare that the anarchists were simply wrong to claim Debord for themselves. There was certainly a clear anarchist sensibility in his work, and Debord did read and know his Bakunin and Proudhon well. I only want to say that we must appreciate the complexities of a rich dialectical relationship here, which I find fruitful and useful in Debord's approach, and which I find also in ours (if it is not too presumptuous for me to say so). I think dialectical developments of Marxism that openly identify their anarchist sensibilities and advances are crucial for the theoretical and political movements we most urgently need today. I know we return to the question of anarchism often in our book, so I will end this answer here for now.

RGO asks: I want to juxtapose two ideas from the final sections of *Singularities at the Threshold*. In Chapter 8, you write about the differential dependencies of newborns and the elderly, about forms of fragility, and about the differential needs of even the healthy in light of accident or illness.[50] In the context of care, and in light of the common of the singular, you suggest it is better to think of *interdependence* where "the carer and the cared-for become part of a new relationship."[51] Several pages later, you sum up your arguments following Simondon, Deleuze and Guattari, and others as follows: "[W]e have actually claimed that the individual as such does not exist and the self itself is a fictional construct."[52] I understand that because of the concept of singularity, there is no contradiction between saying that each one will have different needs *and at the same time* that there are no individuals. However, I still think there remains a problematic tension there.

In *Critique of the Gotha Program*, Marx says that "unequal individuals (and they would not be different individuals if they were not unequal) are measurable only by an equal standard insofar as they are brought under an equal point of view, are taken from one definite side only -- for instance, in the present case, are regarded only as workers and nothing more is seen in them, everything else being ignored. Further, one worker is married, another is not; one has more children than another, and so on and so forth. Thus, with an equal performance of labor, and hence an equal share in the

---

50   Gullì, *Singularities at the Threshold*, op. cit., 129.
51   Ibid.
52   Ibid., 133.

social consumption fund, one will in fact receive more than another, one will be richer than another, and so on. To avoid all these defects, right, instead of being equal, would have to be unequal."[53]

In the above passage, Marx argues that people will need differential shares of "the social consumption fund" (which we may today call the common or the commonwealth), since each should get what they require according to their needs. Accordingly, I have always found Marx's attention to differential abilities and needs to be perfect and conclusive proof that he saw the individual better than liberals or conservatives ever did (or do). Do you agree with this? Is there not a way in which Marx and Marxists like us *see the individual* better than our opponents do? Isn't it dangerous to say that the individual does not exist as such, that the self is itself a fiction? I suppose I want to resist this and to suggest that Marxism does not have a special difficulty with seeing both the individual and the common in the *Gemeinwesen*.

BG answers: I see your point, and I think your criticism is well taken. Yet, I don't think that when I deny the ontological reality of the individual I go too far. First of all, I wish to replace the individual with the singular. That doesn't mean that we have to stop using the word 'individual' and use the word 'singular' instead. What it means, rather, is that we should achieve some conceptual and critical clarity and appreciate the ontological reality of the singular. Indeed, the singular is not individual, but trans-dividual, and this is so because of its ontological constitution. Gilbert Simondon, who coined the word 'transindividual,' speaks of the *relative individual*, which is different from the individual as such, in its independence and absoluteness. For Marx, the individual is always a *social individual*. But the social individual is something completely different from the individual of the liberal and neoliberal tradition, as you note in your question. So, we are on a completely different plane, precisely that of the common. There is an infinite difference between the individual and the social individual, the relative individual, or the trans-dividual. To my mind, in the important passage you quote from the *Critique of the Gotha Program*, Marx is precisely speaking about the singular and singularity. And in fact, Marx's famous slogan, "from each according to their abilities, to each according to their needs," is an enunciation of interdependence and singularity.

---

53 Karl Marx, *Critique of the Gotha Program* (Moscow: Progress Publishers, 1976), 17.

The apparent truth of the individual must be measured against the reality of dependency, which is necessarily a form of sociality and association. I think that it is in this context, where the dependent shows its affinity with the dividual, that we can appreciate the illusory manner of the individual, and especially of the independent individual. However, we do see individuals, just like we see the sunrise and sunset. Even before becoming an institution, or at least a figure, of liberal and neoliberal ideology, the individual undeniably has a place in our perception, and I would even say, perhaps, a degree of reality – just like, once again, the sunrise and sunset do; so much so that we contemplate them and take pictures of them to post on Instagram, Facebook, and so on. The individual appears because its appearance is possible. But it is in abandonment, in death, in our finitude, that both the individual and the dividual show their truth; the former as being a reflection, and the latter as being a threshold, a tear, of the singular. This is so true that when someone who is very dear to us – the dearest perhaps – dies, we experience their death as an amputation. Perhaps we say that a part of us is gone, and this is not just a manner of speaking. It is not a temporary sensation, nor is it a matter of sentimentality. Rather, our singularity is torn apart beyond repair, and we undergo a mutation in the very fabric of our being. Only a ghostly, but existentially necessary presence filled with absence, an aura, remains; only the constant work of the productive imagination, can bring back what cannot be brought back. It is here that we see the force and truth of our interdependence as well as the poverty of individuality.

RGO asks: I am curious about the possibility of communist sovereignty. In *Earthly Plenitudes*, you say that the ability to decide on exceptional cases is a distinguishing feature of sovereignty, and that "the decision itself would decide the sovereign. In making the decision, X would rise to the status of sovereign."[54] The example that best condemns sovereignty is the example of capital. When George W. Bush or some other head of state does whatever is called for by the dictatorship of capital, whatever is desired by and for their own class (the ruling class), they do not care about the permission of the *demos*. They are sovereign and their decision-making establishes this. Yes, but is sovereignty something we might defend if it were that of a "dictatorship of the proletariat?" Let me put this question differently, since

---

54   Gullì, *Earthly Plenitudes*, op. cit., 39.

I do not think that you and I are particularly drawn to that unfortunate (and inaccurately overemphasized) formulation of Marx's: Is it necessary to oppose all sovereignty, as we may do as autonomists, left communists, anti-statist communists, etc.? Or, is it conceivable that we might want a more agreeable sovereign to, for example, disallow exceptions to a vaccination rule, make exceptions in the university, or even in a social movement that follows pacifism only as a general rule (i.e., with exceptions)? I think we agree that it is possible to stake a general position against violence with exceptions to be made in cases of emancipatory counterviolence. If so, is this a form of communist sovereignty? If not, why not?

BG answers: I don't think that by reversing the symmetrical figures that constitute the paradigm of sovereignty as a whole, society makes any real progress, and I certainly don't think that such a reversal would constitute a revolutionary act. Hence, I don't think that there is any possibility for a form of communist sovereignty. Communism should be, to use Marx's expression, *"the dissolution of the existing order of things,"* and that includes, first and foremost, the sovereign order.[55] Of course, the notion of a "dictatorship of the proletariat" is very problematic and, as you say, unfortunate in its formulation and use – and abuse. But let's focus on the notion of the proletariat as a class. Although of course things have changed since Marx wrote about this, some important aspects are still there, namely, the idea that there is a large part of humanity constantly experiencing "the *complete loss* of humanity."[56] This can be the proletariat in traditional Marxian terms, or it can be the colonized, the oppressed, or *homo sacer*, the life that can be taken at will, and so on. What's important is to recognize the existence of a class, a part of humanity, "with *radical chains*," or, if you will, in conditions of bare life, or approximating bare life.[57] The logic of debt, as Maurizio Lazzarato emphasizes, produces precisely this type of situation. However, if we use Marx's superb formulation, not of the dictatorship of the proletariat, but of the proletariat "as a class that is the dissolution of all classes," and if we extend this to all situations of unbearable oppression under any form of sovereignty,

---

55 Karl Marx, "Toward a Critique of Hegel's Philosophy of Right: Introduction," in *Selected Writings*, op. cit., 38.
56 Ibid.
57 Ibid.

be that of the king, the patriarch, the colonizer, the law of surplus value, and so on – we can easily see that revolution is not the substitution of one form of sovereignty with another, but precisely the dissolution, dismantling, or deactivation of the sovereign paradigm as a whole, in all its possible variations and conjugations – including a communist one, which to me sounds like a contradiction in terms.[58]

Perhaps the case of violence is different. I think that counterviolence is not properly speaking violence; or rather, it is and it is not violence. The word 'counterviolence' itself tells us much about it. Counterviolence is a movement, a process, which *counters* violence, the originary or primordial violence which is an extreme and total situation of capture, from which there is no exit. So, everyone is equally (or rather, unequally) caught up in the same situation of violence. Counterviolence is part of a constituent process, constituent not of a different type of government, a different type of sovereignty, but, as Frantz Fanon says, of *a new humanity*. On the other hand, sovereignty is not a process; it is a state. It is not a constituent, but a constituted, form of power. So much so that, differently from counterviolence, we don't speak about counter-sovereignty in the case of a different form of sovereignty, or rather, in the case of a variation on the same sovereignty paradigm. As Fanon says, "decolonization is always a violent event."[59] The same is true, to various degrees, of all movements of liberation, for any form of unfreedom is the result of a violent situation. But sovereignty represents the highest degree of violence, its most sophisticated, if you will, and institutional (institutionalized) form. Sovereignty is countered by a revolutionary process, not by another type of sovereignty. What can replace sovereignty is an isonomic form of the law and political organization of society, that is, a society in which the law and political order are not superimposed, as by definition must be the case with any form of sovereignty.

RGO asks: I want to ask if the concept of singularity is, for you, necessarily communist. In Chapter 8 of *Singularities at the Threshold*, I find what was – *for me* – the most crucial culmination of that study. There, you say: "Singularity is another word for care... singularity is love. It is the opposite

---

58 Ibid.
59 Frantz Fanon, *The Wretched of the Earth*, trans. Richard Philcox (New York: Grove Press, 2004), 1.

of disindividuation and disaffection. However, that does not mean that it is the same as individuality, not even individuation... The question is whether the singular is today possible at all. Perhaps it is if what is uncontrollable destroys the machinery of control: the State, the bureaucracy, the police, the logic of normalization... Antagonistic struggle is care, and care is ethos, namely, dwelling at the threshold of the common gathering."[60] There is a lot more to this, some of which I have already passed over with ellipses. However, we can see that the identification of the common in each singularity is a communist realization. You are talking about unrest and possibly even revolution; you are talking about the possibility of a new regime of the singular. What I am trying to understand better is if singularity is also another name for communism. Because, as you know, while love is for me not communism, there is an irreducible communism of love. In some passages of your book, it seems that you are saying there is a communist tendency in singularity, whereas in others (as quoted above), I am led to wonder if singularity is another name for communism. So, I want to ask for a clearer explication of the relationship of singularity to communism. Can you help with this?

BG answers: If we understand communism in the proper manner, as we have seen above, that is, communism not as a form of government, but as a form of life, then it is very easy to see that there is a communist tendency in singularity, or a tendency toward singularity in communism. I don't know if singularity might be another name for communism. What seems clear to me is that singularity *cancels*, so to speak, individuality. The singular has an intimate relationship to the common; it is an expression of the common; hence, its communist tendency is evident. Singularity is *coexistence*, as Jean-Luc Nancy says. It is a *co-ipseity*,[61] "an ontology of being-in-common."[62] Perhaps we could then even venture to say that singularity is another word for communism, but I wonder whether a statement such as this would really be useful. I would rather say that communism is a singularity (always plural in its constitution), that is, a singular event, a singular individuating process, a constant agitation of *being-many* and *being-with*, where the "with" itself stirs up and perpetuates the agitation.

---

60   Gullì, Singularities at the Threshold, op. cit., 123.
61   Jean-Luc Nancy, op. cit., 44.
62   Ibid., 55.

BG asks: You say that your book *Precarious Communism* is "about communism."⁶³ Later, you also say that "Communism remains in the world in two ways: First, as a scary idea, and second, as a *real* mode of expressing generalized disaffection."⁶⁴ This is very well put, and I completely agree with you. Yet, given the politics and culture of fear today, we should explode that "scary idea," and our work may be a modest contribution to that aim. Precarious communism, as you say, is non-ideological and it points to the contingency of the present. Perhaps we can say that what is scary today is not communism, but its (philosophically concretized) absence. In this sense, communism is a postcapitalist horizon, a ghost, a specter haunting global societies. Communism makes up the ontological substance of that *general disaffection*, and, as Bernard Stiegler suggests, it points to the fire, the uncontrollable "wastelands" of our hyper-industrialized societies. It is a way of saying farewell to obsolete forms of the production of power. Yet, what is at the horizon? What is at the threshold? What is the new orientation?

RGO answers: Communism is one possible postcapitalist horizon. However, postcapitalism need not be communist at all. Unfortunately, I can imagine many other things after capitalism that are not good news. We could face a new form of capitalism that we mistake as postcapitalist, to which we give an altogether different name. It often seems that many scholars misdiagnose "neoliberalism" as "postcapitalist," since they often swap the word capitalism out for neoliberalism. I think it is better, generally, to speak of capitalism instead of neoliberalism so we do not forget what we're talking about. We can trace other variations of this tendency from feudalism to industrialization to post-Fordist and informatic or finance capitalism. All these named stages of capitalism might convince us that capitalism has left itself behind. However, we should call none of these new stages of capitalism "postcapitalist." Let us consider *real* postcapitalism, then, something that is not capitalist (and therefore properly postcapitalist). I argue below that the postcapitalist need not be communist. We must reject the idea that if it isn't capitalist, it must be communist, or even, that it must be something better.

However, let us stick to the question of capitalism for a little longer. I will more fully address postcapitalism in my next response to your more

---

63 Gilman-Opalsky, *Precarious Communism*, op. cit. 9.
64 Ibid. 16.

direct question about it. For now, consider the strange period of the recent pandemic. What capital wants is everyone on airplanes, rich people traveling to resorts, going on vacations, shopping everywhere, working all day, people going out to restaurants, spending their money, etc. What the coronavirus pandemic said to capital is, "No, you have to stop some of those things right now." The pandemic was not bad news for capitalism in general, but it was bad news for many *petit bourgeois*, for all the little shops and restaurants that couldn't make ends meet because people stopped coming out of their apartments or homes to spend money there. Some capitalists made more profit than ever, like personal shopper services, online vendors, mask manufacturers, takeout delivery services, etc., but empty planes, shuttered hotels, and desolate restaurants and malls are bad news for major flows of capital. The virus was not communist. Capital can take a beating from other enemies than communism. There may be forms of postcapitalist life that could make communists long for the capitalism they loved to hate. In Japan, for example, *hikikomori* and *karoshi* – refusal to leave the home and literal death from overwork (respectively) – pose problems for capitalism, so much so that Japan's Ministry of Health, Labor and Welfare declared *hikikomori* a national crisis.[65] These things may be bad news for capitalism, but none of them is communist. This is one reason why I insist on specifying communism.

I think you are right to mention Bernard Stiegler, who was one of the most important philosophers (after Jean Baudrillard) to think about problems of capitalism that are in no way communist. In his book, *Uncontrollable Societies of Disaffected Individuals*, Stiegler writes about *hikikomori* and *otaku*.[66] *Otaku* are a bit like *hikikomori*, in that they want to be cut off from the existing world of work, but *otaku* choose specifically to live in a world of computer games and comic books where they meet other people only virtually and create communities for avatars, invented characters and made-up worlds, which they prefer to the real world. Stiegler says these

---

65 Ministry of Health Labor and Welfare [November 12, 2007]; "wo chuushin to shita 'hikikomori' wo meguru chiiki seishin hoken katsudou no gaidorain" (Community mental health intervention guidelines aimed at socially withdrawn teenagers and young adults), cited in Alan R. Teo, "A New Form of Social Withdrawal in Japan: A Review of Hikikomori," International Journal of Social Psychiatry. 2010 March; 56(2): 178–185.

66 Bernard Stiegler, *Uncontrollable Societies of Disaffected Individuals: Disbelief and Discredit, Vol. 2*, trans. Daniel Ross (Cambridge and Malden: Polity Press, 2013), 88-89.

disaffected youth are "hermetically sealed away from a social environment that is itself largely ruined... perfectly indifferent to the world."[67]

I am not at all confident that what comes after capitalism will be something to look forward to. When I think about a hopeful horizon, I think about a postcapitalism that is better than capitalism. The basic idea of communism is precisely such a postcapitalist idea. However, we need a communist orientation that can account for new social, cultural, technological, environmental, and political developments in the world, such as the things I have been discussing here, including the social and antisocial conditions analyzed by Stiegler.

Without a doubt, we cannot expect to approach a communist horizon in such a state of dilapidated and disintegrated sociality. Communism will not just dialectically appear as the magical antithesis to *hikikomori* and *otaku*. A communism oriented to the psychosocial dimensions of present-day life is going to be a precarious communism. Any communist who proceeds without precarity, and with a strong political confidence, has an inappropriately strident communism fit for the graveyards of the twentieth century. Precarious communism specifies a starting orientation, yes, but we cannot stop there. We only start there. We do have to think about concrete social and political movements from that starting position. For example, what else do we see besides all the awful things? Where do we find communist desires and possibilities? We must look for those things too, and should name them, point them out, and follow their activities and incarnations in the world. Communism guarantees nothing, perhaps, beyond its persistence and necessity.

BG asks: This is a follow up on the previous question, a way to complicate it a bit. I am reading an excellent book by Dave Beech, *Art and Postcapitalism: Aesthetic Labour, Automation and Value Production*. I wonder whether the term postcapitalism might not be a better way to address a series of problems we are addressing here than the term communism. It would be less likely to cause unnecessary and prejudicial hostilities, thus it would be more effective, but, perhaps more importantly, it would be more precise today and more clearly directed toward the horizon of open contingencies. It would also put to rest once and for all the obsolete question of communism versus anarchism, and it would leave the petty ideological

---

67   Ibid.

discussions of the superiority of capitalism over communism to the various kinds of narrow-mindedness that will hopefully be extinct very soon. As I have said earlier, I find your distinction between ideological and philosophical communism very important. We know we are speaking about philosophical communism, and I also said the same in *Labor of Fire*, where I wrote, that "the creation of communism is a philosophical endeavor, and communism itself a philosophical state."[68] Today, I would perhaps add that this philosophical state is itself necessarily in a state of metastability, necessarily contingent and contingently necessary. Thus, this is not a retreat from communist desire (the desire for *genuine communism*, as Marx says), but rather an advancement and a refinement of it, in accordance with the times we are living in now. In the first chapter of his book, in a section called "The Reinvention of Revolution," Beech explains what postcapitalism is, by putting it in its historical context – (the chapter itself is called "What Is Postcapitalism?"). Beech says, "Postcapitalism emerged as a new style of political thought in the wake of Zapatista insurrection, the antiglobalisation movement, anticapitalist street protests, the Arab Spring, the *indignados*, Occupy and the politics of the 99%."[69] He continues, "Although writers such as Paul Mason, Nick Srnicek and Alex Williams have become prominent contributors in the last five years, the agenda was set during the 1990s and the 2000s by writers such as John Holloway, the Midnight Notes Collective, the theorist duo Gibson-Graham and the post-Marxist political philosophers Michael Hardt and Antonio Negri."[70] To this, I can add the name of Mark Fisher and his posthumous book *Postcapitalist Desire: The Final Lectures*. Fisher is very precise and clear about this in his first lecture, titled "What Is Postcapitalism?"

He says, "So, what are the advantages of the concept of postcapitalism? – and just initially I think it's worth thinking about this – why use the term 'postcapitalism' rather than 'communism,' 'socialism,' etc.? Well, first of all, it's not tainted by association with past failed and oppressive projects. The term 'postcapitalism' has a kind of neutrality that is not there with 'communism,' 'socialism.' Although this is partly generational, I think: the word 'communism' has lots of negative associations for people of my age

---

68 Gullì, *Labor of Fire*, op. cit., 30.
69 Beech, *Art and Postcapitalism*, op. cit., 19.
70 Ibid.

and older."⁷¹ He continues saying that the word "postcapitalism," to the contrary, "implies victory" and the fact that "there's something beyond capitalism."⁷² He says, "The concept of postcapitalism is something developed *out* of capitalism. It develops *from* capitalism and moves *beyond* capitalism."⁷³ However, it also develops from Marx's own insights and analysis, or at least it is very much in keeping with those insights and analysis, especially in works like *Grundrisse*. It seems to me that our "Inquiry into the Construction of New Forms of Life" is really about this philosophical and political postcapitalist project, which is perhaps what *genuine* communism, as well as your own *precarious* communism, has today become. I'd like to hear your thoughts on this.

RGO answers: I have already revealed that I do not like the concept of postcapitalism, and provided some of the reasons why. However, I am grateful for the opportunity now to elaborate fully the argument against it. We may begin with the most basic objections. It would be a terrible concession to our enemies to surrender the words and ideas of 200 years of struggle. We must not abandon our words and ideas, and indeed, our history, to those who have besmirched and weaponized their meanings and our intentions. If we abandon our language, let it be to embrace a better language, but that is not postcapitalism. In *The Soul at Work*, Franco "Bifo" Berardi refused to relinquish the concept of the soul to theologians, and in *The Communism of Love*, I refused to hand over the concept of love to poets and the romance industry. We must defend what deserves defending and condemn what deserves condemnation. If communism or anarchism or feminism or any rival vision for a different world has suffered decades of vilification, targeted by propagandistic warfare, this does not mean we exchange a vocabulary full of normative content and positive visions for an anemic vocabulary, which lacks resonances and connections to living histories. Moreover, we should not assume that, if we allow our enemies to take our words and ideas and declare them moot, that they will not try to take the new ones as soon as they too gather traction.

Now, let us confront the main problems. As a replacement for the term communism (or for socialism or anarchism, for that matter),

---

71   Fisher, *Postcapitalist Desire*, op. cit., 50.
72   Ibid.
73   Ibid., 51.

postcapitalism is an empty proposal for a future time without content. "Post" specifies temporality. The term "postcapitalism" specifies the time after the time of capitalism. Beech is correct to acknowledge that there is some promise in the idea of "postcapitalism," because if something comes after capitalism, then postcapitalism also always specifies the end of capitalism. We can agree that imagining the end of capitalism, a time after its demise, is important. However, the term says nothing about what comes after capitalism, and we cannot assume any positivity in the postcapitalist horizon. Is any postcapitalist future preferable to capitalism? One would like to think so, but the word and idea of postcapitalism specify nothing, nothing more than one finds in the words "antiglobalization" or "anticapitalist." Although, "anti" is more reassuring than "post." "Anti" at least designates something that "post" cannot, namely the dimension of being-against.

Richard Falk, in his book *Predatory Globalization*, argues that instead of being against globalization, we should seek to globalize different things than capitalism.[74] He argues for what he calls "globalization-from-below" against the predominant "globalization-from-above," because "antiglobalization" only says what it is against, and not what it is for.[75] Falk argues it is not enough to oppose globalization-from-above. Instead, he claims we must adopt an alter-globalization movement that *wants to globalize* things like human rights, the public good, democratic participation, transparency, and non-violence.[76] We have to say what we are for. Communism is the purposive statement of a *for*, that is, of another form of life, not only a being-against, but a being-to-be. That is also why the word and idea communism remain preferable, for me, to the word and idea anarchism, because anarchism defines itself by an against (*an*), whereas communism implicates commune, the common, community, and other possibilities of the *Gemeinwesen*. These are things we can aim at in multifarious ways when we think about a time after capitalism, and these are variously the aims of global revolutionary struggles throughout history. The notion of "postcapitalism" implicates none of this. This is the heart of the problem, but it gets even worse.

We cannot come along later and pull into the postcapitalist milieu writers like John Holloway, the Midnight Notes Collective, or Michael Hardt

---

74   Richard Falk, *Predatory Globalization: A Critique* (Cambridge, UK: Polity Press, 1999).
75   Ibid., 127-136.
76   Ibid., 148-149.

and Antonio Negri. This seems to me at least a little disingenuous. Writers like John Holloway, George Caffentzis, Silvia Federici, Antonio Negri and Leopoldina Fortunati ground their theorization in Marx and Marxism. Marxists have always strived to surpass Marx. That is what Marxism does. We may call some of these writers "post-Marxist" or whatever else you like, but we cannot erase or minimize their deep commitments to positive visions of a different world grounded in communist imaginations. The process of Marxism exceeding Marx, or as Negri put it, "Marx beyond Marx" already began in 1917 just months after the Russian Revolution when Gramsci wrote his essay for *Avanti* entitled "The Revolution Against *Capital.*"[77] There, Gramsci argues, in the immediate aftermath of the Russian Revolution, that the revolution was a revolution against "*Capital,*" against Marx's book *Das Kapital*. However, he is also clear that none of his observations about the limitations of Marx or Marxist historiography mark a break with Marxism. Gramsci's efforts to renew and centralize the importance of ideas and ideologies, to revive a certain Hegelianism, if you will, never meant an abandonment of Marx. Gramsci was dealing with the question of revolution and thinking about a postcapitalist horizon, but he was doing so *as a communist*, continuing the communist project. Why does this matter?

In McKenzie Wark's book *Capital Is Dead*, she writes: "So the bad news is: this is not capitalism anymore, it's something worse. And the good news is: Capital is not eternal, and even if this mode of production is worse, it is not forever. There could be others."[78] It is crucial to note that Wark's claim is that we are already in a postcapitalist era. *This is postcapitalism.* Capitalists and their communist enemies refuse to see this fact, according to Wark, because capitalists and communists cannot stop thinking about capitalism as eternal. Wark thinks that is a problem, and argues in the book's first chapter, "The Sublime Language of My Century," that we do not yet know how to speak about the world without the language and conceptual apparatus of capitalism. She argues that information has already replaced capital as the central organizing logic of the world, and thus, that we should stop insisting our world is capitalist. We could argue for the rest of this book about the provocative question of what rules over what: does

---

77 Antonio Gramsci, "The Revolution Against *Capital*" in *The Gramsci Reader: Selected Writings 1916-1935* (New York: New York University Press, 2000), 32-36.
78 McKenzie Wark, *Capital Is Dead: Is This Something Worse?* (London and New York: Verso, 2019), 29.

information govern capital, or does capital govern information? However, what I want to focus on is Wark's powerful insight that a postcapitalist reality could be worse than capitalism, as she insists is already the case and aims to substantiate throughout her book.

Therefore, I insist on speaking of communism instead of postcapitalism. Communism specifies something we can say that we want, whereas postcapitalism only specifies a time after capitalism, which could even make us long for the old capitalism we left behind. It is not so hard to imagine; the recent pandemic has made so many communists and comrades pine away for a return to the previous nightmare of "normal" so that, at the very least, we could resume our familiar war footing against it. In the 1960s, "retour a la normale" was a prediction of defeat. However, in pandemic times, even revolutionaries may want to return to the normal nightmare of capitalism, because with capitalism, we have a long history of invested thought, energy, and action in trying to oppose it. Whereas, we did not know how to abolish the reality of the pandemic. Opposition to the pandemic was not a road to postcapitalism, but rather, back to capitalism. What it comes down to, then, is saying yes, we want to live in a time after capitalism, but not just any time… We need to think through new forms of life that are better than capitalism, not worse than it.

Mark Fisher was a very important thinker. I think his work is full of insights and epiphanies that are beautifully stated. He was right about so much, but not about everything. In his lecture "What Is Postcapitalism?" I think he was wrong to suggest swapping "postcapitalism" for "communism, socialism, etc." We need the ideas of communism and socialism to substantiate the kind of postcapitalist reality worth fighting for. It is true that association with Stalin and Tito and Ceaușescu and other villains tainted the words and ideas communism and socialism. However, we can say both that such men are villains *and* what we ourselves mean by communism. That is why I prefer Negri and Guattari's *Communists Like Us* over Fisher or Beech's "postcapitalism."[79] "Postcapitalism" may imply victory, but if what we mean by communism is a real movement to abolish the present state of things, the abolition of capitalist society, then communism implies the same victory, but with other contents we should not be too quick to minimize. As Guattari and Negri put it, "communism is the establishment of a communal life

---

79 Félix Guattari and Antonio Negri, *Communists Like Us: New Spaces of Liberty, New Lines of Alliance*, trans. Michael Ryan (New York: Semiotext(e), 1990).

style in which individuality is recognized and truly liberated, not merely opposed to the collective. That's the most important lesson: that the construction of healthy communities begins and ends with unique personalities, that the collective potential is realized only when the singular is free."[80] Despite our deep and shared suspicions about the notion of community, I would say that you and I are variously committed to this idea.

While I could agree – with qualification – that our present "Inquiry into the Construction of New Forms of Life" is a postcapitalist project, it is also clear that we are not aiming for the postcapitalism of Wark's account, we are not interested in just anything after capitalism, and certainly not in something worse. I can only concede that what we are talking about is a "*communist* postcapitalism," and hence, we should reject Fisher's either/or juxtaposition.

Finally, Fisher also says that the term "postcapitalism" offers a certain neutrality as an advantage. For me, however, this is its most dire limitation. We are not liberals or conservatives or pseudo-objective hosts on cable news. For us, neutrality is not a virtue. Paulo Freire was right about neutrality: We must never be neutral.[81]

BG asks: I'd like to briefly go back to the question about postcapitalism. In *Specters of Revolt*, you say, "We do not live in a 'post-capitalist' world, since most of the whole of human affairs is governed by exchange relations according to the logic of capital."[82] Here, I understand what your position is about this. However, can you connect this with your answer to the previous question?

RGO answers: Yes, but this statement in *Specters of Revolt* does not adequately capture my critique of "postcapitalism" elaborated above. My statement that "we do not live in a post-capitalist world" only asserts the premise that the world is still governed by the logic of capital. But, I see no good

---

80 Ibid, 16-17.
81 I am referring here to the following passage: "'Washing one's hands' of the conflict between the powerful and the powerless means to side with the powerful, not to be neutral." Freire's point was that refusing to stake a clear position for and against may look like neutrality, but such "neutrality" is essentially to take sides with the powerful. See Paulo Freire, *The Politics of Education: Culture, Power, and Liberation* (Westport and London: Bergin and Garvey Publishers, 1985), 122.
82 Gilman-Opalsky, *Specters of Revolt*, op. cit., 192.

reason to assume that a postcapitalist world would be in any way more communist, kinder, or healthier. In the great zombie films (if you agree with me that some of them are actually great), you can find depictions of postcapitalist worlds that make you long for the capitalist one. Take out the zombies, and we move from fiction to fact. A global pandemic, a brutal theater of war, or ecological catastrophe could create a kind of postcapitalist nightmare without the zombies, even if they all originate from capitalist causes. This is why it is not enough to move forward. We have to have some idea of where we are going and where we desire to go.

BG asks: Back to the very important question of ideology, in *Precarious Communism* you say, "Today, we are seeing the slow disintegration of capitalist ideologies."[83] This is of course true, and it is very good news. As you say, quoting Debord, ideologies disintegrate. Are we going beyond communist and capitalist ideologies towards a non-ideological, but philosophical, postcapitalist and communist future? Certainly, the question of disaffection and disindividuation remains central throughout this passage. You say, importantly, "People are more mobile and privatized than ever before, while our unhinged individuation is made coherent by the "social" façade of new media."[84] What you call "*our* mobility" cannot obviously be taken for granted, in both the physical and virtual spheres.[85] From the tragic destinies encountered in the journeys of global migration to segregation and control in the global cities and the injunction to constantly having to verify your identity (both in physical daily life and online), mobility as such is criminalized and often made impossible. Winning ideologies are not willing to go easily, not willing to disintegrate. They do disintegrate, and yet at times they seem to come back with a vengeance. Despite the importance of regulating the public health crisis that emerged with the current pandemic, this is certainly one of the lessons to be learned: that the system will do anything in its power to increase modalities and measures of control. Thus, the precarity of everyday life increases, and this happens, as you say, as a result of "the increasing fluidity and mobility of capital."[86] You continue, "In other words, capital can come and go quickly,

---

83   Gilman-Opalsky, *Precarious Communism*, op. cit., 53.
84   Ibid., 54.
85   Ibid., 40.
86   Ibid. 55.

by surprise, and beyond the command of expert capitalists who may also find themselves tossed about by the unpredictable waves of a crisis they didn't see coming."[87]

This is a very important moment in your book, including for the fact that it provides an eerie premonition of the current global situation with the pandemic. It is also a moment when, in your answer, you can connect the theme of precarity to the practice of radical philosophy made of invented/created situations and ruptures that you describe in *Spectacular Capitalism*.

RGO answers: We will only move beyond communist and capitalist ideologies when we arrive at their real irrelevance in the world, at the point when they are obsolete in political discourse. However, so long as we may continue to understand the existing reality with the help of this discursive apparatus, we cannot abandon the language of communism and capitalism. If we choose a new language, terminology, conceptual framework, the reality will not notice that we have done so, and it will remain just as it was. As Marx wrote in *The German Ideology*, the reality (of the capitalist division of labor) "cannot be dispelled by dismissing the general idea of it from one's mind, but can only be abolished by the individuals again subjecting these material powers to themselves and abolishing the division of labor."[88] In other words, the first and most pressing question is about the world such as it is. For as long as the logic of capital continues to govern the world, for as long as money rules over life as a power of exploitation, a determinant of autonomy, we will have to continue to speak about capitalism. For as long as we want to juxtapose to such a world of capital, the idea of a radically different world grounded in the logic of human health and well-being, the logic of another *Gemeinwesen*, we will continue to speak of communism. If we were not talking about such a world and an opposition to it, then we would not be talking about capitalism and communism, and could adopt a different language.

At the same time, many things have changed since *The German Ideology*. Technology is the obvious example. When Marx gave stock of technology in 1848 in *The Communist Manifesto*, he accounted for "steam-navigation,

---

87 Ibid.
88 Karl Marx, *The German Ideology* in *The Portable Marx* (New York: Penguin Books, 1983), 192.

railways, electric telegraphs" all of which he looked upon with genuine awe.[89] When we consider planes, drones, and smartphones, and the fact that people are more mobile and privatized than ever before, we must acknowledge that our present level of disembodied and instantaneous life was beyond the imagination of a young Marx. Things have certainly changed, but change does not necessarily mean that we need a new language.

I appreciate your mentioning the "tragic destinies" of global migration and segregation in cities. Since the publication of *Precarious Communism*, we have seen new walls erected, refugee crises, ever-growing fatal deportations, and recently ramped up restrictions on human mobility in the context of fascistic xenophobia and COVID-19. We have seen Black bodies targeted for incarceration and scandalized murderous cops who often fear Black bodies in motion, whether in prisons or on public sidewalks. We could say that, in a society that Donatella Di Cesare calls "immunodemocracy," we are more restricted than ever before.[90] That is the other side of our increased mobility. Immunitarian democracy has not forgotten about the regulation of bodies and borders, as it promises to protect everyone from everyone else. That is why Di Cesare juxtaposes immunity to community. You have the separating and social distancing logic of immunity on the one side, and on the other, there is the real-time instantaneity of technologically reconfigured ontologies. This enables us to come apart and come together simultaneously. What are the ontological implications of this being-together-apart?

Yes, winning ideologies cling to life. Capitalists would far sooner embrace a series of capitalisms with prefix qualifiers from "industrial" capitalism to "postindustrial" capitalism to "finance" capitalism, etc. Capitalists are not, as you say, eager to think about postcapitalism because "post" signals the end of *their* era. The pandemic, in a certain sense, was a different kind of good news for capitalist ideology, insofar as people longed for a return to capitalist normality. Only the most callous indifference would fail to account for all the abusive households, overburdened hospitals, challenges of impoverished apartment living, neglected health of entire parts of the world, de-socialization of children, estrangement, isolation, shuttered schools, and

---

89   Karl Marx, *The Communist Manifesto* in *The Portable Marx* (New York: Penguin Books, 1983), 209.
90   Donatella Di Cesare, *Immunodemocracy: Capitalist Asphyxia*, trans. David Broder (South Pasadena: Semiotext(e), 2020).

so much else that made the pandemic worse than the preceding capitalist normality. Many of the most precarious people of capitalist normality experienced their precarity exacerbated even further during the pandemic.

In *Precarious Communism*, I was thinking about the global economic crisis, the so-called great recession, when I was writing about the unpredictability of capitalist catastrophes. I think you are correct to point out that the pandemic was another, albeit very different, shock to the system, though it was also an exposé of what is most shocking about the system.

Part of the problem is that major economic and public health crises that have recently upended life have been crises of capital; they have not been crises brought about by movements against capital. What often interrupts capitalist normality is its own bad news. Therefore, crises are not necessarily indications of communist advances. What we can do in a crisis, or with a crisis, may not be what we would like to do. Capitalists, for example, were far better prepared to seize crises from Hurricane Katrina to COVID-19.

However, this does not mean we can do nothing at all. Ideologically, we precarious communists look for critical points of entry to refute and reveal the problems of spectacular capitalism. We can also look beyond ideology to the global uprisings that directly challenge the existing reality in active and embodied expressions of disaffection that say "no," and we can continue to imagine and share other possibilities in art, writing, and conversation. Even with all the evolving differences of our terrain, you still find in my answer a certain lack of confidence. We can only refute, reveal, challenge, and imagine as precarious communists. From where we are, all strident hope is deceptive. While we cannot give up on hope, we can have no sure confidence in a postcapitalist future favorable to our own rival visions.

BG asks: Coming now to *The Communism of Love*, I am increasingly struck by the similarities between our projects, though we have evidently written very different books. *The Communism of Love* is a true masterpiece. I can't deal here with all the aspects of the book, and I certainly can't comment on the many thinkers and authors you review. I will content myself with reviewing and elaborating on the main ideas you present and questions you raise. That will already be more than enough to enhance and deepen our conversation.

I'd like to start with the title of Chapter 1 of your book, "The Logic of Love as a Communist Power." You already say very clearly, and perhaps forcefully in the Introduction that "love is either a communist power or it is in fact not love."[91] Later, at the end of Chapter 1, you speak of love "as an irreducibly communist power."[92] And again, toward the end of the book, in Chapter 6, you say, "If love is not communist, it is a false form of love."[93] This is perhaps the main theme of your book. I completely agree with you. What you are doing here is not just recasting the concept of love as a practice, but that of communism, too. You say, "We have established that what we mean by communism is no political state in history, no form of government; it refers instead to forms of life, forms of being-in-the-world with others."[94] On the one hand, this goes back to the notion of precarious communism as "*more philosophical, less ideological*" of your third book, *Precarious Communism*, and, in general, to the important difference between ideology and philosophy you underline there.[95] On the other hand, this once again opens up within your work the possibility of an anarchist critique of orthodoxy, or even simply of a dogmatic and generally (and thoughtlessly) widely accepted notion of communism. Love as a practice and communism as an ensemble (perhaps a totalizing ensemble, or a constant gathering) of forms of life make up the ontological structure of your argument.

You do say that you see your book, and your work in general, "as a contribution to new autonomist Marxist theory for the twenty-first century"[96] and, after acknowledging its importance, you distance yourself from the negative character of "an anarchism of love,"[97] negative because of "a lack or absence of an objectionable power."[98] "In contrast," you say, "we are primarily interested in the positivity and establishment of a certain power: the communist power of love."[99] Perhaps there is here a synthesis of your remarks on the relationship between anarchism and communism of your previous books. However, in addition to that, and to your interesting reference to Harry Cleaver's *Rupturing the Dialectic*, what comes to mind here is John Holloway's notion, in *Change the World without Taking Power*, of revolutionary power as a power

---

91   Gilman-Opalsky, *The Communism of Love*, op. cit., 5.
92   Ibid., 59.
93   Ibid., 271.
94   Ibid., 59.
95   Gilman-Opalsky, *Precarious Communism*, op. cit., 5.
96   Ibid., 11.
97   Ibid.
98   Ibid., 12.
99   Ibid.

that is not seized, not power over, but a power that is constructed, constituted, a power-to, closely linked to care, about which you also speak.

Although your book has much about this, can you say more here about the ways in which this positive power is established, this practice made common, and the modality of power as care (power-to) actualized?

RGO answers: I have said enough elsewhere about the relationship between communism and anarchism that I may allow those elaborations to serve as an answer to that part of what you say here. However, it has been very important for me to identify my work as a hopeful contribution to new autonomist Marxist theory for the twenty-first century, and not as anarchist, for exactly the reasons given in *The Communism of Love*. When I think of autonomist Marxist theory, I think of a Marxism that has learned from the failures and impasses of the twentieth century and from the insights of anarchism. The insights of anarchism have made their way into the work of many contemporary Marxists from history, and not by way of expansive bibliographies of anarchist literature. That is OK. Autonomist Marxism is not only a Marxism that takes seriously the logic and problems of a withering state, but goes further to a near-totally withered hope in the state. We are still Marxists because of our centralization of the question of capital – what capital is and does in the world to life and society – and because we prefer to think of communism than to think about the absence of what we despise.

John Holloway is one of the most important Marxists within our milieu, even though he has fiercely criticized the autonomist trajectory's major writers, especially Antonio Negri.[100] Holloway has been more associated with a tendency called "open Marxism" than with "autonomist Marxism," but there is a common sensibility about the state, about the necessity of Marx and the abolition of capitalism. There are also many commonalities regarding communist ontology. Personally, I regard Holloway to be one of our best writers. He writes with a poetic energy that I often find very beautiful and moving, even if not entirely convincing. Indeed, he is sometimes unconvincingly hopeful, which I suppose may also be a feature of poetry.

You mention Holloway's book, *Change the World without Taking Power*, which I think, along with *Crack Capitalism*, are both very important.

---

100 See, for example, John Holloway, *Crack Capitalism* (London and New York: Pluto Press, 2010), 190-196.

Holloway writes about what he calls "other-doing."[101] His idea is that when someone says "No!" this always implies a different way of doing things, and that, in imagining and enacting other-doing, we can experiment with and actualize anti-capitalist practices directly, even if on a very small scale. Another way to get to "other-doing" is to talk about what we *already do* that is not governed by capital. One lesson of such "other-doing" is that there are common non-capitalist, even anti-capitalist, practices that we already engage. However, I hesitate to call these modalities of power. Power entails not only relations of power, but changing those relations, so that we can reconfigure forms of life or social relations, and that new relations of power can be codified. That is how Michel Foucault speaks of power, not as a thing but a relation.[102]

For example, the so-called power of love is only a minor power, which only becomes political at that juncture where it displaces or replaces exchange relations. Imagine that I hired a therapist who only spoke to me because I paid her fee. Then, years later, she left her practice but continued to speak with me, and I was able to take an interest in her life too, finding out for the first time her own trials and history. That becomes a different relation. A friend is not a "service provider." In this story, a relation of mutuality and friendship supplants an exchange relation, and this is a miniature picture of the displacement logic regarding communism and capitalism. However, it is too small of a change to speak of in terms of power. A relation is changed, but social relations are essentially unaffected. I think that the concept of power in politics, culture, and economy requires a certain scale that we could describe as "social" or as implicating society. This is unfortunate, because it is much easier to change small things. I do not demean friendship, but we cannot overextend its implications. Moreover, it is not impossible to change big things in big ways too, such as gender identity and relations between men and women and so forth. There are many other examples.

So, love can exceed the boundaries of our little precarious communes (as I call them in the book), and while love matters even in tiny places, power requires a certain movement from private to public (if one wants to think a bit more about Habermas and the public sphere).

---

101 Ibid., pp. 19 and 29.
102 See Michel Foucault, *Power/Knowledge: Selected Interviews and Other Writings, 1972-1977*, trans. Colin Gordon, Leo Marshall, John Mepham, and Kate Sopor (New York: Pantheon Books, 1980), parts 3, 6, and 8.

BG asks: What does it mean to say that "Communism exceeds what it describes"?[103] This is in *The Communism of Love*, in the section on Maurice Blanchot, where you speak about the power of revolt and the power of love. You go back to this in Chapter 4 when you say that "love sometimes takes the form of revolt."[104] Perhaps communist love always does that insofar as it always "has to do with the subversion of rules."[105] You mention, as an example among others, the queer politics of love, which is subversive by definition, one could say. So, what is this connection between love and revolt? You distinguish revolt from rebellion, going back to the main argument in your previous book, and say that the former, not the latter, is "closer to what is best in the communist idea."[106] Furthermore, there is here a link to the important remark you make in *Specters of Revolt* about writing and revolt, that "revolt is another kind of writing" and that perhaps it is "the writing that matters most."[107] Can you elaborate on this?

RGO answers: We have discussed the famous definition of communism of Marx and Engels in *The German Ideology*, namely that communism is "the *real* movement which abolishes the present state of things."[108] The tricky part of this definition is that the present state of things in 1846 is not the present state of things in 1871 or 1968 or 2023, so communism is an abolitionist movement that targets an ever-changing present. I am completely committed to this definition.

Communism has certain basic features we can discuss, i.e., that it is abolitionist, revolutionary, dialectical, antagonistic, actual, and so forth, but it takes aim at different realities and takes on different forms historically. One obvious example is that, when you look at Hungary or Poland or Romania or China or Russia in the twentieth century, you find real communists aspiring and trying to make a communist reality. China Miéville so beautifully presents the early Russian aspiration to communism.[109] The

---

103 Gilman-Opalsky, *The Communism of Love*, op. cit., 38.
104 Ibid., 206.
105 Ibid., 39.
106 Ibid., 43.
107 Gilman-Opalsky, *Specters of Revolt*, op. cit., 197.
108 Karl Marx and Frederick Engels, *The German Ideology* in *The Portable Marx* (New York: Penguin, 1983), 179.
109 China Miéville, *October: The Story of the Russian Revolution* (London and New York, Verso Books, 2018).

real movement takes a certain form at a certain time, but at a later stage, communists themselves oppose the so-called communist governments and insist on communism against a certain spectacle of "communism" in the world. That is one way to understand my point about "communism exceeding what it describes." If communist movement is good at a certain point, we may and should join that movement, but without signing up to support and claim whatever that movement becomes or does in the future. If a revolutionary movement becomes counterrevolutionary, we have to spot the difference. Because communism relates to the present state of things, and the present always changes, communism must necessarily exceed a fixed form of itself in some one context or another.

Regarding Maurice Blanchot, what is interesting is that Blanchot was very conservative for a long time. He was not even in the distant orbit of communism, but then he saw the form communism was taking in the politics of revolt in his lifetime and that compelled him to think anew about communism and to become a kind of unwitting yet self-conscious communist. I address this with more depth in the book, and I will not repeat the story here. However, it is crucial to my overarching argument in *The Communism of Love* because one of the things I am trying to do is to point out communism in unusual places, in striking distance, in real relations. Blanchot found communism variously in friendship and street protest, and its discovery there made him more inclined to it. That is close to the central question of my book: What if we could find communism in our cherished relationships with friends and other people.

Blanchot also raises the question of revolt in his book *The Unavowable Community*, of which Part II begins with "The Community of Lovers," an essay on the uprising of 1968.[110] I was fascinated that Blanchot thought about a community of lovers in the revolt, I understood the sensibility, and agree with it. However, I wanted to go further than Blanchot. Both love and revolt send people off in search of others with whom to make common cause. Both love and revolt disrupt and discombobulate everyday life, and they often end in frustration and failure. Yet we go into them willingly for their promise, and in pursuit of our aspirations. We try, in both love and revolt, to find others with whom to create a better lifeworld. These are just similarities, and we should not

---

110 Maurice Blanchot, *The Unavowable Community*, trans. Pierre Joris (New York: Station Hill Press, 1988).

make too much out of them. Yet, Blanchot observes that there is also an ecstatic joy in revolt, as if it were a community of lovers. People who felt all alone the day before a revolt feel impassioned with kindred spirits in revolt. Revolt is a form of being-together that shares some of the energy and transformative hope of love, and we might add that there is always something romantic about revolt too. While I do not reduce love to romance, I never deny its romantic dimensions.

More concrete is the point you highlight about love taking the form of revolt. This is part of a crucial counter-narrative to the common liberal reaction against revolts. Liberals generally contend that those who rise up against police violence, when they start to engage in property destruction, damaging gas stations, smashing windows, etc., must hate their community. To the contrary, I argue that what mobilizes these uprisings is a love for the community, plus indignation over the fact that capitalist predators use and abuse the community, and racist policing governs it. One could even say that if they did not love their community, neighborhood, friends, and family, they would not rise up. Love can mobilize hatred of the cops. If a cop kills your brother or sister, you may end up with a hatred mobilized by love. Hatred is not the opposite of love, which is something I explore more fully throughout my work. As you can see, I think that love and revolt are more intimately related than appears in a list of commonalities.

Perhaps we should have recognized long ago, that those who profess to love life on earth, who love their children and friends and comrades to want them to have real futures on this planet, may have no choice but to make sustained global revolt against the ecological catastrophe of capitalism. As Kohei Saito argues, if we do not destroy capitalism, we will soon arrive at the end of the Anthropocene.[111] Saito argues that capitalism requires growth, and that from the growth logic of capital, degrowth appears as a death sentence. Yet, from an ecological perspective, degrowth is necessary for continued life on earth. No one thinks that capitalists will choose degrowth over growth, that capitalists will choose a veritable death sentence for capitalism. Does anyone think humanity can address ecological crisis without sustained global revolt? I cannot imagine what that would look like. This has to do with love because, in order to participate in the other's becoming, we need time, and we have to presuppose a future.

---

111 Kohei Saito, *Marx in the Anthropocene: Towards the Idea of Degrowth Communism* (Cambridge: Cambridge University Press, 2023).

What I prefer in the concept of revolt, over the concept of rebellion, is that the word and idea of revolt is both etymologically and conceptually closer to revolution. I never want to lose sight of the necessity of revolution, and what I write about more extensively in my work is that revolt is closer to revolutionary possibility than rebellion. Whatever plays with revolutionary possibility holds a closer proximity to the communist idea.

As to the question of writing, writers may play with revolutionary possibility too. There is what we can call "revolutionary writing," and writing by writers interested in and committed to revolutionary possibility is out there. Returning to a central point in *Specters of Revolt*, I maintain that, inasmuch as a writer wants to send new thinking about possibility, a critique of the existing reality, and pose provocative questions out into the world, no writer can accomplish those things as well as a revolt. People who have written about white supremacy for a long time, like Angela Y. Davis and Ruth Wilson Gilmore, were quickly and intimately aware of how much the uprisings of Black Lives Matter aided and abetted their aims and interests as revolutionary writers. We must never pit revolutionary writers against revolts. Moreover, we should also include other creative energies, such as those of artists, musicians, etc. We are all capable of placing what we do in the service of some common revolutionary aspirations.

BG asks: This leads to the interesting question of what you call the "humanism of *Grundrisse*."[112] You clarify this by saying, "Those who categorically reject the basic premises of Marxist-humanism do not do so only by selectively reading the *Economic and Philosophic Manuscripts of 1844* but also by failing to read *Grundrisse* well or even at all."[113] I agree with your humanist interpretation of Marx and the *Grundrisse*. However, I wonder how this may go together with your claim that your book is in line with the work of "some other communists," such as Michael Hardt and Antonio Negri, who "have recently thought about the communism of love."[114] You make similar claims throughout your work. Personally, I also feel that there is an important connection in my own work with that of Hardt and Negri. However, would you say that they recognize the "humanism of

---

112 Gilman-Opalsky, *The Communism of Love*, op. cit., 102.
113 Ibid.
114 Ibid., 280.

Grundrisse," especially if you think of Negri's important and great book on the Grundrisse, *Marx Beyond Marx*? As I mention above, I like the fact that you recognize Marx's continuous concern with the question of alienation, and I think it's great that you quote the passage from *Grundrisse* on the commune as "a *coming-together* instead of a *being-together*."[115] So, although I don't think you explicitly say this anywhere, it seems to me that you reject so-called theoretical anti-humanism. Can you say more about this?

RGO answers: I should begin by saying what I mean by humanism and by Marxist-humanism, none of which is terribly original. However, because many anti-humanists misunderstand humanism, it is worth the effort to clarify. The fundamental premise of humanism is an ethical claim about others than one's self. Humanists reject any delineation of ethical obligation only to those who share nationality, religion, race, class, language, etc. A humanist refuses to treat a fellow Jew or fellow Chilean as "worthier" of moral regard, or of ethical obligation, on the basis of that common trait. In other words, a Jew in Israel who refuses to see that a Palestinian child is of equal moral worth to an Israeli child cannot be a humanist.

Humanists do not deny that real differences matter. Indeed differences do matter, and we should neither minimize nor ignore them. Rather, humanists try to cut through – *not erase* – ideological, cultural, national distinctions to consider the human condition in varying contexts and contingencies. Some have suggested that humanism is too narrow still, because it centers the human being over the non-human animal, but I think that is not precise. If humanism implicates ethical obligation to others than one's self, the non-human animal is also a being unlike one's self, and humanism is indeed capable of thinking about ecology and animal life from radically unlike perspectives. This is one dimension of humanism, a broadening of the sphere of affection and of ethical regard. The other fundamental part of humanism involves thinking about what the human being may become, centering on questions of human flourishing, the realization of human powers.

That is a very basic definition of humanism, which we may find in non-Marxist theories from Diogenes to Immanuel Kant to Martha Nussbaum to A.C. Grayling. Then, you have the Marxist dimension, which seeks to understand very specific impediments to human flourishing and

---

115   Ibid., 102; Marx, *Grundrisse*, op. cit., 483.

regard for others inside and against the capitalist reality. What makes a humanism Marxist is that, when it considers the human condition in one or another context, it focuses especially on the effects of exploitation, alienation, class power, political economy, and revolutionary forms of life and becoming. When you get to the Marxist side, you find many other figures like Raya Dunayevskaya, Maurice Merleau-Ponty, Erich Fromm, Herbert Marcuse, and I would even include writers like Frantz Fanon, C.L.R. James, and perhaps more controversially, Rosa Luxemburg. We could add many other names to our lists of humanists and Marxist-humanists. I find a lot of the above humanism and Marxist-humanism agreeable, though I have many deep disagreements with a lot of this literature too. Like you, I am not interested in choosing a camp.

In some ways, the whole history of Marxism is a history of partitioning Marx against Marx (we can discuss Marx against Marx before getting to Marx beyond Marx). For example, in Eugene Kamenka's famous volume, *The Portable Marx*, he divides Marx's work into "political writings" and "economic writings," which is absurd. According to Kamenka, *Grundrisse* and *Capital* are "economic writings," a partitioning that obscures their political, philosophical, and other content, not to mention that it betrays the basic premise of "political economy." It is worth mentioning that Kamenka was himself a well-known Marxist-humanist. Then, there are those who are hotly opposed to all Marxist-humanism, and there are humanists who hate anti-humanists, and much more in the partitioning of Marx and Marxism that weaponized Marx against Marx in ways that remind me of how Southern Baptists and Unitarian Universalists can read the same Bible in opposing directions.

I am a Marxist who insists that Marx has written no sacred texts. That is why Antonio Negri's ideas in *Marx Beyond Marx* never offended me, and why I like many other heterodox and creative efforts to read Marx in very open ways, and not in the service of a church around which one has to erect barricades. I do not staunchly identify as a Marxist-humanist who then sets out to attack Louis Althusser or Georg Lukács or to pick fights with those who do not adopt a humanist orientation. I love reading Althusser and Lukács and I think we still have so much to learn from them. I think we have to criticize all of our great philosophers, and indeed, such critical engagement is one of the best ways of taking them seriously. We know this well as authors. To have your work read closely for critical engagement by the serious interests of other people is a great honor.

What I am responding to in the passages you cite has to do with a tendency to incorrectly say that, after Marx broke with the religious and spiritual encrustations of Hegel and Feuerbach, in other words, in the years after 1844 and certainly by the time of *The Communist Manifesto* in 1848, he had totally abandoned any earlier humanist concern. *Grundrisse* shows that this claim is not true, although in order to see that, we cannot read *Grundrisse* as a merely economic text. Marx never abandoned his early concern about *species being*, or what it means to be human, as that concern runs through his entire body of work in various ways.

An open approach to Marx means precisely that I can say this and, at the same time, appreciate Michael Hardt and Antonio Negri and many others continuing to think about the problems of capitalism from diverse points of view. Hardt and Negri write a bit about love, especially in *Commonwealth*, and Hardt has lectured on the subject independently.[116] I think it is safe to say that Hardt is the author who carried consideration of the communism of love into his co-authored work with Negri.[117] Although, we must assume from the co-authorship that Negri did not object very strongly. What I find in Hardt and Negri, even with supplemental lectures by Hardt on the question of love, is only a very preliminary and fleeting encounter with the subject of my book. That is one reason why I offer my book as an attempt, among other things, to more fully study and think through the communism of love.

Certainly, I do not think Hardt and Negri recognize or appreciate the humanism of *Grundrisse*, or perhaps, even the humanism of what they themselves are saying about love. I think Negri's much earlier solo authored *Marx Beyond Marx* is one of the most important studies of *Grundrisse*, largely because in it, he fully clarifies the revolutionary

---

116 In *Commonwealth*, for example, see the section 3.3 "De Singularitate 1: Of Love Possessed," though the topic recurs throughout the book. Hardt and Negri, *Commonwealth* (Cambridge, MA: Harvard University Press, 2009). See also Michael Hardt and Leonard Schwartz, "A Conversation with Michael Hardt on the Politics of Love" in Interval(le)s II.2-III.1 (Fall 2008/Winter 2009), 810-821.

117 For example, Michael Hardt gave a lecture at European Graduate School called "About Love" in 2007.

character of Marx's work in one of the fiercest phases of Negri's own writing. The text is impassioned and insistent on revolution, and offers many insights we can still benefit from. However, Negri's reading is certainly not humanist, and in the section on "Communism and Transition," he stridently articulates a hard anti-humanism. Let us look at what he says there.

Negri recognizes that the early Marx appears compatible with a generic humanism, but that by the time of *Grundrisse*, it should be clear that "in this science where contradiction becomes antagonism, there is no place for humanism."[118] He further argues that Marx's theory is "in no sense a restoration of an original essence. Here, humanism has no place."[119] Later on, Negri concludes: "The universal individual *can no longer appear* as the fruit of a humanist nostalgia: he/she is the product of a materialist process and we must connect to the materialist character of this analysis, every leap of every qualitative deepening of the subject."[120] These passages present the basis on which Negri attacks humanism; they also reveal that he fundamentally misunderstands or intentionally mischaracterizes humanism, for reasons that are not altogether clear to me.

Notice that Negri understands humanism as a restoration of some generic human *species being*, what he likens to "an original essence." He further says that the universal individual (or subject position) is not proof of an essential human being of some kind, but rather of a subject position produced by class relations and born from antagonism. He seems to think that humanists claim some kind of essential generic commonality that would soften or oppose antagonistic class struggle. As much as I have learned from reading Negri, and as much as he himself cites Dunayevskaya in the book's bibliography, his portrayal of humanism is an egregious misrepresentation. If one considers the basic definitions of humanism I began with, one will find that none of what I say contradicts materialism, and none of it treats the human being or human flourishing as anchored to some original essence that denies antagonistic class relations. Most humanists and possibly all Marxist-humanists retain Feuerbach's notion of *species being*, but like Marx himself, strip

---

118 Antonio Negri, *Marx Beyond Marx: Lessons on the Grundrisse*, trans. Harry Cleaver, Michael Ryan, and Maurizio Viano (New York, Autonomedia: 1991), 16.
119 Ibid., 32.
120 Ibid., 181.

it of Feuerbach's metaphysical contents and set it down in a materialist context. This means that we are humanists who consider the human being in processes of development and becoming that occur in real social relations. Dunayevskaya, for example, does not argue for any restoration of some mythical-harmonious pre-capitalist human essence. To the contrary, she seeks the emergence of a new human being in a new human society – and a new set of relations – arrived at only through major struggles and global uprisings born from antagonisms.[121]

If humanism meant what Negri claims, I would reject humanism alongside him. However, if anti-humanism looks like his attack on humanism in *Marx Beyond Marx,* then I would have to reject anti-humanism. A more generous conclusion is possible, and as follows: Negri has long had different axes to grind and his more recent work is largely consistent with, and expansive upon, what I take to be the best humanist readings of Marx.

BG asks: I particularly like and relate to Chapter 3, "The Love of Communists," starting with the first section on the *Grundrisse*, perfectly titled "Capitalist Disfiguration: *Grundrisse* and the Community of Alienation." First of all, I want to say that, even before that section starts, I completely agree with your critique of the concept of community, and it would be nice to hear more about that.[122] Here, you also use the expression "post-capitalist," "the imaginaries of post-capitalist future."[123] I wonder if you can elaborate on this as well.

As you know, the *Grundrisse* was a crucial text for me when I wrote *Labor of Fire*, still is, of course, and I am happy to say that I totally agree with your interpretation of it, your elaboration on it, in this section of your book. To begin with, I like your focus on the concept of alienation in Marx, too often understood as an interest of the early Marx only. But you say that Marx "remained focused on various forms of alienation from that young age until his death."[124] It is also important that you look at the concept of alienation in Marx and his critique of

---

121 This is clear in all her work, but see especially, Raya Dunayevskaya, *Women's Liberation and the Dialectics of Revolution: Reaching for the Future* (New Jersey, Humanities Press, 1985) and *Marx's Philosophy of Revolution in Permanence for Our Day* (Leiden and Boston: Brill, 2018).
122 Gilman-Opalsky, *The Communism of Love*, op. cit., 90.
123 Ibid., 91.
124 Ibid., 90.

the concept of community in the same place. And, as I have said, I agree with you in both instances. You state very clearly and categorically, "In 1857 and 1858, Marx produced the massive work of *Grundrisse*, in which he carried forward his earlier theories from the *Manuscripts of 1844*, *The German Ideology*, and *The Communist Manifesto*, moving his thinking in the direction of the final masterpiece that would ultimately (and posthumously) emerge as the volumes that comprise *Capital*."[125] I think that this is absolutely correct. You also say that "the very concept of 'community' was always suspicious to [Marx]."[126] So, I like your position on Marx, and I also like your remarks on solitude versus isolation, which you go back to a few pages later. You say, "Being alone is not the issue";[127] rather, "Isolation is a real problem."[128] You return to the concepts of alienation and isolation in your section on Erich Fromm, and you of course remind us of Hannah Arendt's important and famous distinction between solitude and loneliness.[129] Then, you make some very important remarks on the question of loneliness itself. I quote two short passages: "Not only can loneliness not be abolished; its abolition would also be bad for us."[130] You prepare this by saying that the problem in loneliness is not the *presence of others*, but the *relations to others*. The other short quote is, "the solution to loneliness cannot be *not being alone*."[131]

I would here be tempted to speak, not about intersubjectivity, but trans-dividuality, the theme of my latest book. But let's stay within the limits of your section on Karl Marx and the *Grundrisse*. Here, you deny the concept and reality of the individual as independent. You do say that no one is independent, something I also maintain in my latest book, that the independence of the individual is "at bottom merely an illusion," and you speak about care and caring.[132] Perhaps this is the most important lesson of the *Grundrisse*, for care is time (as well as power), *disposable time*, and that is, "real wealth," "the wealth of all" against the disfiguring logic and the poverty

---

125 Ibid., 92.
126 Ibid.
127 Ibid.
128 Ibid., 103.
129 Ibid., 104.
130 Ibid., 186.
131 Ibid., 187.
132 Ibid., 96.

of exchange value.[133] Again, "love is a tendency contrary to that of the system of exchange."[134] And you speak of the "natural necessity" that communism is as a form of caretaking.[135] Perhaps you want to respond to this.

RGO answers: I completely agree with your observations and comments here. I appreciate that we share a deep suspicion about the concept of community, and at the same time, that we are deeply suspicious of the individual. For us, it is not a question of choosing the community or the individual, but rather, of undermining both sides of this oddly pervasive equation in various ways. Community and individual are problematic, but for too long, philosophers have accepted that they must choose one or the other. In "The Humanism of Existentialism" Jean-Paul Sartre addresses a criticism he frequently faced from Marxists who claimed that his philosophy chose the individual over society.[136] The common argument against Sartre, especially from Marxists, was that, because existentialism calls for a subjective reflection on the meaning of one's life it leads to a solipsistic rejection of collective action and revolutionary politics. Although it turns out that the Marxist critics were right in the narrow historical sense that existentialism never did move from a philosophical disposition to political movement, Sartre himself aligned with political struggles and always insisted that beginning with the individual does not require staying there. Ultimately, Sartre was himself one of the great Marxists of the twentieth century.[137] However, Sartre's insistence that we need both individual and community did not go far enough insofar as it preserved both sides, and instead of choosing one side or the other, Sartre chooses both. Whereas, we want to challenge both sides.

Marxists have to be critical of the concept of community, following especially Marx and Engels's discussion of "the illusory community" in *The German Ideology*.[138] Often, the concept of community is a counterinsurgent

---

133 Marx, *Grundrisse*, op. cit., 708.
134 Gilman-Opalsky, *The Communism of Love*, op. cit., 101.
135 Ibid., 105.
136 Jean-Paul Sartre, "The Humanism of Existentialism" in *Essays in Existentialism* (New Jersey: The Citadel Press, 1965).
137 See, for example, Jean-Paul Sartre, *Between Existentialism and Marxism*, trans. John Matthews (London and New York: Verso, 2008) and *Critique of Dialectical Reason*, trans. Alan Sheridan-Smith (London and New York: Verso, 2004).
138 Karl Marx and Frederick Engels, *The German Ideology* in *The Portable Marx* (New York: Penguin, 1983), 191-193.

force. People believe they are part of one big human community, that the human community includes everyone, or that the national community is a real thing, and all of this obscures a class analysis that would bring to light lines of antagonism between different generations of haves and have-nots. According to the mythology of community, or illusory community, if we love our country and are part of the national community, we should find no class enemies here. The answer to this cannot be to juxtapose the real community to the illusory community because the so-called real community, or the one which embodies and reflects an ideal *Gemeinwesen*, does not exist either. In what sense, then, is the community of our dreams real? If we merely imagine it, what is its reality? How is the community of our dreams not just another illusory community?

In my discussion of community, I am offering a critique of Peter Harrison who idealizes indigenous community and rejects, at the same time, the entire persistence of the community as a feature of emancipatory politics.[139] I will not repeat my critique of Harrison here, but simply say that I think Marx's idea of community in the *Gemeinwesen* was more complex than an uncritical acceptance or a total rejection. Marx's work offers a fraught relationship to the concept of community. Marx's concept of the revolutionary *Gemeinwesen* of from each according to ability and to each according to needs is critical to any aspiration of healthy society, and he even uses the concept of community to demarcate the point at which capitalist exchange relations begin.

Towards the end of *Grundrisse*, shortly before the manuscript breaks off, Marx writes, "Exchange begins not between the individuals within a community, but rather at the point where the communities end – at their boundary, at the point of contact between different communities."[140] This is a crucial line because Marx recognizes capitalist exchange relations as alien to the *Gemeinwesen* of our aspirations, and even claims that the alien logic of exchange to community is a historical fact.

Rosa Luxemburg took up this latter point about capitalist exchange being alien to the community in her important essay "The Dissolution of

---

139 Peter Harrison, *The Freedom of Things: An Ethnology of Control* (New Jersey: TSI Press, 2017).
140 Karl Marx, *Grundrisse*, trans. Martin Nicolaus (New York: Penguin Classics, 1973), 882.

Primitive Communism."[141] Luxemburg traces communist social relations, not capitalist exchange relations, as the normal comportment of mark (or so-called "primitive" communities) in Germany, North and South America, Greece, Spain, India, Russia and other locations. She argues that imperialism and slavery variously caused and accelerated the dissolution of communist forms of life. This is the complexity. We cannot discuss community as if we may build or reach it as a benign destination. Nonetheless, we can retain a core notion of being-together, an ontology or form of life within which we are not cut off and opposed, within which we relate to one another for different reasons than exchange, and where being-for the other in exchange for some commodity (directly or indirectly) is regarded as an insult or a threat. Inasmuch as community implicates forms of being-together, forms of life ungoverned by the logic of capital, we cannot simply dispense with the word and idea. Instead, we approach it with caution.

As to the question of solitude, loneliness, isolation: I think we have to begin with the basic insight that one may be alone in a crowd, and that one may be healthy alone. The basic premise of David Riesman in *The Lonely Crowd* still stands, which is that a person who suffers from a lack of human connection is not going to find the antidote on a packed subway train.[142] Healthy people with rich social relations, with deep and meaningful connections to others, can and often do seek out being alone as a part of their health and well-being. Then, the question becomes not one of how many people are nearby or sitting beside you, but rather, it becomes a question of real relationships, of human relationality. We cannot flatly deny that human relationships have nothing to do with community. This is another reason why we cannot dispense with the notion of community altogether.

This leads to the question of trans-dividuality. After studying your work, I agree. I do not use your conceptual language in my writing, but we are after something similar in the idea that each one only becomes a singularity in the becoming of trans-dividual relationality. There is no individual to speak of without other people. "Individuality" only ever appeared because of other people. The individual, inasmuch as we may still entertain

---

141 Rosa Luxemburg, "The Dissolution of Primitive Communism" in *The Rosa Luxemburg Reader*, trans. Ashley Passmore and Kevin B. Anderson (New York: Monthly Review Press, 2004).
142 David Riesman, *The Lonely Crowd* (New Haven: Yale University Press, 2001).

the idea, only appears "individualistic" by way of distinction from others. What we are doing is questioning whether we should go on speaking of the individual as such.

Independence is an illusion. People resist this statement, I think, because they incorrectly believe that without independence there can be no freedom, no human autonomy, as if independence were synonymous with freedom. We do not accept that notion. The very notion that the independent individual is a prerequisite for freedom owes its existence to modern capitalist thinking, certainly traceable (at least) to John Locke's chapter on private property in *Two Treatises of Government*.[143] No one gets free alone. You cannot leave a young child alone in the woods with Locke's labor theory of private property to fend for herself for the first years of life. No, a young child only moves towards a certain independence by way of the care and caring of other people, and specifically, by way of a care and caring outside of the system of exchange. The mother does not feed her young daughter, or offer her safety, only in exchange for chores or a fee. Before you get to private property in the life of any person, there is already a substantial prehistory of natural and necessary communism.

You ask, again, about my position on "postcapitalism." I have already elaborated my position more fully above. I will only add the following here: As a communist, I insist on postcapitalist futures of particular kinds. If by postcapitalism we mean something communist, then I can agree. My resistance to postcapitalism is a resistance to the idea that any postcapitalist future would be better than the capitalist present. Like so many fiction writers and filmmakers, I can imagine many dystopian nightmares we may call postcapitalist that I would never want to calibrate our aims.

---

143 See Chapter V. Of Property in John Locke, *Two Treatises of Government* (Cambridge, UK: Cambridge University Press, 1988).

CHAPTER 5

LIMIT POINTS AND STRATEGIC DEPLOYMENTS

Bruno Gullì (BG) asks: In *Unbounded Publics*, dealing with the paradigmatic case of the Zapatistas and their ability to concretize the 'double occupancy' of the neither/nor of transgression – retaining "a particular nationalist rhetoric and orientation" while managing "to recast indigenous politics as transnational and cosmopolitan at the same time" – you highlight the importance of modern technologies.[1] You say, for instance, "And indeed, the Zapatista public sphere could not have achieved its transgression without the use of Internet communications."[2] I think this is intimately connected to your idea that, "In Gramscian terms, the Zapatistas have been fighting a war of position more than a war of maneuver."[3] It would be nice if you could elaborate on this tactical (and strategic) aspect even beyond the specificity of the Zapatista experience, especially in relation to the recent developments in the digital technologies of communication and their impact on the state of the world today and on the potential for new struggles under the pandemic. In other words, what is potentially the danger in the widespread use of these technologies and what instead is their potentially positive, and even revolutionary, use for a future society built on true knowledge, connectivity, and care?

Richard Gilman-Opalsky (RGO) answers: As soon as one begins to criticize technology, for example, to focus on its subordination as an instrument of capital, especially when one does so within the milieu of

---

1   Gilman-Opalsky, *Unbounded Publics*, op. cit. xv.
2   Ibid., 321.
3   Ibid., 254.

critical theory, it is almost as if to announce oneself as a reactionary curmudgeon and luddite. Critique of technology is not always right. Neil Postman, who was not a critical theorist, had a deep streak of conservatism in his thinking, and he has perhaps left the worst of all anti-tech caricatures to inhabit.[4] Having made these provisos, I do think it remains necessary to keep the capitalist governance of technology in mind, but to avoid simply repeating conclusions from Theodor Adorno and Max Horkheimer's *Dialectic of Enlightenment*.

Paul Virilio had a better approach to the question of technology, I would say. His basic premise was that a logic of speed governs technology more than the logic of capital, which is not to deny that capital has nothing to do with speed. However, Virilio made a dromological analysis, which is to say, he focused centrally on acceleration, racing, and speed. I would tend to tweak this position a little, since it seems to me that acceleration, and even Virilio's own account of it, is a feature of the capitalist organization of life. In fact, when one thinks about quotas, mass production, overnight shipping, fast food, slowing down may possibly even appear as anti-capitalist. Famously, Virilio said, "When you invent the ship, you also invent the shipwreck; when you invent the plane you also invent the plane crash; and when you invent electricity, you invent electrocution... Every technology carries its own negativity, which is invented at the same time as technical progress."[5] Everyone knows that Virilio was not opposed to ships, planes, or electricity, and indeed, that he liked all three. His observation was simply that we should not be stupid about their possible or inevitable – *even accidental* – catastrophes.

I share a similar general perspective. On the one hand, we lose some things and risk some things. On the other hand, we find certain applications that can have some emancipatory power. I would say that the emancipatory side of technology is the narrower side. Catastrophic outcomes have outstripped the emancipatory ones, and it is not entirely out of the question that one of technology's catastrophic outcomes may be human extinction. Perhaps this aligns too much with a predictability of critical

---

4　See Neil Postman, *Technopoloy: The Surrender of Culture to Technology* (New York: Vintage Books, 1993) and *Amusing Ourselves to Death: Public Discourse in the Age of Show Business* (New York: Penguin Books, 1985).

5　Paul Virilio, *Politics of the Very Worst*, trans. Michael Cavaliere (New York: Semiotext(e), 1999), 89.

theory going back to Marcuse, Adorno, and Horkheimer. However, it is nonetheless true, and the observation does rightly belong to the critique of capital, since capital defines and determines so much of what happens in the world of technology, from development to deployment.

War of position is essentially a communicative politics, so communications technologies inevitably affect it. For the Zapatistas, the 1994 rebellion took place during the early stages of the internet, and the main way that they could wield technology as a weapon was through e-mails and listservs. In *Unbounded Publics*, I attend to the important work of Oskar Negt and Alexander Kluge, who wrote about the revolutionary necessity of proletarian public spheres to produce, circulate, and work on the reception of their own analysis. Kluge, of course, is well-known in Germany as a TV and film director. Kluge has wanted to wield the media for purposes that are more radical for a long time, and to some extent, has been able to do so in Germany. Today, however, times have changed, and everyone who wants to be a director is a director, and a producer, and a host too. You have a phone and a YouTube channel and you can have your own show, or your own podcast. Anyone who is not paying attention might claim that these shows are "not real shows." But, look up what are some of the most popular channels on YouTube (they are always changing, but the data is easy to find online) and you will discover that massive audiences flock to channels that begin with one or two people in a family, made – often originally – with a small digital camera or even a cell phone. Children unboxing new toys have their own toy lines and occupy space on shelves in major stores across the United States, and some of these "hosts" and "stars" are among the richest people working in new media environments.

When I was growing up, if a punk band made a 7" record with three songs on it, they could tour the entire US and Canada on the popularity of those three songs alone. They would not make any money in most cases, but the difficulty of recording, producing, and releasing a record was such that the music achieved a certain visibility just for appearing on a commercial format. Things have changed very fast, and largely because of technology. Today, anyone can record and release anything and very little of it stands out. With everyone publishing everything, music has never been so inaudible, so invisible. It is something like being lost at sea, where if someone launches a small boat or dinghy into a vast ocean, there is almost no chance it will be visible from most people's location on Earth.

It is because of developments like this sheer volume of invisible and inaudible communication that I cannot place too much faith in our ability to take up counterhegemonic wars of position today. On the other hand, movements like Occupy Wall Street and Black Lives Matter did utilize new technologies for their international resonance. Personally, too, my reconnection with old friends through Zoom technology during the pandemic has been authentic and meaningful. To some extent, the pandemic has shown us that friendship really can make use of new communications technology, really can facilitate sustained active relationships. We have to appreciate such things.

Nonetheless, a philosopher cannot recommend tactical or strategic deployments of communications technologies. The fact is that people rise up and confront what has to be confronted in their own times and ways, and people rising up will make use of what they can. People who rise up in Palestine or Minneapolis know what to communicate about their causes, and young people in the squares of Turkey or Egypt have more technological practical understanding than I have. We see the uses of technology by witnessing its deployments. These deployments are not always in our favor. In any case, we must never wish to relocate social and political struggles to cyberspace. One cannot take refuge in a house made in Minecraft. However much technology may aid and abet our struggles, we must not technologize struggle as such. We should speak instead about technological dimensions of struggle and human life.

You asked also about "true knowledge, connectivity, and care." My reconnected and rekindled friendships, where we look at each other through screens, nonetheless enable us to listen to one another, to gather in collective real-time, and those meetings are full of real knowledge, connection, and care. In many regards, my obligatory interactions with professors I see in the hallways at my university are far less authentic. Many of them are fake, functional aspects of "getting along." There is no real depth or feeling to them.

When you ask about knowledge, I also want to make a distinction between information and knowledge. They are not the same, of course. Many people think new technologies are increasing knowledge when in fact they are only increasing information. Information is like raw data. It can come to you as if you are a passive receptor, it can scroll before your eyes on a screen. You can repeat information, share it, and tell a friend that you saw some bit of news. You may or may not think about it, you can forget it, etc. Knowledge, on the other hand, is produced by the knower (the *subject* of knowledge), and integrated into a functional human understanding. To be precise, the only way for information to become knowledge is if we do something to it and with it. We take in information, yes, but knowledge requires that we think about it, integrate it into a part of our understanding, and then proceed to act in the world with that understanding. Knowledge is not passive. It is an active production, and one of the greatest dangers of the present technological reality is the conflation of information with knowledge. There are certain situations where we could say that people are both more stupid and informed than ever before.

BG asks: In relation to the issue of communication, and communicative power, you say in *Unbounded Publics* that for Hannah Arendt "communicative power is the opposite of violence" so that "wherever real power exists violence is unnecessary."[6] You disagree with Arendt insofar as, you say, "we cannot think of power and violence as simple oppositions, for there are degrees of each one that admit for degrees of the other."[7] I think this is very interesting, and it would be nice if you could elaborate a bit on this, both in relation to some of your arguments in *The Communism of Love* and to your recent reading of *Humanity and the Enemy*. Power can be seen as domination (power over) or as a capacity, or ability, to do something (power to); in the latter case, power is intimately connected to care. You also say that, if one follows Arendt, "communicative power" is redundant.[8] It would be nice if you could elaborate on the relationship between communication and power on the one hand, especially in relation to the Zapatistas as a paradigmatic example of your idea of transgression, and, on the other hand, on the relationship between power and violence.

RGO answers: Hannah Arendt made some very important interventions on the question of violence, most obviously in her book, *On Violence*, but I would also add her important essay "What is Authority?" from *Between*

---

6   Gilman-Opalsky, *Unbounded Publics*, op. cit., 37.
7   Ibid.
8   Ibid., 39.

Past and Future: Eight Exercises in Political Thought.[9] Arendt refused to allow our enemies of the twentieth century – mainly, fascists and totalitarians – to claim the concepts of power and authority for themselves. Arendt argued brilliantly well that we must distinguish authority from authoritarianism. We even need authorities, as can be seen during a pandemic, so we must defend authority from conflation with authoritarianism. This was her way, in the 1950s and 60s, of criticizing a certain "anti-authoritarianism," which was rising in vogue and seemed to her to be against all authority writ large. Arendt's discussion of "communicative power" appears in *On Violence*, and in it, she wants to stop political theorists and social scientists from confusing other things than power for power. For example, we should not confuse force, authority, violence, or strength with power. None of those is power. Force is like a natural or social force, like the energy generated by a hurricane or a mob action. Authority needs only to be established, and then recognized by others, such as the authority of a priest or professor in ceremonies of absolution or conferring a degree. Strength is a private property, for example, when we compare the variable abilities of two people to lift weights or to speak well in public. Each individual possesses, like a personal property, some differential strength of body or character. Then there is violence, which for Arendt, rests on implements like tanks, guns, armies, etc. Violence may secure obedience by way of implements and threats, but actually, it indicates a lack of power. OK, but how and why does this matter?

Arendt was not a feminist, but I prefer a feminist approach to her point about violence and power through the example of rape. Feminists have long pointed out that rape is about power, not about sex. More precisely, there is a powerlessness of the rapist, which he seeks to compensate through a violent abuse of physical strength. One only "needs" violence to get what they want when the other from which they want something does not agree to it. Whatever a rapist wants – and that is *not necessarily sex* – he cannot get by agreement. In the absence of agreement, someone may be held up and robbed, may be raped, or a rebel city can be bombed, can become the target of violent militarism. If, on the other hand, you agree to hand over your wallet, your body, or a whole city, then violence may not come into play. This is how Arendt distinguishes power from

---

9   See Hannah Arendt, *On Violence* (New York: Harvest Books, 1969) and *Between Past and Future* (New York: Penguin Books, 1968).

violence. If I appeal to a crowd, and they agree with me that we should go on strike tomorrow, the plan is empowered by that agreement. There is a long history of meeting strikes with violence when striking workers do not *agree* to go back to work. To avoid the violence, there could be an agreement of the bosses with their workers. Following this, power cannot be domination. Domination enters the stage in the absence of power. Arendt claims there is no other form of power than communicative power, that is, the power of communication that leads to agreement. Everything else that is commonly mistaken for power should be called by a different name. With domination, we may be looking in fact at some combination of strength, authority, or violence, none of which is power. When we understand Arendt, there is no other defensible concept of power than whatever is empowered by our agreement.

My problem with this is twofold: First, I was always surprised that the author of *The Origins of Totalitarianism* could so stridently defend communicatively produced agreement. A whole lot of agreement that may appear to be communicatively produced is in fact a product of various forms (and there are many forms) of propaganda. We cannot claim that Arendt misses propaganda. She studied it. However, she saw propaganda as something more akin to coercion than power. I do not think people can so easily discern whether what they themselves think is communicatively produced, or manipulated. In the United States, for example, people really believe that Trump won the 2020 election. People really believe that COVID-19 is made-up, a total fraud meant to control civil society and ready us for some even worse dystopia. What if you told such people they were victims of propaganda? They simply retort that *you* are the victim of propaganda. There is no easy way out of this trap. This is why we cannot simply accept that what Arendt calls power does not already smuggle in various forms of violence, coercion, etc. Frankly, I do not trust agreement. Sometimes, fascists talk to each other and agree on a final solution. Sometimes, people agree simply because they do not want their disagreement to marginalize them. Agreement is not to be trusted.

My second objection is that, when Arendt thinks of violence, she thinks – as I said – about tanks, guns, other implements, and armies, but she does not think about the everyday violence of the capitalist reality. I call the everyday violence of capitalist society "quotidian violence," by which I mean that it is the violence we are so accustomed to that it appears as perfectly normal and not as some kind of aberration or violent event. What is included in the quotidian violence of the capitalist reality is all of the normal things we come to expect, from poverty to racism to mass incarceration to police brutality. So many legal things are violent, like wars, and economic and foreign policy. C.L.R. James was correct to say, in *The Black Jacobins*, that "The cruelties of property and privilege are always more ferocious than the revenges of poverty and oppression."[10] Simply put, those of us concerned with violence should be equally – if not more – repulsed by the quotidian violence of existing poverty and oppression, than by uprisings against them. Whereas Arendt thinks of tanks and wars, I want to think too about everyday violence in capitalist society. What is the status of violence when those who send in the tanks find the tanks turned on them instead?

Frantz Fanon wrote about the concept of "counter-violence" in the "Concerning Violence" chapter of *The Wretched of the Earth*.[11] He argues that victims of colonization are in fact opposed to the violence of their situation, and only oppose the violence of colonization with counterviolence because no other form of opposition is legible to the colonizer. In the example of the Zapatistas, central to *Unbounded Publics*, the Mexican government and international press vilified the rebels as violent terrorists. However, we cannot accept the vilifications of governments: we must ask what they were opposed to instead. The Zapatistas gave an answer to that question. They were opposed to the violence of the new era of post-Cold War neoliberal capitalism. Violence is complicated. That does not mean we can say nothing about it. It is precisely because it is complicated that we have to philosophize about it. It is the reason why Arendt wrote *On Violence*.

Some of the above complications would suffice to explain why I am not myself a pacifist, and why I am both suspicious of and nervous about Arendt's categorical schema, her defining analytical rubric, in *On Violence*. Arendt was not a simple pacifist either, so that is not the disagreement. Everyone will choose to be a pacifist for as long as possible. Historically, however, there are moments where it makes no sense to be a pacifist, and where one should even say that not fighting back by any means is immoral. I want to

---

10   C.L.R. James, *The Black Jacobins: Toussaint L'Ouverture and The San Domingo Revolution: Second Edition* (New York: Vintage Books, 1989), 88-89.
11   See Chapter 1 of Frantz Fanon's *The Wretched of the Earth*, trans. Constance Farrington (New York: Grove Press, 1963), 88 and *passim*.

be clear that I am not arguing for a Utilitarian position on violence. I am just trying to always appreciate and remember the observations of Frantz Fanon and C.L.R. James. In *The Black Jacobins*, James says, "When history is written as it ought to be written, it is the moderation and long patience of the masses at which men will wonder, not their ferocity."[12] This is true. When we think about violence, we should not think about revolutions, riots, revolts, social movements, crime, or more broadly, civil society. We have to think instead about capital and the state, for violence is primarily *their* thing... Everything else appears moderate and patient by comparison.

BG asks: Before your interesting paragraph on E.P. Thompson's position on the actual existence of nonbourgeois public spheres – which, as you say, "in itself challenges Habermas's contention that nonbourgeois public spheres shared their orientation and aims with the bourgeois public sphere[13] – you write: "Nonbourgeois public spheres therefore are those that fight against exclusion, for inclusion, and for the capacity to hold sway in politics."[14] This is done with an implicit reference to Gramsci, who is then quoted soon after in relation to the concept of hegemony and the idea of "wars of position" fought by nonbourgeois public spheres.[15] In particular, you are here speaking of the case of the feminist, suffragist movement. But I think this can be generalized to all fights by the nonbourgeois public spheres, as your endnote #33 on the difference between Gramsci's ideas of *war of maneuver* (or war of movement) and *war of position* makes clear.[16]

What is interesting is that for you, against Habermas, social movements, which you beautifully call "extra-institutional projects,"[17] are "a major component of the approach that distinguishes the nonbourgeois from the bourgeois public sphere,"[18] and just like acts of civil disobedience, they function "between civil war and civil society."[19] This is soon repeated with a specific reference to the Zapatistas.[20] All this produces what you call a

---

12   James, op. cit., p. 138.
13   Gilman-Opalsky, *Unbounded Publics*, op. cit., 92.
14   Ibid., 91.
15   Ibid., 94.
16   Ibid., 111-112.
17   Ibid., 98.
18   Ibid., 97.
19   Ibid., 99.
20   Ibid., 101.

philosophy from below, which I think is an idea that is found throughout your work, perhaps one of the most basic ideas. This is part of a philosophy of praxis, we might say, and a transformative philosophy. In this sense, the insurrectionary element of nonbourgeois public spheres is essential. First of all, we have here "a multiplicity of public spheres," which are transgressive by definition, even simply because they do not address the state, but posit themselves beyond its borders.[21] However, by doing this they are not simply transnational, but transgressive, as they also go beyond the national/transnational false dichotomy. Here, too, it would be nice if you could elaborate, tell us more about these *extra-institutional projects*, and the prospects for them today.

RGO answers: I received most of my academic training in philosophy programs, which mostly avoided Marx and Marxism, almost entirely in my experience. Early in my philosophy Ph.D. program, I decided to switch over to political science because, at The New School for Social Research, one could continue to do philosophy there, but also because I could find more support for the study of social movements and global uprisings there. In philosophy, the Zapatista rebellion was not viewed as a philosophical event. Whereas, in political science, people were studying the Zapatistas, like Courtney Jung who chaired my dissertation committee. At the same time, I was surprised by how much of the attention of political science was fixated on the behavior of states, institutions of governance, policymakers, constitutions, legal rights, public policy, and reform. In North America, academic philosophy marginalizes Marxism and its permutations in Continental and critical theory. Political science marginalizes approaches to politics that do not focus on the professional political class, or what I would simply call the ruling class. When most people think about political science, they think about the world of professional politicians, elections, procedural politics, and the varied activities of the branches of government. Perhaps sociology or anthropology do better, but they have their own problems and limitations. Personally, I was always interested in the politics of other places, always drawn to a more Foucauldian notion that power is not a place or possession but a social relation, which we can recodify and challenge in the active relationships of everyday people.

I am a political scientist working in my university's College of Public

---

21 Ibid., 102.

Affairs and Education. Here, regular media inquiries that ask me to comment on national elections and legislative politics are frustrating. Every local newspaper assumes I will have something to say about laws and politicians, but not about the George Floyd Rebellion. I find it maddening that people still think about heads of state as soon as they think of politics. Regardless of the approach, politics is fundamentally about power. To think about politics, one has to think about power. People often assume they know what power is, without bothering to define it. The assumption typically views power as the domain of the ruling class, and the effects of power are typically regarded as whatever that class does with its money and military. That is why, despite criticisms of her work in my own, I continue to reference Arendt's conception of power from her *On Violence,* where she insists that those who can only get what they want by bribery, war, or other coercions, are revealing their own lack of power.[22] Tanks and soldiers only come in to compensate for deficits of real power.

Instead of tanks and states, I have always been interested in the politics of everyday people who act outside of and against conventional politics. This grounds my early interest in the Zapatistas, which we can trace – as you correctly note – all the way through my entire body of work, perhaps most clearly in *Specters of Revolt.* In short, I am interested in those moments when presumptively "powerless" people mobilize and realize other powers than the powers of the institutional apparatus of politics, an apparatus that includes the police, prisons, courts, and military. I would wish to see political theory truly and finally break with its long historical fixation on the professional political class, a fixation that goes back to antiquity in the canons of Western philosophy, and which was already well established by the time of Thomas Hobbes's theory of the sovereign in the middle of the seventeenth century.

In 1977, Michel Foucault expressed a sentiment that I share when he said, "What we need is a political philosophy that isn't erected around the problem of sovereignty, nor therefore around the problems of law and prohibition. We need to cut off the King's head: in political theory that has still to be done."[23] This means that those of us interested in politics

---

22 Hannah Arendt, *On Violence* (Orlando: Harvest Books, 1970).
23 Michel Foucault, *Power/Knowledge,* trans. Colin Gordon, Leo Marshall, John Mepham, and Kate Soper (New York: Pantheon Books, 1980), 121.

should see and appreciate power in other places. Foucault held that we should study relations of power between and around us, and not only look up to the political sovereign as the locus of power. Over forty years since Foucault's plea, the social and political sciences have yet to do this, and neither have mainstream discussions of politics. This is easy to see in 24-hour news that hangs on every presidential tweet or utterance and centers its attention on heads of state. This is what I mean when I speak about "extra-institutional projects." I want to shift our focus to different fields of power, different terrains of politics.

This is the field that Enrique Dussel called *potentia*. Dussel distinguished *potentia* from *potestas*. In his excellent book, *Twenty Theses on Politics*, Dussel claims that *potestas* is the whole procedural and policing apparatus of institutional politics, from elections to prisons, whereas *potentia* is the social field outside of that, where we find everyday people, their everyday lives and struggles. Dussel also specifies a third term, *hyperpotentia*, which indicates moments of revolt and rebellion.[24] He argues against the fetishization of *potestas* and for a concept of the political that centers *potentia* and *hyperpotentia* instead. I agree with Dussel, and in my work, "extra-institutional projects" refer to the activities that move *potentia* to *hyperpotentia*. The shortcoming of Dussel's framework is that there are not only the two positions of civil society he discusses, not only passive society (*potentia*) and open rebellion (*hyperpotentia*). The term "extra-institutional projects" may be able to capture some other positions, such as those of the more rhizomatic activities that are *neither* passive, *nor* (*yet*) open revolt. Beyond that example, there are many ways that artists take up the question of power, that schools or jazz musicians may challenge power relations, that feminists renegotiate power in the family, or that punks deal with power in counterculture. Take a look at certain figures of history too, such as Benjamin Lay.[25] Lay was one person. He was not himself *potentia* or *hyperpotentia*. Yet, he was not a passive member of the Quaker community. He was a radical abolitionist, an incredible troublemaker.

All of these things must be included in a good concept of politics. In so many ways, people seek to realize power in other places. This is what I am after with the notion of extra-institutional projects.

---

24   Enrique Dussel, *Twenty Theses on Politics*, trans. Geo Maher (Durham and London: Duke University Press, 2008).
25   Marcus Rediker, *The Fearless Benjamin Lay* (Boston: Beacon Press, 2017).

BG asks: You often speak of the "in between," a phrase that I particularly like. You say, for instance, "Specters of revolt haunt in between, that is, both before and after, realizations of revolt."[26] In a sense this relates to the previous questions I ask in this section. However, here I want to complicate it a bit. It seems to me that although you use the both/and formula, there is here a link to the neither/nor logic of *Unbounded Publics*. I don't mean to push this too far, but I think it's there. Am I correct in this? If I am, this would highlight once again the idea of transgression, so important in your first book. But I would also like to ask how this might relate to the concept of threshold I develop in my most recent book, *Singularities at the Threshold*.

RGO answers: I confess that I did not see the relation of the "in between" to "the transgressive," but I find what you say convincing. The basic sensibility you observe in my work comes from my experience as a student of Jacques Derrida, who was always warning against on/off binaries. "Both/and" along with "neither/nor" strike me as a different way to approach a choice one does not want to accept. From the very start, I was interested in questioning boundaries, originally expressed in the concept of transgression. I wanted to challenge the boundaries of national and political identity, the boundaries of ideology, the boundaries or limit points (and yes, we could say thresholds) of communism. In *Specters of Revolt*, I challenge the boundaries of historical events, the beginnings and ends of political action. Philosophy has relied too much on categorical and analytical rubrics, and often retains old definitions necessary for preserving systems of understanding. Of course, philosophers who took nothing for granted started from scratch, and doubted everything, every logic and every premise, just to arrive at first principles.[27] Meanwhile, many others did not want to reinvent the proverbial wheel, so they stuck to the categories, rubrics, and delimitations produced by previous hard efforts.[28] I have always been inclined to look for in-betweens and boundary transgressions, which seems to me more Derridian in some ways, than Cartesian, Kantian, or Marxist.

However, I want to talk about you here, Bruno. In your book, *Singularities at the Threshold*, Chapter 4: Borders and Vortices (Life and Work)

---

26 Gilman-Opalsky, *Specters of Revolt*, op. cit., 17.
27 The iconic example is Descartes.
28 Many examples in Marxism.

is one of many places in your writing where I see our similar approach to boundary transgression. There, you engage Balibar's essay "What is a Border?" In the discussion, you say, "what matters is not subjectivity or identity, but singularity, which retains within itself the ontology of its plural and common constitution and remains open to the common and plural. In this sense, the border becomes a threshold."[29] In this, we see how transgression is generative of new thinking and subverts bad categories. What you are saying about singularity here is a transgressive "in between." In philosophy, there is the old border between the individual subject and the plural collectivity. Usually, philosophers have to specify whether they are discussing the one or the many. Nietzsche, in *The Will to Power*, treats individual and collective as opposites. The individual even dies in the collective, and the collective is broken to pieces by the individual.[30] The individual's will to power, when no longer suppressed, rebels against the weaknesses of herd mentality, whereas the collective is nothing more than compensation for individual weakness. Nietzsche opposes socialism, anarchism, political parties, and all hope for democracy on precisely that basis.[31] Even though some philosophers, including so many faithful Kantians, regard Nietzsche as a kind of misfit anti-philosopher of philosophy, Nietzsche reproduces that very old rigid opposition of the one to the many.

Contrary to that, you are refusing the choice, and even, if I may say so, calling out the surprising stupidity of such an opposition. You do this by the border-crossing transgression of your concept of singularity. Singularity says that each one is here and can assert one's self, but that the one's being-in-the-world (and this is the ontological point) imbricates plurality and a common constitution. Every assertion of the singular is sensible only in relation to others, and in each human person, there is a connection to the common and the plural. This is because each one is a relation to others, and one's desires are never *only* the desires of the one. When we recognize this, you argue, the border becomes a threshold because a singularity is *neither* one *nor* many, and yet it is *both* one *and* many.

---

29   Bruno Gullì, *Singularities at the Threshold* (Lanham: Lexington Books, 2020), 65-66.
30   See Friedrich Nietzsche, *The Will to Power*, trans. Walter Kaufmann and R.J. Hollingdale (New York: Vintage Books, 1968), especially "Part III: The Will to Power as Society and Individual."
31   Ibid., pp. 397-398.

I have simplified your argument here, but I think it suffices to show that transgression is crucial to our work because of what it creates not only because of what it subverts. For example, in your work, it creates the possibility to reject Nietzsche's choice between the one or the many (a choice that also appears in Plato and Hannah Arendt and for many others unlike Nietzsche), a choice that still plagues political thinking. Indeed, we still live in a world where individualists and collectivists have their own political parties, suited for their variously individualist or collectivist tastes.

In my theory of revolt too, the revolt does not eradicate the individual and the individual does not contradict the revolt. The revolt is itself an example of what you call "trans-dividuality" (which you introduce as another way of saying singularity) in that it is intersubjective and interindividual.[32] It would be a peculiar and coercive move to insist that the collective action of revolt erases individuals, or that individuals appear only outside of the revolt. Approaching the border as a threshold exposes the choice between individual and collective as a certain kind of nonsense, and then what is most surprising is only how long the nonsense has persisted. A stupid choice, the one or the many, a choice that demands a dangerous ontological reduction. So yes, I think we should always find ways of asking what is in between the two positions, what is beyond the threshold.

BG asks: I like what you say in *Precarious Communism* about cellular time obliterating time "after work."[33] You put "after work" in quotation marks and I wonder what you mean, really. What is indeed this "after work" time for many people today in the 24/7 economy? You do speak of "the structural transformation of everyday life in the interests of capital," and this in a sense already answers my question.[34] But I would like to hear more about this. You say that it is not about technology, but about intersubjectivity,[35] "about being-in-the-world."[36] This is great, and in some ways, it anticipates themes you deal with in *The Communism of Love*. You say that "we are not talking

---

32 Gullì, *Singularities at the Threshold*, op. cit., p. 2.
33 Gilman-Opalsky, *Precarious Communism*, op. cit. 25.
34 Ibid.
35 Ibid.
36 Ibid., 26.

about technology, but being."[37] Can you say more about this even in relation to Heidegger's essay on the question concerning technology?

RGO answers: The phrase I use in the book is "technontology," by which I mean to think about how the technologizing of life, including work and social relationships, changes our being-in-the-world. Part of this has to do with the seizure of our wakeful energies by capital, which has many uses – and far more than at any previous point in history – it would like to make with our time and attention. Capital has always captured and colonized time and attention, and of course, physical labor too. However, in a 24/7 predatory and increasingly virtual society, attention and purchasing have somewhat displaced the central physicality of production. Despite this relative displacement, I oppose interpretations of post-Fordist society that focus so much on cognitive labor that they appear to forget the ongoing necessity of production centers for mass produced commodities of every kind. Even if we shift our attentions to technologically mediated life, we must not forget the continuing reality of physical centers of mass production. The cellular dimension of technontology is, however, a development that needs special attention. It functions mainly through the colonization of our wakeful attention, near-totally seized through screen interfaces today.

Heidegger, in "The Question Concerning Technology," writes, "The manufacture and utilization of equipment, tools, and machines, the manufactured and used things themselves, and the needs and ends that they serve, all belong to what technology is. The whole complex of these contrivances is technology. Technology itself is a contrivance, or, in Latin, an *instrumentum*."[38] Heidegger is correct to consider what he calls "the whole complex," what it serves, and the instrumentality of technology. Technology is not just the tool or the machine, but the way it changes human activity and relations, and what those activities and relations serve. To think about how technology develops is, to some extent, also to think about what we are becoming.

In our lifetimes, there has been too much quickness in the instinct to celebrate the emancipatory possibilities of technology. Revolutionaries

---

37 Ibid
38 Martin Heidegger, *The Question Concerning Technology and Other Essays*, Trans. William Lovitt (New York and London: Garland Publishing, 1977), 4-5.

have also seen some hopeful hijacking, rerouting, and subversion, not only from predictable places, like in the practices of hackers, but in the milieus of organizing activists as part of the infrastructure of social movements. Cellular technologies have increased surveillance, yes, but not only in predictable repressive directions. They have also increased surveillance of killer cops, neo-Nazis, racial profilers, and white supremacists. We see them better than ever, and thus, cannot so easily deny them as the liberal order has preferred to do. Cell phone cameras irrefutably documented many recent cases of police brutality, of cops killing unarmed Black people. More recently, we have seen how Zoom and other social media have helped people stay "connected" with beloved friends and family during periods of social distancing and pandemic. Only the most reactionary critical theorist could declare all of that to be techno-fascist bad news. Catching killer cops, exposing the violence of white supremacy to everyone everywhere, and enabling a degree of human community in times of estrangement; none of that is bad news.

However, Heidegger does help us see how this good news is exceptional to a mostly uniform application of technology, which has not been very good news at all. One should wonder if Heidegger could have appreciated this in the film and radio technologies so integral to Nazi propaganda. Apparently, Heidegger failed to extend his analysis in certain political directions. Today, the psychological damage wrought on young people by a screen-mediated social life – the constant screen pathology – is not so easy to assess in real time. Intersubjectivity itself may be a casualty of the present form of life. We have shifted from an embodied intersubjectivity with metatopical supplements (such as when we used telephones and televisions) to a *disembodied* intersubjectivity with periodic topical supplements. Both sides remain, but we can mark a shift in our "being-in-the-world" here. The ontological shift transfers so much of what we do in *the world* to a *private lifeworld* that is in many ways cut off from the world. The *private lifeworld* is nonetheless a meta-world unto itself, and many increasingly favor and choose the *private lifeworld* over the social world of embodied relations outside.

I am deeply worried about this as a human being and from a political point of view, which are, of course, imbricated concerns. As a human being, I worry that our new modalities of being-in-the-world are simply not consistent with our psychosocial health and well-being. Politically, the ruling classes could only have dreamt of a future where their enemies would oppose them in 26 characters or less, using only their thumbs and shared images that people may (or may not) scroll past without any disturbance or interruption. In contrast, a highway stopped by bodies that obstruct it, the sabotage of ecologically destructive machinery, the overtaking of public squares, workplaces, and schools by means of occupations, or the stoppages of work in strike activity, are all things that cannot happen on a screen with the thumbs of any person. Now, that screen activity may or may not support the embodied politics we need, but it cannot replace it. What is most troubling to me in the shift towards disembodied politics is the extent to which we are helping the ruling class make its dreams come true.

BG asks: You focus a lot on insurrection, more than on revolution. In *Specters of Revolt*, you say that insurrection is a fragment of revolution.[39] Yet, obviously, fragments are very important. Then, speaking of the transition from "what is" to "what ought to be," you thematized revolution as such. I would suggest that "what could be" is a much better way to think about this than "what ought to be." What do you think about this? I believe that speaking about the "could" modality, rather than the "ought to," gives much more room to the contingency of true revolutionary activity. You do speak of revolution as "an open-ended process of transformation that can address its own failures through further transformation," a metastable and never-ending process.[40] So, insurrection, as "the actual exercise of revolutionary activity," makes sense. You speak of insurrection everywhere, and you end this chapter by saying "Revolution betrays its own logic when it claims to have reached the end."[41] Some people might think that this is self-defeating, and yet, there is something here that goes beyond that, so much so that it comes in a section (which only has one sentence) titled "Epilogue (after the end)."[42] So, the end is not the end, as if the beginning were not the beginning. This goes back to the spectral and ghostly modality you discuss in your book, the in-between, the tension, or, as the title of your Chapter 4 has it, "The Eternal Recurrence of Revolt." My question is, is this an empty space and a false

---

39   Gilman-Opalsky, Specters of Revolt, op. cit., 148.
40   Ibid., 172.
41   Ibid., 190.
42   Ibid.

movement, insurrection after insurrection with no end in view, or is it rather a constant and concrete subversion of the miserable reality we are forced in to begin with?

RGO answers: You may be right about "what could be" as a better formulation than "what ought to be." Obviously, I choose to say "ought" deliberately, but I confess that it always makes me nervous when I do. Sometimes, however, I do use "what could be and should be," which can be found more frequently in *The Communism of Love*. Perhaps "could" and "should" do not need to be presented as either/or. Still, it is true that I only retain the "ought" with some trepidation. I want to get into this point a bit more fully. I completely agree with you about the "could" modality as a mode of contingency, centralizing the fact that something else is possible. Indeed, that is our shared ontological hope. So, then, I should explain why I remain connected to the "ought" modality.

The most common answer has to do with normative theory as a point of resistance against decades of postmodern philosophy in which I (and many others) steeped. However, there is also something in the "ought" modality having to do with revolution. A revolutionary does not only condemn what is, but also, imagines how things could and should be. This is what Raya Dunayevskaya calls "the second negation."[43] We have to oppose everything worthy of our condemnation, but we also have to move from that abolitionist position to a positive consideration of what "ought" to be, and that positive movement is the second negation, or the negation of the negation. Dunayevskaya talks about needing to overthrow the post-revolutionary Russian ruling class in the positive movement of a second negation. She argued, "The negation of the negation" is "the destruction of the existing system which had destroyed the previous system. That is what the Russian ruling class trembles at, as well it may, for it knows this movement *not* by the name of 'negation of the negation,' but by the reality of revolution against it."[44] There is no way to approach this second negation without moving from is to ought, and considering what could be and should be.

Here, I want to return to and appreciate the relation of this "ought" to the intellect of the insurrection itself, to philosophy from below. In the

---

43 Raya Dunayevskaya, *Marxism and Freedom: From 1776 until Today* (New York: Humanity Books, 2000), 10.
44 Ibid., 66.

open-ended processes of revolt too – not only in full-blown classical revolution – the "ought" is considered, approached, and even tested in various ways. Marina Sitrin and Dario Azzellini have discussed this particularly well in the ways that uprisings work through what ought to be, or could be and should be, in experimental and prefigurative ways. In *They Can't Represent Us!*, Sitrin and Azzellini discuss how *horizontalidad* in Argentina and various experiments with popular power, assemblies, and practices of direct democracy are real activities of exploring what could be and should be that happen everywhere in recent global uprisings.[45] People want to try to do things differently as part of testing out the practicality of what they think ought to be done.

Finally, to the point you raised about insurrection in contrast with revolution. I am thinking about revolution, contributing to revolutionary theory, and consider myself more of a revolutionary than an insurrectionist. The explanation is very simple. This is because I think we need revolution more than we need insurrection, and because inasmuch as revolution means the structural transformation of the world, from what it is in the direction of what it could be and should be (there is that ought again), I argue that revolution is necessary. Insurrection is not a structural transformation of anything, beyond possibly the psychology of the insurrectionist. The problem is that there is far more insurrection than revolution in the world. I am a philosopher, but also a materialist who insists on thinking from the point of the actually existing movements of my time. These movements are essentially revolts, insurrectionary interruptions of everyday life, and they very rarely approach anything we may call revolution. A materialist philosopher has to think about what is happening, and a revolutionary theorist has to think about the relationship between insurrection and revolution; that is largely what I am trying to do in *Specters of Revolt*.

However, my point about revolution betraying its logic when it claims to have reached its end is not defeatist. That is an idea that goes back to the concept mentioned above, the concept of permanent revolution so important to Marx and Dunayevskaya and many others. The apparent end is usually not the end, in fact, and we have to keep on going. I do not think this means that the insurrection has no aims. Insurrection has

---

45   Marina Sitrin and Dario Azzellini, *They Can't Represent Us! Reinventing Democracy from Greece to Occupy* (London and New York: Verso Books, 2014).

various goals, and what those goals are often depends on whom you ask about them. We cannot move from the miserable reality of the present to a communist utopia in a swift fell swoop and we should beware all claims of victory. We need to take some lessons from the twentieth century. We cannot only defend "the real revolution" if that means putting down or denigrating real revolts against the existing state of affairs.

RGO asks: I understand that, for you, sovereignty must be opposed writ large because servility is its necessary corollary (if not precondition). In *Earthly Plenitudes*, you describe this as "the problem associated with all forms of sovereignty" and you insist that when one renounces either side of this divide (sovereignty or servility), the other side collapses.[46] I like this conceptualization, but would nonetheless pose a Gramscian challenge here. For Gramsci, in his discussion of the art and science of politics in *Prison Notebooks*, the point of counter-hegemonic politics is NOT to oppose all hegemony, but rather, to replace one hegemony with another. For Gramsci, politics is essentially about the war of position, where socialists and revolutionaries must try to make a particular worldview hegemonic. Of course, *hegemony is not synonymous with sovereignty*. Politically, however, hegemony is connected with sovereignty inasmuch as every sovereign requires its supportive hegemony. What happens to politics if we are not allowed to establish sovereignty on top of a new hegemonic order, let us say, in the ideological war of position? In other words, I believe that we want a certain point of view about healthcare, human rights, ecology, capitalism, etc., to be established as hegemonic on the ruins of the existing capitalist hegemony. Gramsci's political theory seems to insist on the clash of actual and possible sovereigns and their different hegemonic interests. Socialists would declare victory if socialism were established as the ruling worldview, for example. Does Gramsci's art and science of politics challenge what you say about sovereignty, or do counter-hegemonic wars of position have no implications for your critical theory of sovereignty?

BG answers: I see your point. However, the main question is, ruling over what or whom? I don't think that a counter-hegemonic process is one in which a type of hegemony, a socialist or communist hegemony, replaces the previous dominant one, the capitalist and bourgeois hegemonic order.

---

46   Gullì, *Earthly Plenitudes*, op. cit., 91.

Rather, the victory of a counter-hegemonic movement and process signals the end of the previous one, and thus the end of hegemony as such. Once again, I would think of the isonomic order I have mentioned above – isonomia as *no rule*. This doesn't mean that anything goes, but rather that there is no superimposed rule, typical of any sovereign order. Furthermore, a war of position cannot last forever, just like any war can't. The *end* of the revolutionary, counter-hegemonic process is not imposing a kind of new *hegemony as domination* over a defeated subject; rather, it is a transformative process whereby the old dominant forms of power cease to exist – and in which there are no longer *subjects*.

In a sense, this is similar to the question of the relationship between violence and counterviolence. The latter is not a modality that is supposed to last forever; it is not another type of violence – a better kind of violence. That would be rather strange. The *end* of counterviolence is to end violence; the *end* of counter-hegemony is to end a (any) hegemonic order of one group over another or others. I know that this sounds utopic, but there must be a utopic element in revolutionary discourse, in communism – or perhaps better, a heterotopic one. In a critical remark on Hegel's conception of the state – the ethical or cultural state, but really the bourgeois state with its ideological and repressive apparatuses, Gramsci, implicitly recalling Marx's conception of the proletariat as the class that is the dissolution of all classes, says, "But, in reality, only the social group that poses the end of the State and its own end as the target to be achieved can create the ethical State – i.e., one which tends to put an end to the internal divisions of the ruled, etc., and to create a technically unitary social organism."[47] Of course, there is also Gramsci's celebrated notion of the *interregnum*, in which "the old is dying and the new cannot be born."[48]

However, the new cannot be another version of the old. Rather, it is a situation in which the division between the rulers and the ruled is abolished – no sovereignty and no hegemony as domination.

RGO asks: I would say that both you and I seek to radicalize certain aspects of Kantian philosophy. I am, for example, clearly interested in a radicalization of Kant's public use of reason, and in your work, we find a

---

[47] Antonio Gramsci, *Selections from the Prison Notebooks*, ed. and trans. Quintin Hoare and Geoffrey Nowell Smith (New York: International Publishers, 1971), 259.
[48] Ibid, 276.

radicalization of the kingdom of ends.[49] Perhaps we also agree that a radicalization of Kant's cosmopolitan idea could be achieved in some form of Marxian internationalism or Marxist-humanism. In any case, the question of Kant (not to mention your insistence on working with Heidegger and Schmitt, despite their conservatism), leads me to wonder what you think about the radicalization of liberal/conservative thinking, as opposed to a total opposition to the whole monopolized system of liberal/conservative politics. What do I mean? Well, democratic socialists from Eduard Bernstein and Erich Fromm to Bernie Sanders and the latter's *de facto* magazine, *Jacobin*, maintain that radicals can win crucial battles by way of a radicalization of liberal positions. Opposed to this, communists from Rosa Luxemburg to Antonio Negri insist on a politics of total opposition to the liberal/conservative field, because they are convinced of inevitable failure there. Whereas other communists, like Jodi Dean, have been ready to campaign for democratic socialists on the main stage of capitalist elections. How do you think about these things politically? If we can make communist arguments from Kantian philosophy (not to mention from Heidegger and Schmitt), then can we extract some socialist victories from a liberal/conservative politics that is decisively capitalist?

BG answers: To begin with, for me this is part of my eclectic method in thinking, researching, and writing. Some people may take issues with eclecticism – basically because their concern is narrowly ideological – but I think it's the correct method both historically and philosophically. To answer your last question, I don't think we can extract socialist victories from a liberal/conservative politics as such, but we can (and should) critically engage that type of thinking. A case in point, before even thinking of Kant (or Heidegger and Schmitt), is the thought of Hobbes. I regularly teach the central chapters on sovereignty from *Leviathan* and engage them in my writing. Of course, I'm very critical of Hobbes; yet, his importance (and greatness) cannot be overlooked. So, it depends on what you are doing. You can't address the question of sovereignty without looking at Hobbes and Schmitt. The case of Heidegger might be different. Perhaps you can avoid engaging his work in a direct and explicit manner. However, he remains one of the greatest thinkers of the twentieth century, so I don't see how one can (or should) avoid him altogether. Moreover, there

---

49 Gullì, *Humanity and the Enemy*, op. cit., 49

is today the risk of falling into that malaise known as "cancel culture." I think what's important is not whose work you use, but *how* you use it. I don't think it's an either/or between a radicalization of liberal and conservative positions and a politics of total opposition to them. I actually think it's something completely different from that.

To elucidate this a bit, I'll briefly turn to some important pages from Sartre's *Search for a Method,* where he speaks about Paul Valéry and Gustave Flaubert. The key sentence here is, "Valéry is a petit bourgeois intellectual, no doubt about it. But not every petit bourgeois intellectual is Valéry."[50] Ultimately, it is a question of singularity. For Sartre, "living Marxism is heuristic," analytic and synthetic at the same time.[51] This is what, I believe, an eclectic method, a gathering, makes possible. In his perhaps exaggerated criticism of Lukács, Sartre addresses the importance of the complexity of a situation, not reducible to some type of preestablished understanding of it. Interestingly, Sartre also says that he read Heidegger in 1933, "when Heidegger should have been at the height of his 'activism')."[52] Indeed, not only Kant with his kingdom of ends and public use of reason, but Heidegger, too, with his creative (if problematic) rereading of the history of Western philosophy and his indictment of our loss of thinking – of our *stupidity*, in Bernard Stiegler's sense – can help us with the project of a communist future.

BG asks: I find your idea of going beyond struggle intriguing. Of course, you maintain the *reality* of struggle, but you say that "the virtue of struggle must be refuted and overcome, and pleasure must play a part in displacing the worn-out logic of paying for everything with pain."[53] I couldn't agree more. Struggle, you say, "must be decentered."[54] And you clarify that it is desire that "displaces and decenters struggle."[55] In a sense, this chapter is a call for autonomy against sovereignty, for struggle and pain are intrinsic to the logic of sovereignty. The liberatory politics you trace,

---

50 Jean-Paul Sartre, *Search for a Method,* trans. Hazel E. Barnes (New York: Vintage Books, 1968), 56.
51 Ibid., 26.
52 Ibid., 38.
53 Gilman-Opalsky, *Specters of Revolt,* op. cit., 68-69.
54 Ibid., 96.
55 Ibid., 95.

which, as you say, "follows Guattari's principle of transversality,"[56] abandons "the fetishization of struggle" and opens up the field of indeterminacy and contingency, the realm of possibility.[57] Revolt, you say, is often "the joyful interruption of struggle, a reaction against (and not an expression of) struggle."[58] Obviously, by overcoming struggle, you don't mean that all activity ceases. In a sense, perhaps, you are here already thinking of your next book, *The Communism of Love*, where you see love precisely as activity.

What is liberatory is rather the movement away from coercion (the sovereignty paradigm) toward pleasure and play (the autonomy paradigm). In the *Grundrisse*, speaking against Adam Smith, Marx says that the "overcoming of obstacles is in itself a liberating activity."[59] But this is not the damnation to struggle and pain that makes people's lives miserable and creates the precariat, which, as you say very well, "is the class of people who lead precarious lives, whose everyday life is set within an ongoing state of anxiety about an increasingly uncertain future."[60] How can this (institutional and externally imposed) uncertain future become the autonomous indeterminacy of open contingencies, the transversal movement (the line of flight) toward a future that is still uncertain (as that belongs to the very concept of the future), yet sustained by an ontological potency of subversion, a subterranean fire of transformation? I guess that's my question here.

RGO answers: Listen to the music of Sun Ra! You can hear in Sun Ra's music, and in the history of the mostly Black, impoverished members of his bands, that we must never forget about joy. For Sun Ra and his group, the struggle was real and deadly serious. For people living in the face of war, poverty, torture, exploitation, and other forms of marginalization, the struggle is not only real, but it is inevitable, simply unavoidable. People struggle because they have to, not because they want to. Therefore, we must not treat struggle as if it were itself a virtue. Those who now struggle in Yemen, Palestine, the US, Ghana, etc., struggle because the material conditions of the world demand it. I try to address the common idea that we should be happy to join struggles, when in fact, the ideal of

---

56   Ibid., 109.
57   Ibid., 95.
58   Ibid., 67.
59   Marx, *Grundrisse*, op. cit., 611.
60   Gilman-Opalsky, *Specters of Revolt*, op. cit., 89.

happiness hides in the hope that struggle may come to an end. You are right to say that struggle and pain are intrinsic to the logic of sovereignty. We must always ask, wherever there is sovereignty, who are the subjects of the sovereign? It is no surprise that the historical passage from subject to citizen was a long one. However, we should never forget that "subject" is the root of "subjection" and etymologically connected with "subjugation." We could think about sovereignty in the capitalist workplace, or the example of a worker fired for insubordination. When fired for any form of insubordination, we should stop for a moment to think about the opposite of insubordination, which is the virtue of the capitalist workplace. *The opposite of insubordination is subordination*; no one is fired for subordination. We should also note that insubordination is closer to fun, that there is joy in breaking the rules. Sun Ra understood that profoundly.

Revolt opens up a field of indeterminacy and contingency, a space of possibility, a bit like Sun Ra's music, which is also a joyful interruption of struggle, a response to a life of struggle. I wish I could say that I was already thinking of my next book, *The Communism of Love*, but I was not aware of what I would do next at the time of *Specters of Revolt*. Now it is easy to see that they are intimately connected. I am always interested in emancipatory activity, forms of action and life that break with coercion, sovereignty, and put us in touch with pleasure and play. If one does not like Sun Ra's music, they may find similar things in love relations with beloved friends, family, and comrades.

Now, back to the question of precarity. Its defining feature is that we do not know what will happen in the future. We generally regard that as bad news because an uncertain future means insecurity, anxiety, essentially no reliable reassurances. However, global recession, pandemics, the ends of Mubarak and Morsi, the insolvency of banks and the auto industry, are just some of the many things that expose an often-neglected flipside of precarity. This other side of precarity is that existing sovereign institutions, and capitalist power, are also precarious in various ways, albeit different from the precarity of everyday people. There is an important insight in the fact that even our enemies may be precarious. It means that we cannot simply assume the indefinite permanence of the capitalist reality. I even think the smartest capitalists have always been aware of this, perhaps more than many of their critics, even if only secretly. We should think more about the precarity of imperial and colonial power, which saw defeat in many struggles of decolonization. We are precarious, but so are they.

Recently, Costas Panayotakis wrote a beautiful little book documenting the many ways that capitalism is not only bad for people, ecology and democracy, but also destructive of the grounds of its own functioning.[61] Panayotakis is no optimist or utopian, and his catalog of present and looming crises would convince any reader of the instability of the capitalist system. "It is these forces underlying the operation of the capitalist system that account for the seemingly paradoxical coincidence of an advance of the forces of production and the forces of destruction alike."[62] The history of capitalism is not only a history of production, but of destruction too, and especially in the ecological sphere, such destruction undermines the future of production. This is not good news, but it means that indeterminacy and contingency are not our sole private property. There are many things upon which our enemies also depend, which they cannot count on forever.

What might we try to do if we understood there was a chance that our capitalist enemies or the enemy of humanity (as you may call it) was not permanent? In some cases, precarity is our friend, because belief in the permanence of the capitalist reality is one of capital's greatest ideological achievements. I do not believe in the permanence of capitalism. The impermanence of capital lends an ontological potency to a politics of subversion. Subversive autonomous activities that do not ask permission can be – and are – undertaken without knowing what will happen. We do not know where things will lead, and sometimes everything appears closed until one discovers an opening. There are concrete examples. The first Black Lives Matter protests, coming out of the murders of Trayvon Martin (2012) and Michael Brown (2014) could not have predicted the George Floyd Rebellion (2020) almost a decade later. Black liberation politics in the US has a long history, and it is far from finished. For as long as white supremacy continues, regardless of its form, from slavery to mass incarceration, liberation struggles will continue and we cannot presuppose success or failure in advance.

There is no epitaph for revolt. We can only declare things impossible until they start happening. Therefore, we must not only dwell on our

---

61 Costas Panayotakis, *The Capitalist Mode of Destruction: Austerity, Ecological Crisis and the Hollowing out of Democracy* (Manchester: Manchester University Press, 2021).

62 Ibid., 75.

own precarity, but on that of our enemy too. We must not only dwell upon struggle, remember that joy is also in our reach, and that many people find joy in the uprising, or in the music of Sun Ra (which is also a kind of uprising).

BG asks: Another important concept I'd like you to comment on is that of personality. You speak about this in *The Communism of Love* in the section on Rosa Luxemburg. The way you frame it, speaking of the different personalities of both the human and nonhuman animals, you obviously equate personality with singularity, *thisness*. This is particularly interesting to me because, as you know, that's exactly what I do in the last chapter of *Singularities at the Threshold*, where I see personality as a kind of schematism or glow or aura cutting across the various gathering of dividual moments, not in the sense of unifying them, but rather as a process whereby both meaning and memory are produced. What I like in your treatment of this concept and reality is the fact that you see it in a dialectical fashion. Already in the introduction to *The Communism of Love*, speaking of "the possibility of a real collective subject that is *not* secondary to the individual," you say that "the individual's personality is realized only in dialectical relations with others around her."[63] I couldn't agree more, and I think that you are here touching on the concept of transindividuality, or my version of it, trans-dividuality. I hope that you also see the affinity here between our works as I do. Then to go back to your section on Rosa Luxemburg, there is a reiteration of this relational and dialectical constitution of personality when you speak of what it means "to know the personality of the other."[64] This is very important on so many levels, of ontology, epistemology, and, perhaps above all, politics and ethics. In fact, speaking about the "proximity between beings," you say that "*at the affective level of feeling for the other* – this proximity is *not* merely imaginary."[65]

A few pages later you speak of the question of vulnerability, which is often a result of someone opening up completely to us (and obviously we can very well be that someone, the other, another one, or perhaps more or less than one), in total reliance.[66] It is in this sense that your remarks on cruelty

---

63 Gilman-Opalsky, *The Communism of Love*, op. cit., 6.
64 Ibid., 121.
65 Ibid., 122.
66 Ibid., 125.

are also very important from an ethical point of view. You say, "Often, the problem of cruelty to others is a problem of insufficient imagination,"[67] and you footnote Elaine Scarry's essay "The Difficulty of Imagining Other People."[68] But of course, this also relates to Hannah Arendt's important concept of *the banality of evil*, which is rooted in and caused by *thoughtlessness*. All this opens up a profound ethical problematic on which you may want to comment. Basically, the question you yourself ask about "the effort to see the world from the other being's perspective, especially for those on the losing end of power."[69] We find empathy again as well as love as a practice, and really as work, a lot of work, often very difficult work.

RGO answers: The defining attribute of a person is a personality, which means that we may speak of both human and nonhuman persons. It is important to increase our affective regard for the suffering of nonhuman animals, as Luxemburg often expressed. I argue that such affective regard broadens our regard for human beings. Deep respect and affection for the nonhuman is also a means of resistance against dehumanization, since humans have long targeted other humans for cruelty by likening them to animals, to a subhuman status. I agree that we should connect personality with singularity, and even that, I would argue, is applicable to the personality of nonhuman animals. Anyone who has lived with two or three different cats or dogs can attest to each one as a singularity. Animals of the same species and breed have a diversity of temperaments, ways of being, of relating to others, different fears, different favorites.

I like the way that you, in *Singularities at the Threshold*, regard personality as a kind glow or aura. I would put it in slightly different terms, though not contradictory.

When my father died, I remember going with my mother to the facility that was going to do his cremation. The woman working there told us that they would cremate him later that day, and she offered us the opportunity to go and see him one last time. I remember vividly what I said in response to this: "No, I want to see my father, not his body." My point was perfectly materialist and I could easily articulate it without allusion to the celestial or metaphysical. My point was that my father was, for me, his

---

67   Ibid.
68   See Martha Nussbaum, *For Love of Country?*, op. cit., 98-110.
69   Gilman-Opalsky, *The Communism of Love*, op. cit., 123.

active being-in-the-world. To see my father is to hear his voice and share his humor, to know the gait of his large lumbering body, the way he carried that body through a house, always a bit more loudly than others, and with a distinctive sound. My father was the way he sat and laughed at his own jokes, the way he hugged, and the sweetness with which he tried to be friends with his children, despite many challenges. All of that and more is what my father was, and a lifeless body exudes none of it. That is what I meant when I said I wanted to see him, not his body. We could speak of my father's aura or glow. It was certainly a singularity, like a unique voice on the saxophone, you could tell it from just a few notes.

At the same time, none of this means he was some kind of individual apart from others. To really understand my father, which I did not fully achieve, would require understanding the whole story of his social and historical development on the lower east side of Manhattan, his fatherless working class childhood, his formative experiences, and education, which was not acquired in a college or university. I can remember in the final years of his life a few notable times when he wanted to tell me stories about his life, and he wanted me to sit down and listen and I did. Though not enough. In any case, this was an effort to tell me who he was, which is to say, to explain how he emerged as a singularity in and from relations with others. His singularity, like singularity more broadly, is a matter of trans-dividuality. I certainly see our affinity here.

I do think a deeper understanding of how each singularity is a trans-dividual would diminish cruelty, because we could then appreciate a certain connective tissue, which I write about often. However, we should be cautious to remember that some singularities emerge from physically or verbally abusive and violent relationships, from experiences of war, displacement, exploitation, discrimination, and other abuses and tortures. Some trans-dividual singularities take their shape in much worse situations than in situations of healthy love relations. We still need a good concept of the enemy. We can be full-blown humanists and still have to oppose some people, to fight against oppressors and exploiters, if not by the force of a physical conflict then by way of opposing what they stand for, what they represent and enact in the world. I think that your book, *Humanity and the Enemy*, offers the insight we need. The enemy is real, but is not so much a person or personality as it is a certain logic (in this case a capitalist logic) materialized only because people actively carry it into the world. Logics of domination, like those of patriarchy, capitalism, white supremacy, are problematic because they are logics that organize relationships, govern institutions and practices, and have real histories of brutality and bloodshed. The logic of racism survives when a racist dies, as do the logics of patriarchy and capitalism when individual patriarchs and capitalists die. If only the real enemy was Jeff Bezos, Derek Chauvin, or someone else. If that were the case, we would at least be facing mortal enemies.

In this, there is a little reproduction of Arendt's concept of "the banality of evil." Like her, I do not believe in the bad seed, i.e., the idea that Adolf Eichmann was born evil. There are pathological people who have no feelings of remorse and cannot think with any concern about others, and that is a dangerous thing. However, even that does not make such people "evil." In general, I think Arendt is right about the question of evil, though I also think that, as communists, we need to draw some battle lines. Even if evil is a matter of *thoughtlessness*, the fact is that no one can make everyone think. This is not to say that people are not *capable* of thinking, but look at politics today. What you see is that people are perfectly capable of only thinking about what they want to think about in precisely the ways that support their claims, or in only those ways that corroborate their ideology. What happens when the employer thoughtlessly rejects the very reasonable demands of the workers? What happens when even the most rational arguments – complete with an abundance of evidence – fail to convince? What happens when a whole course on Marxist philosophy ends with a student who continues to insist that Marx was wrong because of Stalin? What happens when capitalists cannot see or take responsibility for their role in the ecological catastrophe? We cannot simply go on forever trying to help the mortal representatives of enemy logics think in different directions. At some point, there is always a struggle, confrontation, conflict, revolt, and if we are fortunate, there is revolution.

CONCLUSION

MOVEMENTS TOWARDS NEW FORMS OF LIFE

Bruno Gullì (BG) asks: You make a very important point about revolt as the motor of political/ontological unrest. This is really the meaning of the two phrases in the subtitle of your *Specters of Revolt*: "the intellect of insurrection" and "philosophy from below." First of all, you state the superiority of revolt over professional philosophy.[1] Importantly, you say, "To theorize revolt as 'philosophy from below,' it is necessary to refute its conventional vilification as irrational and violent."[2] Indeed, if anything, the violence comes from the system; it is state violence bent on repressing and crushing any expression of revolt (an expression of reason!). You say that this is what your book is dealing with, and it does that beautifully. In this sense, you cite Michel Foucault and Gilles Deleuze and Félix Guattari.[3] That's very good. However, when I read this, I also think of Marx's wonderful section on the emancipation of the senses in the *Economic and Philosophic Manuscripts*, "The *senses* have therefore become *theoreticians* immediately in their *praxis*."[4] To me, if there is a 'revolutionary alternative to revolution,' to play with the title of one of your sections from *Spectacular Capitalism*, this is it. Perhaps we find ourselves again in the territory, on the plane, of transgression, the neither/nor, the threshold. Insurrection, rebellion, and revolt, do not simply belong in the instinctual realm, the blind senses (so to speak), as if there really

---

1 Gilman-Opalsky, *Specters of Revolt*, op. cit., 18.
2 Ibid., 26.
3 Ibid., 18.
4 Marx, *The Economic and Philosophic Manuscripts of 1844*, op. cit., 74.

were a separation between reason and unreason. It is rather the recuperation of the senses as theoreticians in their praxis that might yield a different type of thinking and acting and doing. In your engagement with détournement and epiphany (an important concept in *The Communism of Love*, too), you say that "we must look centrally at the critical and philosophical content of revolt."[5]

Can you elaborate on this subversive ontology, the subversive writing you already speak about in *Precarious Communism*? Am I correct in thinking that this is what a philosophy from below is about, what it engenders? Am I correct in thinking that the intellect of insurrection lies at the level of the concept, not in the sense that it is an abstraction from reality, but rather that it becomes reality's (subterranean) ontological movement and volcano? In other words, revolt is the potentiality, the potency, that in the "There is no alternative" ideology is given as nothing; and yet, it is perhaps this *nothing as philosophy* (what is merely taken as nothing) that, as you say, "produces epiphanies about the world, suggesting its transformation."[6] And you add that epiphany is "a crucial part of what is called revolution."[7]

Richard Gilman-Opalsky (RGO) answers: That is a beautiful line from Marx about the *senses* becoming *theoreticians* in *praxis*. I agree with the sentiment. When we consider the dominant historiography of Marx's time and his juxtaposition of collective action to philosophy, such as one finds in "Theses on Feuerbach" and *The German Ideology*, the sentiment makes perfect sense. It is incomplete to say that Marx was simply confronting German idealism with materialism. He was also dealing with problems posed in and by Hegel's *Lectures on the Philosophy of History*. He also wrote a PhD dissertation in philosophy, and it is in the context of all of this that one has to grapple with his purported disdain for philosophy. For all of his criticism of philosophy's limitations, Marx remained a philosopher who devoted himself to major works of theory. Had he lived in a different epoch (perhaps the present one) it is easy to imagine that Marx may have championed theory and philosophy, especially in a period of its relative

---

5 Gilman-Opalsky, *The Communism of Love*, op. cit., 20.
6 Gilman-Opalsky, *Specters of Revolt*, op. cit., 28.
7 Ibid.

absence. In his young days in Berlin, Marx felt surrounded by too much philosophy. It is hard to imagine feeling anything like that today.

We must not only ask, *What is Philosophy?* as Deleuze and Guattari did, but also, "what are philosophy's aims in the world?"[8] That is not a question about what philosophy actually does, but rather, about its aspirations. It is not too difficult to draw some basic conclusions about that. If philosophy is not a silent, private inquiry one keeps to one's self, then it goes out into the world and confronts something, questions ideologies, concepts of truth and justice, and authoritative discourses in politics, science, etc. Over its course of encounters, philosophy gives birth to new understandings. This is, perhaps, its epistemological side. However, philosophy at its best is also an ontological project inasmuch as it wants us to think deeply about actual and possible forms of life, different ways of being-in-the-world, and the moral, social, and political imperatives shifting forms of life. Epiphany is a big part of this. Philosophy goes into the world and aspires to be an epiphanous force. Philosophy aims to accomplish epiphany, or else it would stay in the private skull of the philosopher; the philosopher would publish nothing.

Now, I claim that these epistemological and ontological aspirations are also – at the same time – the discernable aspirations of a revolt. I understand how one could say that insurrection, rebellion, and revolt are instincts of indignation. I agree, but that is not all that they are. One has a survival instinct, but one does not only have that. There are also some ideas about what kind of survival would be best. It is not that I want to separate reason and unreason per se, but rather, that I am trying to abolish a very specific idea (with a long history) of revolt as unreasonable. Therefore, when I say that we must look at the critical and philosophical content of revolt, this implicates, as you rightly note, a subversive ontology. Why? First, I argue that we have to appreciate knowledge, understanding, and insight in other places than in the heads and words of professional thinkers. This has both ontological and epistemological content. Ontologically, I want to subvert the idea that certain forms of life only yield emotional reaction, while other forms of life position people for serious thought. A state of revolt is a being-in-the-world that generates serious critical understanding and analysis, it is an active mode of cognition, a mode of life

---

8 Gilles Deleuze and Félix Guattari, *What Is Philosophy?*, trans. Hugh Tomlinson and Graham Burchell (New York: Columbia University Press, 1994).

that implicates becoming, a movement towards the not-yet. Epistemologically, Stevphen Shukaitis and I refer to this as "riotous epistemology."[9]

We may contextualize all of this, as you say, with the concept of philosophy from below. Insurrection is material. It happens in the world and disrupts the world. Capital and state may suppress revolt only for some time before it breaks out again, picking up its unfinished business. The specter of revolt is not about history repeating itself. Nothing like that. Again, continuity is not repetition. The idea of the specter is that when revolt appears to have ended, it is not really over. Revolt is – among other things – an expression of disaffection about material conditions of life, and as long as those material conditions remain in place, even if they have taken a new shape, then revolt will recur. It is a part of reality, an engine of historical change, and operates in a philosophical modality too, which we see when we are willing to wrest the concept of philosophy from the philosophers and find it elsewhere.

Finally, I want to appreciate your use of the word "volcano." I have not thought about this, but I like the idea of an eruption we are waiting for. There appears to be "nothing happening" when the volcano sits dormant. However, those who live next to a volcano, certainly at any time after Pompeii in 79 CE, would dare not describe "nothing happening" as "nothing." The fear of living beside a volcano is that *nothing* is a prelude to *something*. Something is happening inside the volcano that one does not see until it appears. It is perhaps a bit like Deleuze and Guattari's rhizome. Something is growing underground that only shows itself at certain moments. People want the roots to stay buried, the volcano to stay dormant. The longer you can live without an eruption, the better, they say. Not so with revolt. We need more eruptions of that kind. You can spot the difference between the volcano and the revolt when you look at who fears each one and wants to keep them down. Those who make revolt do not see their eruptions as bad news. That is where the analogy breaks down.

BG asks: I particularly like your discussion in *Spectacular Capitalism* of what is perhaps Debord's most important contribution to revolutionary philosophy (and you portray it as such): *the practice of theory*. First of all,

---

9   Richard Gilman-Opalsky and Stevphen Shukaitis, *Riotous Epistemology: Imaginary Power, Art, and Insurrection* (Brooklyn: Autonomedia, 2019).

you present Debord's work "as a corrective to and an extension of Marx's political philosophy,"[10] and you stress Debord's *difference*[11] as "a revolutionary who had no hope for revolution."[12] Thus, something must be invented –that's his situationist stance in politics: "we must create situations, unexpected ruptures."[13] This is what you call Debord's "atypical" notion of revolution.[14] And you explain what that means when you speak of Debord's idea of "revolution as a never-ending process that destabilizes dominant ideology."[15] One way to do this is through art, or perhaps it is an artistic, esthetic, endeavor throughout.[16]

I'd like to hear more about this, especially given my interest in this respect. In fact, in the final chapter of *Labor of Fire*, on the relationship between art and labor, I deal with Debord's thinking in a somewhat similar way. Here, you could say more about what you name Debord's "special importance" for us today.[17] In particular, in addition to the question of art, you could say more about your remarks around the idea of Debord's "practice of theory," which you consider, in agreement with Debord himself, "of primary importance."[18] At this point, you stress the necessity of philosophy. Differently from Marx's time, "today, there is not too much philosophy, and we are far from overwhelmed by it. Rather, there is too little philosophy, and its absence is debilitating."[19] I completely agree with you. So, we have art and philosophy as tools for the practice of theory and as revolutionary alternatives to revolution. Do I understand you correctly? If so, what role would they play in the construction of new forms of life, to play with the subtitle of our conversation?

RGO answers: We very much agree on the social and political dimensions of art, which I noticed in reading your concluding focus on art in *Labor of Fire*. However, since you are asking about the practice of theory, I

---

10   Gilman-Opalsky, *Spectacular Capitalism*, op. cit., 64.
11   Ibid., 68.
12   Ibid., 67.
13   Ibid., 81.
14   Ibid.
15   Ibid., 81-82.
16   Ibid., 81.
17   Ibid., 63.
18   Ibid., 95.
19   Ibid.

would like to begin with the meaning of that term, and more fundamentally, with what I mean by theory in this context.

Let us start with distinguishing philosophy and theory. I would say that theory is one of the things philosophers do. All theory, one could argue, is a philosophical activity, but some philosophical activity is not theory. Therefore, I regard philosophy as the broader field, which includes various pursuits of truth, even pursuits that are not undertaken theoretically. This view seems to me consistent with the view of philosophy in Bertrand Russell's *The Problems of Philosophy*, where he observes that all of the social and natural sciences began as philosophy, whether we are talking about mathematics, physics, history, psychology, economics, etc.[20] It is worth recalling Pythagoras and Thucydides and Aristotle. In addition, we could think of men like Adam Smith who thought of himself as a moral philosopher (and not an economist) when he wrote *The Wealth of Nations* (not only when writing his *Theory of Moral Sentiments*). Russell observed that only after a certain line of inquiry gathers up a body of confident facts does it separate itself from philosophy and announce itself as a new discipline like physics or economics. I think Russell is mostly right about this history, but we should note the implication. The implication is that philosophy works best where there is uncertainty, *before* there are confident answers to our questions. I agree, and that is why I also insist that philosophy is an antidote to ideology, because the latter is too confident to be properly philosophical. To get a fuller – and I would say better – idea of philosophy beyond this basic distinction vis-à-vis Russell, I recommend Gilles Deleuze and Félix Guattari's *What Is Philosophy?* There, Deleuze and Guattari begin with the question of what is a concept, and they slowly approach the notion that philosophy is a painful process of creating concepts that may help us confront the chaos of human life.[21] In any case, for Deleuze and Guattari, it may take one a life of philosophizing before one may even approach an answer to the question of what philosophy is.

As I said above, theory is something we find in philosophy. When we do theory, we are working with concepts to understand the world, and more critically and politically, we are introducing concepts with an

---

20   Bertrand Russell, *The Problems of Philosophy* (New York and Oxford: Oxford University Press, 2017).
21   Gilles Deleuze and Félix Guattari, *What Is Philosophy?*, trans. Hugh Tomlinson and Graham Burchell (New York: Columbia University Press, 1994).

intention of altering understandings of the world. Ultimately, theorists want to change the way we understand the world and our relationship to it, and they often do this by introducing and substantiating troubling thinking or interpretations and analyses that threaten to undermine already-established understandings. When we talk about the practice of theory, we are talking about the activity of a conceptual confrontation. You can write a book or an article that becomes an occasion for that confrontation. Because philosophers who have defined what theory is, from Immanuel Kant's famous intervention on the question of theory and practice to Jürgen Habermas's insistence on the political practices of theory identifying norms and reconfiguring political identity, have themselves been authors of books and articles, their main mode of practicing theory is to write. One of the terrible limits of philosophy has been its text-centric concept of theory.

With Debord, however, one finds a different sensibility about non-textual modalities of theory. Debord was close to artists and poets, to painters and surrealists, to fellow travelers like André Breton, and to subversive filmmakers like René Viénet. Debord appreciated that subversive theory on limited and marginal visual or performative terrains could not compete with the sprawling architecture and advertising of a spectacular capitalist society, so he advocated the Situationist method of détournement. This is essentially a hijacking, derailment, repurposing, where we take the materials of others and make them say something else. One excellent example of cinematic détournement is Viénet's movie "Can Dialectics Break Bricks?" There, Viénet takes a martial arts film and overdubs actors with a different script converting the movie into a heavy-handed (and rather funny) Situationist and Marxist critique of capitalist society. This approaches what I call the "special importance" of Debord. We have to think about all of the terrains on which we can do theory, and now, with social media, podcasts, YouTube, and the latest me-centered media forms, we are learning that our shrewdness with terrain requires constant updating.

Above all, we must find new ways to practice theory because we still live in a world where the first problems we encounter as revolutionaries are often ideological ones, problems having to do with simulated, assimilated, delimited, or otherwise blocked thinking. This means a kind of topsy-turvy for Marxist materialism, because he used to say to philosophers, for example in *The German Ideology* and in his "Theses on Feuerbach," that changing the world is much more important than changing people's understanding of the world. Marx's concept of revolution requires a real transformation of the material conditions of life. Today, I might half-jokingly retort to a call for such a difficult world-historical task: "If only it were so easy!" Yes, we need to change the material conditions of life, but unfortunately, it is much harder than that because we also have to confront the fact that so many people do not think so or do not think doing so is possible. We now know that ideological opposition is a theoretical problem. We have seen impoverished working class people rallying to the end for Donald Trump. Their class position does not dissuade them.

What is crucial about art is its affective power. Philosophical texts and theoretical arguments, as much as I love them myself, do not move people as reliably as great events, experiences, and real human dramas. There are other ways of doing theory. There are different ways to practice the questioning that got Socrates in so much trouble so long ago. Again, we should remember that Socrates never wrote a single word. Moving people by way of conceptual confrontations is one of the central aims of theory. I would therefore argue that art, which includes movies, music, theater, and even the political theater of street protests and occupations, is generally and more reliably powerful than journal articles and books.

Only such unconventional theory can help us think through revolutionary alternatives to revolution. This is because the theory of events and experience and art help us to imagine and see real alternatives, different forms of life. Therefore, in a most fundamental way, we are talking about the ontological work that interests us both. With regard to revolution, the role of theory is to help us explore the desirability and possibility of new forms of life. Revolution depends on the desirability and possibility of new forms of life, new ways of being-in-the-world. We have to think about the forms of life we prefer, and we have to keep on thinking about the question of possibility. However, I am convinced that we will not move to the possible and desirable by way of international proletarian rebellion. I would welcome news to the contrary, but no one should hold their breath for this. Although it reveals a certain desperation, my real hope comes from smaller and more rhizomatic activities, which nonetheless retain an old-fashioned commitment to the necessity of global revolution. The Zapatistas were an example of that, but they are not the only one. We have seen new permutations of anti-fascist and anti-racist politics that are small in practice but global in aspiration. We may prefer to start somewhere else, as if with hope in our hearts before the Paris Commune, but that is not where we are. We have to start where we are.

BG asks: This question closely relates to the previous one. It also goes back to the initial and fundamental point of the critique of ideology. You say, "There are critical differences between the spectacle of socialism (or socialism as ideology), on the one hand, and socialism as philosophy or political theory, on the other."[22] And you add that the spectacle of socialism "is *not* really socialist."[23] You also say what this spectacle really is, or was: "bureaucratic state capitalism."[24] In a sense, we are back to one of the main questions here: the question of the state, of sovereignty, and the necessity of an anarchist solution, or perhaps, more than a solution, a threshold of sort. "The world needs a kind of humanism," you say.[25] You already address this question elsewhere in our book. However, what is the humanism that you are proposing? With a reference to Marx's "Theses on Feuerbach," you say that this humanism cannot be based on the abstract and isolated individual. Can you say more about this, especially in light of the pandemic that seems to have shattered some commonly accepted frameworks? At the outset of your book, you say that praxis needs to be rescued "from the wreckage of Baudrillard," the rhetoric of simulacra.[26] I agree with this. Yet, what kind of praxis can we imagine and envision today? How can the practice of theory deliver us, not only from the spectacle, but from all ideological distortions, the source of so much confusion, which at times seems to stall revolutionary desire?

RGO answers: I am opposed to keeping old stupidities alive, such as those once-fierce oppositions between Marxist-humanists and Marxists of other kinds, or as we have already discussed, those old stupid hostilities between anarchists and Marxists or of class politics to identity politics, etc. We must never take the bait and go to war with other anti-capitalists and revolutionaries. We have to learn something from that history of failure.

---

22 Gilman-Opalsky, *Spectacular Capitalism*, op. cit., 89.
23 Ibid.
24 Ibid., 93.
25 Ibid., 119.
26 Ibid., 24.

Moreover, our real enemies would prefer us to remain hostage to those internecine squabbles. Therefore, I do not declare a full-faith alliance with humanism in order to attack those Marxists who reject humanism. That said, humanism – as I have argued above – indicates for me getting down to the question of human health and well-being, to the question of human flourishing. Humanism is a means of cutting through national and linguistic identities to get to what Marx called, following Feuerbach, "species-being."[27] This does not involve any erasure of linguistic, national, ethnic, sexual, or gender identity, but rather, it means an insistence on considering the whole range of processes of dehumanization. Exploitation at work can be dehumanizing, which was how Marx approached estranged labor in 1844. Marx considered problems of estrangement from one's actual labor, from the products of one's labor, from other workers, and from one's self as a part of humanity. The concept of "species-being" reveals how dehumanization is the result of any mode of estrangement.

I think it is crucial to confront dehumanization from a sensibility that opposes the brutal reduction of the human person to an instrument of capital, a sex object, a criminal, an exchange value, etc. Anyone who regards the other as a tool, commodity, virus, or threat carries out a certain dehumanization because we can reduce no human person to a singular despised trait without stripping him or her of the breadth and complexity of singularity, of his or her being-in-the-world. Those of us who oppose the dehumanizing realities of our imperialist white supremacist capitalist patriarchy must aim at fuller understandings of the other. One way to go about this may be to dehumanize the dehumanizers, which would perhaps follow Marx's famous notion of "expropriating the expropriators."[28] As fun as that may be, I think it is far more important to humanize the dehumanized. Dehumanization is a distinctly human process. A humanist cannot say that everything human is good. Capitalist exploitation does not come naturally out of the soil of the Jurassic age. Capitalism comes out of a human history of production, exploitation, and accumulation. Some of the worst things humans face are distinctly human things, not only things like white supremacy and capitalist exploitation, but also things like nuclear

---

27 See Karl Marx, *The Economic and Philosophic Manuscripts of 1844*, trans. Martin Milligan (New York: Dover Publications, 2007), especially the chapter on "Estranged Labor."
28 See, among other places, Karl Marx, *Capital, Volume 1*, op. cit., especially the end of Part 7, Chapter 24.

fallout and mass incarceration. Humanists must confront the special horrors of distinctly human things.

The COVID-19 pandemic has been far more dehumanizing than humanizing. For all the talk about being "in it together," the emergency atomized us to a breaking point. It was an emergency of the other as threat to our health and well-being. My first-grader said many heartbreaking things during the pandemic. Getting ready to go somewhere, he wanted to know if other people would be there. He would say he was afraid of other people and did not want to go around them. Of course, he would say that! He goes to school in a mask and is smart enough to know why he does that. Early in the pandemic, he learned that every person is a biological threat. More broadly, it is difficult to humanize people when you reduce them to a vector of disease. In the biological reality of a pandemic, we cannot pretend that other people pose no threat. No, but a humanist can insist that the other is not *merely* a danger, and can try also to appreciate that there is sociological and psychological suffering in a pandemic which has distinctly human dimensions and which goes beyond the problem of biological transmission.

In the midst of a pandemic, it is difficult to make any recommendation that contradicts the advice of virologists and infectious disease specialists. Giorgio Agamben (and some others) tried to do that, and although Agamben made interesting and often very good points and analyses regarding the state of exception, I did not share his confidence in dissenting from what appeared to me an imperfect but nonetheless pragmatic scientific consensus.[29] To think against the grain takes courage, but that one thinks against the grain does not mean one is correct. I found activism centered on getting people what they needed during the lockdowns far more compelling. I witnessed many examples locally in Illinois, with food pantries and social media orchestration of activist responses to pressing needs in the community. An exemplary initiative came from comrade organizations like Woodbine in New York that activated mutual aid programs. How Woodbine repurposed itself as a kind of communist response unit

---

29   One can find much of Giorgio Agamben's thinking on this subject in his book, *Where Are We Now? The Epidemic as Politics*, trans. Valeria Dani (Lanham: Rowman and Littlefield, 2021). However, his original hot takes and diatribes on the COVID-19 situation appeared first online as the pandemic was breaking and rapidly evolving.

during the pandemic was truly inspiring.[30] The example showed that we can and must move through a pandemic in ways that resist its dehumanizing tendencies; sometimes people can do this through relief efforts, art, conversation, and even electronically, using available technologies to establish, rekindle, and maintain connections with friends and family.

Having said all of this, the pandemic pushes us away from imagining and envisioning different forms of life. It does not bring us closer to the communist ontology we need. It forces a new form of life upon us, and that is not the one of our dreams. A pandemic (and one could imagine here, too, an ecological emergency, Russian invasion, or massive comet) does not create a form of life that springs from our aspirations or revolutionary desires. Our orientation shifts to surviving the pandemic, to biding our time even more than we are already accustomed to as revolutionaries. COVID-19 is unequivocal bad news. However, there is a role for theory here. We can use theory to learn some things about ourselves, about our society, work, and everyday life. While we are masking up, we can unmask certain conceits of the spectacle. For example, we at least see that other forms of life are possible, even if they are not the ones we desire. The importance of realizing that possibility should not be underestimated. The deep ideology of spectacular capitalism wants us to think indefinitely that nothing is possible but what we are doing. However, when what we are doing changes, when how we teach and gather and study and work changes, that marks an opening for theory. Therefore, even though a pandemic is bad news, it may shatter that dangerous lie of the spectacle that tells us we can only live one way.

When you ask about revolutionary desire in pandemic times, the hopeful side of the question is to consider what happens to revolutionary desire during a time when people discover that others forms of life are possible. Even in dark times of backwards motion, we may discover new hopes and possibilities that seem, if not more hopeful than before, perhaps more possible.

RGO asks: Art occupies the final attentions of *Labor of Fire* as it appears in the final analysis as the example *par excellence* of living labor. Fantastic! I wanted to ask you a question related to Albert Camus's *Resistance,*

---

30   Woodbine documented and discussed these activities on their website (https://www.woodbine.nyc/) alongside their slogan, "Against the End of the World."

Rebellion, and Death. That collection also offers a concluding section on art as an activist terrain for social transformation. Camus's section, The Artist and His Time, consists of two pieces, "The Wager of Our Generation" and "Create Dangerously." Camus conceives of social and political action and movement in terms of creative works of art that reflect upon and condemn the ugliness of the era in which they are made, yet at the same time, imagine hopeful pathways out of that. I like Camus's view – *and yours* – that involve fighting wars of position in diverse venues of culture, creativity, and artwork. What always impressed me was Camus's understanding (in 1957) of the capitalist cooptation of art, the ways that art and artists are bought up by commercial interests to produce "artworks" that are celebrated and proliferated by capital, that become accomplices to our exploitation. Since Camus's essays on art-activism in the 1950s, we have seen major developments in music, film, social media, and cyberspace more broadly, which create *both* new opportunities for art to revolt against capital *and* new opportunities for art to be further coopted by capital. What are some examples today of art as living labor that give you hope, or art as productive labor that may be new causes for concern?

BG answers: I have always appreciated Albert Camus as a novelist – and as a playwright (*The Stranger, The Plague, The Fall, Caligula*, and so on). But I have never been particularly taken by his essays. The ones you mention, on "The Artist and His Time," I find them a bit confused, idealistic, and perhaps simplistic. Of course, it is important to say, as he does, "To create today is to create dangerously." That is true. It is also important to underscore the fact that "the strange liberty of creation is possible" in the midst of repressive and sovereign violence, "the police forces of so many ideologies."[31] And of course, as you say, Camus's understanding of the capitalist cooptation of art is also important. However, in my answer, I would like to take a different approach and briefly speak about the question of the politics of work in art. This is what Dave Beech, in a wonderful book on the separation between art and handicraft – a book which is rightly and constructively critical of my positions on art and labor in *Labor of Fire* – asks us to do. Beech's book ends with the following sentence, "Despite all of its failings, therefore, art, along with its distinctive social form of labour

---

31 Albert Camus, *Resistance, Rebellion, and Death: Essays*, trans. Justin O'Brien (New York: Vintage Books, 1961), 251.

must be defended against commodification, financialisation, empire and patriarchy partly because it has shielded itself from the capitalist mode of production for so long but mainly because everything should be fortified against capitalism in order to do away with it."[32]

Art still has a revolutionary role to play, despite capital's sinister power of cooptation. Art remains a form of living labor against dead labor, i.e., capital. I would, once again, name anonymous art, graffiti art – as I did in *Labor of Fire* – as a paradigm of rebellion and resistance. In a sense, this would be a paradoxical, and completely transformed, return of the idea of 'art for art's sake' – though the return is not individualistic, nor is it truly self-referential: the real aim is perhaps hidden, but totally revolutionary, facing the increasingly violent power of capital and its euphemistic expressions, such as democracy, tolerance, wellness, and so on. I remain convinced that art is labor, and we have to fight for a time when labor can be art. Obviously, the commodification and financialization of art (and of life) is undeniable today. Can we change that? That's our task, our challenge, and our aim.

BG asks: In your introduction to *Spectacular Capitalism*, you also anticipate what in Chapter 2 becomes the idea of "Revolutionary Alternatives to Revolution," a wonderful section title. You say that your interest in Guy Debord has to do with the possibility of "a new philosophy of praxis."[33] You continue, "My overarching aim is to address wrong turns in socialist theory and praxis, to develop a radical critique of the current era of spectacular capitalism, and to think through the prospects for countervailing forces to capitalism and its culture."[34] Indeed, given the power of the spectacle, it seems difficult to find and implement an alternative. You speak of "a seemingly intractable problem," for "the crises of capitalism call for the remedies of capitalism."[35] In this sense, you make an important reference to Naomi Klein's *The Shock Doctrine: The Rise of Disaster Capitalism*. You call attention to the a priori importance of the ideological/mythological dimension and the compliance and subservience of people in general, their giving in to authority.

---

32 Dave Beech, *Art and Labour*, op. cit., 275.
33 Gilman-Opalsky, *Spectacular Capitalism*, op. cit., 21.
34 Ibid.
35 Ibid., 22.

This is a very important problem, with a long tradition in philosophical thinking. Famously, in the Preface to *Theological-Political Treatise*, Spinoza asks why it is that people often fight for their servitude as if they fought for their freedom. You see in the new philosophy of praxis a way of undermining the spectacle and its ideological formation – an ideology, as you importantly says, that "matters precisely because it can be materialized."[36] As I have already mentioned, you go back to this important problem when you say that "capitalism has developed ways to provide capitalist alternatives to itself."[37] This can also be understood according to the logic of the real subsumption of labor and life (really, of everything) under capital. Yet, Debord, seeing "the necessity of a revolutionary transformation of society,"[38] even when this transformation is often preempted by capital's own spiral of madness and arrogance, will "theorize revolutionary alternatives to classical conceptions of revolution."[39]

In your book, you do give a sense of what these (situationist) alternatives are. But can you elaborate on this a bit more here, especially in light of the events of the past ten years, that is, since the publication of your book, including these last two years of the COVID pandemic? In other words, what can be done in order to disrupt and deactivate the ability of capital to subsume everything under itself and normalize everything?

RGO answers: This is a very important question. I wish I could say things have improved over the decade or so since I wrote *Spectacular Capitalism*. It is perhaps fair to say that some things have improved in terms of the general prospects for thinking about revolutionary alternatives to revolution throughout civil society internationally. However, there is no way around the fact that things have gotten much worse, and demonstrably so. Let me begin with the bad getting worse, and then we can look at some of the more hopeful developments after that. It is always better to end with some hope.

For most of my adult life, I have identified as – among several other more pressing identifications – an activist, and even during periods of scarce opportunity to join in actual protest or social movement activity, I

---

36 Ibid., 23.
37 Ibid., 77.
38 Ibid., 78.
39 Ibid., 80.

always insist that activism is good. Activism demarcates modalities of political action undertaken by people outside the professional political class. Activism is, in other words, a political field for those outside the ruling class. That is the sense in which I say that I am for activism. Today, however, it is not enough to say one is for activism, but also necessary to specify what the activism is for. Now, we must note immediately that this was, to some extent, always the case. Nonetheless, activism has also always signified to me the practical effort of trying to change things, distinguished from an opposition to activism in defense of the status quo, an opposition of those who did not want things to change. So far, so good. However, over the weekend of January 22 and 23 in 2022, there was a large demonstration in Washington DC of people marching together and chanting with their children. Some held signs that said "My Body, My Choice." Others held signs of declaration against tyranny, and for human and political freedom. From these signs, you might think this was a "pro-choice" or "abortion rights" rally, a rally of activists trying to change things. However, most of the participants were defending the pre-COVID status quo as pro-life conservatives. Zooming in on the protest signs, you find that their invocation of "My Body, My Choice" was not about women's rights, but was an opposition to vaccine mandates in response to COVID-19. Those at the demonstration also invoked the idea that people who get vaccines are sheep suffering from a dangerous form of herd mentality. If you watched it on a screen with the sound muted, you might have assumed that these were scenes from a liberal or left-wing protest demonstration. Since not a single person I saw in photos from the event was wearing a mask, one might also assume that it took place years ago.

Let me clearly state that I am reluctant to condemn the occurrence of people gathering and shouting together, with their children joining in, against the state. I am all for that whole phenotype of politics. However, that is precisely the problem. A dangerous spectacle is at work there. We cannot simply trust the modality of this phenotype of politics, an apparent rising up against the existing reality. Yet, if its content were different, we would endorse that form of politics for sure.

We could see the spectacle of which I speak more clearly in the so-called "insurrection" on January 6, 2021 on the confirmation day of Joe Biden's presidency. What is the meaning of a "protest" that demands going backwards to restore a preceding normalcy? The answer to that question is part of the reason why I'm inclined to think of the January 6, 2021 upheaval at the Capitol Building more as a paramilitary deployment *of the state* – indeed, as a neo-fascist reaction of a particular head of state and his disaffected base – than as any hopeful revolt against oppressive state power. We should not mistake the form for its content, just as we cannot mistake every marriage or family as some kind of haven of love. An armed temper tantrum of Trump's supporters after Biden's electoral win is not the same thing as a revolt or an insurrection, despite the consistently careless language of media coverage. We must never equivocate backward looking right-wing reactions against change with the future-oriented freedom struggles of women and Black people from radical suffragettes like the Pankhurst women to Black Lives Matter.[40]

It is necessary to ask about the status of various spectacles at work in the world. My book focused mainly on spectacular capitalism, that is, capital's own mythology about itself, which still organizes dominant understandings of capitalism in the world, and on spectacular socialism and communism, which are essentially unchanged from their Cold War caricatures. Now we have the ascendancy of a powerful new spectacle of freedom according to which right-wing capitalists declare human freedom tempered by humanist, ecological, or any other kind of responsibility utterly destroyed. Anti-vax and anti-mask politics have appeared as a full-blown Hobbesian concept of liberty centered on the body, which says that any regulation of the movement of human bodies in the world is a cancellation of human freedom. Beware! We used to own that discourse on the radical and revolutionary left! The resistance of bodies against the regulatory power of the state was *our weapon* against religious fundamentalism, capitalist management of labor, reactionary gender politics, and xenophobia. Many who are today declaring for the freedom of the body are simultaneously opposed to transgender politics, immigration, and abortion. Now we find our arguments in the mouths of our enemies. At some point, we may have to ask: "Will the real spectacle please stand up?"

This is not entirely new. However, its current deployment makes it difficult to speak about what actual freedom could be (and that difficulty signals the triumph of a spectacle, because the spectacle always makes it

---

40 The suffragettes of the Women's Social and Political Union, an organization led by Emmeline Pankhurst, included radical women who smashed windows of government buildings, deliberately damaged property, and even made protests by means of arson.

hard to speak of the real thing; that is, in many ways, its task). The same is true about the so-called "insurrection" of January 6. In 2016, I wrote about the "specter of revolt," but on January 6, 2021 we saw something like the "*spectacle* of revolt." How can we on the left claim our old heroic figure of the insurrection after it has come to mean a paramilitary operation of Trumpist reactionaries? We should not abandon insurrection to its spectacle form any more than we should surrender communism to its spectacle, or allow capitalism its spectacle, its "uninterrupted monologue of self-praise."[41] How much harder it is to speak about revolutionary alternatives to revolution when spectacular "revolutionaries" appear as right-wing insurgents fighting police while calling for retrenchments of white supremacist chauvinism, Christian fundamentalism, and a fully unfettered capitalism. Unfortunately, the world is not in a better position to think about revolutionary alternatives to revolution. We cannot discount the real possibility that our enemies may lead the next revolution with their reactionary and vengeful capitalism, fascism, racism, sexism, etc. Okay, so that is what we may call "the bad news," and it is only a small part of it.

However, some other things have happened that we may count towards hope. Before mentioning some examples, I should briefly explain my idea of revolutionary alternatives to revolution. I want to insist that there could be a third pathway from a confrontation with the impasses of post-World War II capitalist society. The usual pathway – especially after the Algerian struggle did not result in existential losses for capitalists – was to choose one of two directions. If you were a disaffected revolutionary who could finally see, as Jean-François Lyotard did, that the metanarrative of Marxist historical materialism was a dead end, that no proletarian revolution was inexorably on any horizon, you might recoil to some form of democratic socialism, becoming essentially a reformist undisguised by Eduard Bernstein's pretensions about the self-proclaimed Marxism of "evolutionary socialism." Defeated and hopeless, the first alternative to revolution was opportunistic leftist reformism. In the second half of the twentieth century, it was not so easy to assert Luxemburg's refutation of Bernstein because revolutionaries looked at a far bleaker horizon for revolutionary possibility. The second alternative direction was some form of the abandonment of the political. We may see this in what

---

41 Debord, *The Society of the Spectacle*, op. cit., thesis 24.

Raoul Vaneigem called the person of *"ressentiment,"* a disaffected, hopeless person, teetering on nihilism.[42] Vaneigem wanted to overcome this defeatist nihilism, unlike Jean Baudrillard who later embraced it in a more Nietzschean way.

What attracts me to Debord is the rejection of both of these paths. He was committed to revolutionary politics, which for him meant no abandonment of the political writ large, but also, no strident reformism. The way he imagined revolutionary alternatives to classical revolution, nihilism, and reformism, in the 1950s and 60s, was to imagine creative activity on diverse terrains, utilizing film, art, exhibitions, theatrical acts of civil disobedience, poetry, proletarian theory, graffiti, humor, and scandal. For himself, he still held onto writing because, even with all these options, Debord was really best at writing. He was a brilliant writer.

With Debord, I want to destroy spectacles in multifarious and creative wars of position. One may locate this same interest in my earlier attention to the Zapatistas. Revolutionary movements anywhere on earth today will inevitably need to think about all tools and terrains. We certainly need more than philosophy and conventional forms of protest demonstration, the latter of which activists still reproduce with too little imagination from the era of Vietnam anti-war activism. My hope comes from the irrepressible and global uprisings we have seen from roughly 2008, in Greece during the economic crisis all the way up to the series of Black Lives Matter upheavals running into the 2020 George Floyd Rebellion. In between Greece and Floyd, we have seen the Arab Spring and Occupy Wall Street, the Indignados in Spain, and we have seen Nuit Debout in France and massive revolts in Hong Kong and elsewhere. I especially appreciate the fact that the George Floyd Rebellion happened at the height of pandemic fear during COVID-19, and thus, was not a repressible phenomenon. There were millions of people with reservoirs of psychological disaffection and sadness exacerbated by COVID-19. This, I fully expect, will inevitably show itself in future upheavals. These energetic ruptures with everyday life (and I have only mentioned some of them), including impassioned and illegal expressions of disaffection, show us that revolt always comes back until its work is done. Given the material conditions of the world, in all of their differences and stratifications, I think it is safe to

---

42 Raoul Vaneigem, *The Revolution of Everyday Life*, trans. Donald Nicholson-Smith (London: Rebel Press, 2006), 173-177.

say that we will live with revolt for a very long time.

With regard to the society of the spectacle, the question is whether these revolts can marshal the creative and critical resources to mobilize epiphanies in the social body that can change the ways people see and think about the existing reality. I do not know the answer to that question. As should be clear enough by now, my approach to revolution comes from Marx, and primarily centers on the abolition of the existing capitalist reality. What Debord adds to this is the fact that abolitionists today must also arm themselves with imagination and artistic sensibilities capable of aiming at widespread resonance. Enough epiphanies can turn every spectacle into a corpse.

Easier said than done, but there is hope in this because people will never stop trying, and I place my theory in the spirit – if not the service – of such efforts.

RGO asks: In *Humanity and the Enemy* you claim that, behind its ideological mask, the friend-and-enemy logic "is the struggle between the oppressors and the oppressed (i.e., class struggle)."[43] However, I am wondering about other lines of opposition today, for example, the safe-and-sound versus the dangerous other. In *Immunodemocracy*, Donatella Di Cesare juxtaposes "community" to "immunity." She claims that immunity is the opposite of community. The being-together of community is undermined by the logic of immunity, since the latter favors each one to be protected (immunized) against the threat of the other. This was already true at national borders vis-à-vis undocumented workers and the mobility of migrants and refugees, and now, we can see the preference for immunity over community in the face of global pandemic. We even see that many people call for immunity in the name of community. I am not convinced that this opposition of the healthy and sick is simply one of class struggle. Do you think so? Of course, the rich continue to be threatened by the poor and movements of exploited and despised classes are suppressed in the name of a certain immunity. However, what do you think about new compositions of conflict having to do with refugees (i.e., from Afghanistan or Syria), those who are thought of as carriers of disease, and the state's protection of its own from "outside threats?" Do these permutations of the "friend-and-enemy logic" move beyond the logic of class struggle? If so, how?

---

43 Gullì, *Humanity and the Enemy*, op. cit., 35.

BG answers: I'm glad you ask this question about Donatella Di Cesare's remarkable book, especially the first half of it. I believe that the logic of class struggle remains there even as we speak of immunity versus community. Of course, it depends on how we understand the class struggle today, at the global level. For instance, Maurizio Lazzarato sees it as "unfolding and intensifying … around the issue of debt."[44] Coincidentally, the issue of debt is also an important element in Di Cesare's book. In addition to that, there are in her study various moments that can be related to the logic of class struggle, though, as she says, it is risky to use "twentieth century lenses to decipher what's going on."[45] Yet, the distinction between the poor and the elite is a distinction that belongs in the general paradigm of the class struggle as a struggle – or at least, a divide – between the oppressor and the oppressed. Even in the age of immunodemocracy and biosecurity the real opposition is not between the unqualified healthy and unqualified sick. One might say that the sick are the poor; most of them certainly are, and perhaps they all are, one way or the other. What really counts here is the logic of exclusion. If we can't speak of class struggle in traditional terms – and we are under no obligation to do so (see my answer above for a different take on the question of class) – we can certainly see in poverty, disability, old age, illness, foreignness, and so on, forms of otherness and exclusion, forms of life that have become undesirable. They are certainly a nuisance to the ideal of health and wellness defining the sphere of immunity, the society built on immunity. In a word, we can see here new figures of exclusion and oppression approaching bare life (if they are not already completely in it), resembling the figure of *homo sacer*.

What comes to mind is Frantz Fanon's powerful description of the colonized world as "a world divided in two."[46] I recall here some moments of that description: "The colonist's sector is a sector built to last, all stone and steel. It's a sector of lights and paved roads… The colonist's sector is a sated, sluggish sector, its belly is permanently full of good things." On the other hand, "The colonized's sector, or at least the 'native' quarters, the shanty town, the Medina, the reservation, is a disreputable place inhabited by disreputable people. You are born anywhere, anyhow. You die anywhere, from anything. It's a world with no space… The colonized's sector

---

44   Lazzarato, *The Making of the Indebted Man*, op. cit., 7.
45   Di Cesare, *Immunodemocracy*, op. cit., 8.
46   Fanon, op. cit., 3.

is a famished sector..."⁴⁷ A type of *cordon sanitaire*, a border, is in place here. Obviously, this is not only true of the colonized world in its historical specificity, but of today's global apartheid, of the megacities of the Global South and also of those of the Global North. It is then not a surprise that a health crisis, a pandemic, affects people in different ways. Hence, the immunitarian (irrational) injunction to be healthy at all costs cannot be equally conformed to by everyone everywhere, because, yes, class division persists, and thus the class struggle.

Di Cesare mentions the tragic case of the victims of the sudden COVID lockdown in India. They were mainly "internal migrants, in their hundreds of thousands," unable to go back home from the megacities to their rural areas of origin, and the Dalits.[48] But this has happened everywhere: in New York, for instance, where working-class and migrant families living in small, poorly ventilated units did not have the opportunity – contrary to the wealthy New Yorkers who contracted the virus – to properly social distance and quarantine. When I went to Manhattan after months of lockdown during which I was confined to Brighton Beach, in Brooklyn, I was struck by the desolation, the emptiness on the streets, save for the greater number of homeless people, their makeshift shelters, their scraps of food. It didn't look like they had been shielded and looked after by the immunitarian State during the time when New York had become the epicenter of the pandemic.

The question of *essential workers* also highlights another important aspect of a division within the population that very much relates to the issue of class. Yet, at the same time immunitarian politics – obviously present before the pandemic, but brought to an extreme degree by the pandemic – did change a lot, reshaping without canceling the logic of class struggle. New groups of people have become part of the enemy. For instance, many have pointed out the constant discrimination against the non-vaccinated, seen as an enemy and a danger to society. The idea was (and still is) to retreat from the common and singular to the narrow and pale privacy of individuality and identity. As Giorgio Agamben said, "What is at stake is nothing less than the abolition of public space."[49] Indeed, even more than public space, the attempt is to abolish the common, as the only

---

47 Ibid., 4.
48 Di Cesare, op. cit., 37.
49 Agamben, op. cit., 19.

common thing seems to have become the virus itself. Thus, the injunction to conform and be docile for the sake of mere (biological) survival became thousandfold. As Di Cesare says, xenophobia and exophobia – the fear of anything external – clearly revealed "the disease of identity."[50]

But all this remains within the general paradigm of the class struggle that, as Marx and Engels say in *The Communist Manifesto*, is "a now hidden, now open fight" between – in a word – "oppressor and oppressed." The oppressed today – oppressed to various degrees and in various ways – the sick, the poor, the migrants, and so on, constitute the vast majority of humanity.

RGO asks: I love how you take up the question of violence in *Humanity and the Enemy*, which you do consistently throughout that book. I also think it is crucial to distinguish violence from counterviolence, as you do, and to understand that "resistance to violence (i.e., counterviolence) cannot be violent."[51]

Paulo Freire made a similar point in *Pedagogy of the Oppressed*. Freire agrees with you when he writes: "Never in history has violence been initiated by the oppressed. How could they be the initiators, if they themselves are the result of violence? ...There would be no oppressed had there been no prior situation of violence to establish their subjugation... Violence is initiated by those who oppress, who exploit, who fail to recognize others as persons."[52] I find this discourse on violence crucial and convincing (and I develop a similar argument in my book *Specters of Revolt*). I even wonder if this should be the main immediate objective of political struggle: namely, to expose the violence of everyday life in capitalist society. What do you think could follow from a shift in popular understanding about violence? Most people claim to oppose violence, even if they do not. What may come from seeing the violence of everyday life? I think movements like #BLM have been trying to expose the violence of everyday life in Black cities in the US, for example. Do you think that epiphanies about violence are a major part of present struggles? How so? Has this always been true?

---

50   Di Cesare, op. cit., 27.
51   Gullì, *Humanity and the Enemy*, op. cit., 101.
52   Paulo Freire, *Pedagogy of the Oppressed*, trans. Myra Bergman Ramos (New York and London: Continuum, 2005), 55.

BG answers: Perhaps the key moment in your quote by Paulo Freire is to understand what it is to be "the result of violence." It is here that we can understand that counterviolence, resistance to violence, is not really violence, that is, not violence as violence. Perhaps a more proper way to say this is to point out that *the question of violence does not apply to counterviolence*. For instance, Fanon says, "Violence among the colonized will spread in proportion to the violence exerted by the colonial regime."[53] And he adds: "Terror, counterterror, violence, counterviolence."[54] But this doesn't mean, of course, that violence and counterviolence, terror and counterterror are on the same footing. Certainly, this is not so ontologically, and it is not so historically and politically. Fanon also says that colonialism – but the same is true of any other system of oppression – "is *not a machine capable of thinking, a body endowed with reason*. It is *naked violence and only gives in when confronted with greater violence*" (emphasis added).[55] But how can we show that this "greater violence" is not violence as violence and that the question of violence does not apply to it? I am well aware that it is difficult to do so.

What comes to mind is Angela Davis's answer from a 1972 prison interview to the question as to whether she approved of violence. She says that she finds the question itself "incredible." As she also says at one point in her autobiography, "We seemed to be caught in a whirlpool of violence and blood from which none of us could swim away."[56] Indeed, the question of violence, or rather, the question "Why violence?" does not apply to a situation where violence seems to be an unsurpassable given. In other words, the question of violence does not apply to the oppressed, but to the oppressors. It is the latter, as Freire says, who initiate violence. However, it is not simply a matter of initiating it. The oppressor's aim is to establish a total and never-ending regime of violence. The oppressed, on the other hand, in resisting violence, in countering violence, engage in a process and movement of liberation, seeking to bring about a world of freedom and joy. So, the oppressed have no interest, no stake, in violence, though they have to confront the *naked violence* coming from and imposed on them by the oppressor. This is as true today as it has always been. Perhaps, instead

---

53 Fanon, op. cit., 46-47.
54 Ibid., 46.
55 Ibid., 23.
56 Angela Y. Davis, *An Autobiography* (Chicago: Haymarket Books, 2021), 87.

of counterviolence (or even nonviolence), we should think in terms of *antiviolence*, "of a politics conceived as 'antiviolence,'"[57] antiviolence as political innovation," as Étienne Balibar suggests.[58] He stresses the importance of "the prefix 'anti-,' as in antithesis, antipathy, or antinomy"[59] as "the most general modality of the act of 'facing up to' ... or of measuring oneself against that which is, doubtless, enormous or incommensurable."[60]

Perhaps this way of thinking relates to the epiphanies you are referring to. But real changes will happen only insofar as struggles are able to bring about a total dismantling of any oppressing mentality and entrenched logic of violence.

BG answers: My first impulse would be to leave this last question unanswered. Not because it isn't a good question. In fact, it's an excellent and very important question. But because, to go straight to the point, the place of despair is growing. And yet, I don't want to end this work on a totally negative note. Certainly, we still need hope, and perhaps we can still find it; or rather, it is our task, perhaps our duty to keep hope alive and continue working for it. As John Holloway says in his very recent *Hope in Hopeless Times*, with an important reference to Ernst Bloch, "It is time to re-learn hope."[61] This is so precisely because despair is growing.

There are many reasons for despair. In the last few years, two situations have developed that are paradigmatic of the time and regime of fear in which we live – times of anxiety, loneliness, and stupidity. They are also times in which the enemy thought has not disappeared at all, but it has become stronger. I'm thinking about the COVID pandemic and the war in the Ukraine. In both cases, the idea of the enemy seems to be the driving

---

57 Étienne Balibar, *Violence and Civility: On the Limits of Political Philosophy*, trans. G.M. Goshgarian (New York: Columbia University Press, 2015), 22.
58 Ibid., 75.
59 Ibid. 23.
60 Ibid., 23-24.
61 John Holloway, *Hope in Hopeless Times* (London: Pluto Press, 2022), 15.

force: the virus, the "Chinese" virus, Dostoyevsky, the Russians.[62] This is of course ridiculous, but also very disheartening and dangerous. I believe it remains our task to try to build a new humanity and turn the world upside down. But the times are trying, and perhaps we are growing weaker and discouraged. And yet, movements of resistance are possible; they are real, and they are everywhere: from the US to Europe, from Iran to China. The regime of capital has to end. The paradigm of sovereignty, patriarchy, supremacist and identity thinking has the same existential status as the 'Ndrangheta, the utmost of human stupidity.

Yet, movements of resistance today must be reshaped; they have to find a new language, a new organizational structure, and a new *telos*. Today, they are often steeped in the politics of identity, which is just an expression of liberal ideology. In light of the COVID health and political crisis and of the war in the Ukraine, the constant demands for greater democracy become risible, because democracy itself has become a risible concept. What comes to mind is an essay by Mario Tronti, one of the most radical and inspiring political thinkers of our times. In an essay called "Towards a Critique of Political Democracy," he says, first of all, that "the moment has really come to undertake a critique of democracy."[63] I couldn't agree more. What's really important for us here is that he says that democracy has become "the tyranny of the average man." And he adds that "this average man constitutes a mass within the Nietzschean category of the *last man*."[64] To be sure, this relates to the question of class discussed above, but it relates to it in a different way. Tronti says, "Western society [but one could correct that as 'global society'; brackets added] is no longer divided into classes... but into two great aggregates of consensus."[65] This consen-

---

62   The question of the Russian invasion of the Ukraine is too complex to be dealt with here. I just want to highlight the persistent and pernicious rhetoric of the enemy, which only serves particularistic – and often nefarious – interests. The reference to Dostoyevsky relates to the cancellation of a course on Dostoyevsky at a university in Milan, Italy, in March 2022. The course was later reinstated. However, this does not cancel the incredible and disturbing wave of Russophobia we have witnessed since the start of the war in February 2022.

63   Mario Tronti, "Towards a Critique of Political Democracy" in *The Italian Difference: Between Nihilism and Biopolitics*, ed. Lorenzo Chiesa and Alberto Toscano (Melbourne: re-press, 2009), 97.

64   Ibid., 104.

65   Ibid.

sus will have a reactionary or progressive character, but it is underlined by the same logic of the apolitical, known as the system of democracy. In what he calls "a *democratic Empire*," the "web of a neo-imperial power,"[66] which is antipolitical and antirevolutionary in its very constitution,[67] the only form of resistance is to "remain in the condition of a strong and intelligent minority."[68] Hopefully, new movements will emerge – new forms of life – out of the rubble of the present.

BG asks: If I remember correctly, you once told me, over a Zoom meeting, that you write about things that frighten you. So, what about love? What is the fear here? You speak of its worldly character, and you criticize Arendt, who thinks of love as unworldly.[69] Indeed, you write about the political ontology and ethics of love. Perhaps at times you also point to the conception of cosmic love. But fundamentally, at the center of your book, one finds the practice of love, the politics of love as "a politics of insurgency."[70] And this is perhaps the main motif of all of your books so far.

RGO answers: It is not so strange, my dear friend. I only want to study things that I do not know much about. For any research, I try to find something I would like to think about and possibly have something to say about one day. Why study anything if it is already something you know inside out? That is a missed opportunity. Because I am ignorant about most things in the world, I have a lot from which to choose! How, then, to decide? One part of the answer is interest, that is, to identify a topic of interest with – and this next bit is especially significant – interesting literature to read. Another part is energy. I am attracted to something daunting, something scary, yet something that interests me, something important. Research requires energy and energetic attention. So-called dispassionate research seems to me also joyless. This is partly why I write about what frightens me. Fear takes courage, and excitement generates energy. With Habermas, who can appear very dull indeed, I remember reading his book

---

66   Ibid., 106.
67   Ibid., 104.
68   Ibid., 105.
69   Gilman-Opalsky, *The Communism of Love*, op. cit., 302.
70   Ibid., 317.

The Philosophical Discourse of Modernity.[71] I was mystified and felt I could not understand it at all. Later on, I thought: why not write a book on Habermas? That is one way to get on top of things, to demystify them. A similar approach mobilized my interest in Debord, though I agreed more with Debord's theory and politics, and regarded him as more of a kindred spirit than Habermas. After that, for *Precarious Communism*, I wondered who would have the audacity to detourn *The Communist Manifesto*. It seemed to me almost like an obnoxious thing to do, maybe a little presumptuous, and for me, it took quite a bit of courage as well as humility; it was frightening, energetic and fun.

So, what about love? Love is frightening largely because it appears as a giant vaporous idea mainly taken up by theologians, poets, and philosophers, and before I began, I was afraid to claim to know anything about it. The fear of saying something about love almost drove me away, as if attempting to write about love was like attempting to write about God or the soul, which many philosophers have done, but not me. There is also the fear that one might find out enough about love that it may throw into question one's own ability to love, one's own ways of loving. When I first started to read this book with my son, who was interested in what I wrote after the book's publication, he became afraid that he might find out that he does not really love anyone. In the early stages of research, the instinct to run away turned into and instinct to try.

I think the critique of Arendt is crucial for overcoming fear. She claimed love was unworldly, and I reject that. I insist that love is a thing of this world, and that we can study it in the material relations of real people and real lives. In studying frightening things, we demystify them. Racists are always more vicious the more ignorant they are of the lives of the Black and Brown people they hate. Many others do not want to learn about class and race and some even organize and fight against using critical race theory in school. Conservatives fight tooth and nail against teaching children about institutional racism and white supremacy, and in terms of naked fear, we witness something approach terror in the face of teaching kids about gender and sexuality. Right-wing reactionaries do not want to learn or teach about any of this precisely because they want to go on fearing the people they hate. The less you understand transgender and

---

71 Jürgen Habermas, *The Philosophical Discourse of Modernity: Twelve Lectures*, trans. Frederick Lawrence (Cambridge, MA: The MIT Press, 1990).

non-binary gender identity, for example, the easier it is to fear them. For me, to approach love required overcoming fear.

Love is not ineffable. Understanding love is possible, though it takes courage to confront what love really is and does in the world. Understanding love is also a way of understanding a universal communist aspiration. That is one of the chief reasons we need the resolve to understand it.

Finally, you are correct that, fundamentally, everything for me (including love) returns us to a politics of insurgency. That is because, while all the contingency and complexity matter, the bottom line (if we can speak of such a thing) is always the same: We must rise up against the existing reality. We must rise up for a different reality. That is the communist identity. We have to participate in multifarious ways in ongoing efforts to abolish the world such as it is. We have to try to participate in the becoming of new forms of life. Because of the universality and inconceivable vastness of this theory, communist ontology does indeed have cosmic dimensions.

At the same time, it is and must be earthly.

Milton Keynes UK
Ingram Content Group UK Ltd.
UKHW010659100724
445094UK00003B/3